Narratives from the Nursery

This accessible and timely book builds upon and contributes to ongoing debates surrounding professionalism in the early years workforce. In a sector where policy is rapidly changing, Jayne Osgood challenges existing assumptions concerning professional identities and questions what broader lessons might be learnt about race, ethnicity, social class and gender in early years research and practice.

This engaging text:

- offers a thematic overview of the concept of professionalism in an increasingly critical area of study;
- includes unique autobiographical contributions alongside new and compelling empirical evidence;
- stimulates wider debates within a clear theoretical framework;
- provides an in-depth examination of the individual views of early years practitioners.

Addressing new debates and policies from a focused academic perspective, *Narratives from the Nursery* provides inspirational and enlightening reading for practitioners, researchers, policy makers and students.

Jayne Osgood is Reader in Early Childhood Education at London Metropolitan University.

Narratives from the Nursery

Negotiating professional identities
in early childhood

Jayne Osgood

Routledge
Taylor & Francis Group

LONDON AND NEW YORK

First published 2012
by Routledge
2 Park Square, Milton Park, Abingdon, Oxon OX14 4RN

Simultaneously published in the USA and Canada
by Routledge
711 Third Avenue, New York, NY 10017

Routledge is an imprint of the Taylor & Francis Group, an informa business

British Library Cataloguing in Publication Data
A catalogue record for this book is available from the British Library

Library of Congress Cataloging in Publication Data
Osgood, Jayne.
Narratives from the nursery : negotiating professional identities in early childhood / Jayne Osgood.
p. cm.
Includes bibliographical references and index.
1. Early childhood educators--Professional relationships--Great Britain--Case studies. 2. Nursery schools--Employees--Great Britain--Case studies. I. Title.
LB1775.6.O84 2012
372.210941--dc23
2011027269

ISBN: 978-0-415-55621-7 (hbk)
ISBN: 978-0-415-55622-4 (pbk)
ISBN: 978-0-203-14306-3 (ebk)

Typeset in Galliard
by GreenGate Publishing Services, Tonbridge, Kent

MIX
Paper from
responsible sources
FSC
www.fsc.org   FSC® C004839

Printed and bound in Great Britain by
TJ International Ltd, Padstow, Cornwall

Contents

Tables

Acknowledgements

First, I would like to extend heartfelt thanks to the participants of this study. Their commitment and passion to working with children has been inspirational. Furthermore, their willingness to speak so openly, and their investment in this study, reinforces my belief that it is a worthwhile endeavour.

I would like to thank Professor Becky Francis for her inspirational support throughout. Her expertise and knowledge, not to mention her humour and encouragement, have been invaluable. I would also like to express my gratitude to Professor Merryn Hutchings for her guidance, encouragement and meticulous proofreading.

I also appreciate the support, sustained interest and thougtful guidance offered by Alison Foyle at Routledge. And to the production team for keeping me to time.

I also wish to express my appreciation to my partner, Ben, and to my family and friends for their unwavering belief in me, and, importantly, for their patience. I dedicate this book to Noah and Sylvie, who have given me more joy than I could have imagined possible. Furthermore, their existence has provided me with another identity, and a maternal subjectivity, which have undoubtedly influenced the reflections offered in this book.

Earlier versions of some of the material in this book have appeared in the following journals:

- Parts of Chapter 4 have appeared in an earlier version as 'Childcare workforce reform in England and the "early years professional": a critical discourse analysis', *Journal of Education Policy*, 24 (6), 733–751 (2009).
- Parts of Chapter 7 have appeared in an earlier version as 'Negotiating professionalism: towards a critically reflective emotional professionalism', in *Early Years: An International Journal of Research and Development*, 30 (1), 119–134 (2010).

Abbreviations

CWDC Children's Workforce Development Council
ECEC Early Childcare Education and Care
EYPS   Early Years Professional Status

Chapter 1

Introduction

It is simply not a profession that you can't care about. It requires a high level of emotional investment; you need to have a love for the job and a love for what you do and realise that everything that you do in this job has far-reaching consequences; it can be totally exhausting to invest so much of yourself into this work but if you don't then you are doing everyone a disservice: yourself, your colleagues, the children and ultimately their families. This is the bedrock to what we do, but I suppose it's kind of hidden from view, it's...implicit I guess would be the word.

(Natalia)

Professionalism is a widely contested and variously constructed term. Yet the fact that it is gendered, classed and 'raced' is readily obscured from public debate. This book argues that professionalism is a very personal issue. Whilst policy discourses promote particular forms of professionalism, the way in which this is taken up, resisted and negotiated by women working with young children has been largely neglected. This book offers a theoretical exploration of the processes by which (principally working-class) women negotiate and understand themselves in relation to their professional identities. Through exploring the autobiographical accounts of women from the front-line of nurseries, the book argues that professionalism within this context is necessarily emotional.

The book is based on research conducted in three London nurseries, over five years, including 18 months of in-the-field data collection and observation. It was borne of a growing interest in the dissonance between authoritative, policy-driven notions of professionalism and that which routinely plays out in nursery settings: between nursery staff and their colleagues and through encounters with other professionals, parents and children. It contributes to a growing body of literature that seeks to reconceptualise childhood and early childhood services. By using a feminist, poststructuralist approach, informed by other social theories, including critical, cultural and postcolonial theories, this book explores the possibilities for methodological, theoretical and political concerns to become critically informed by empirical data. The book explores constructions of identity, and the negotiation of power that shapes relationships and reinforces social inequalities.

It is intended that, through processes of deconstruction and unsettling, new ways of knowing become possible.

The research described in this book aimed to explore nursery worker constructions of 'being professional'/doing professionalism; to examine the ways in which nursery workers negotiate the intersection of a 'professional' identity with their classed, gendered and 'raced' identities; to compare and contrast the ways in which public discourses position nursery workers; and to examine the extent to which practitioners resist/draw upon these public discourses to (re) position themselves as more or less 'professional'. In order to address these aims a re-reading or problematisation of hegemonic discourses was undertaken to unsettle and provide alternative discursive understandings of nursery staff. It is contended that nursery workers are refashioned through discourse in certain ways to satisfy societal and political goals (Foucault, 1980, 1983, 1994; Cannella, 1997). Further, such constructions manifest in forms of class/gender domination (Skeggs, 1997, 2003; Reay, 1998). In tracing the scope, nature and function of nursery provision, the highly politicised value that is attached to this marginalised group of largely working-class women becomes apparent.

It is important to recognise that the theoretical position in this study is not concerned to identify an authentic truth, since the fundamental unifying characteristic of poststructural approaches is that there is no one, single truth but rather a realm of possibilities dependent upon the subject position of the researcher (Davies, 2000). Through this investigation the aim is to present an alternative 'truth' to that offered and sustained through hegemonic public discourses. In this book certain discursive 'truths' are privileged over others to achieve emancipatory goals by offering insights into the marginalised lives of nursery workers. In rejecting positivism, the approach adopted does not conform to the enlightenment research tradition of making generalisations based upon a discovered truth (Parker, 1998).

The theoretical position emphasises the social construction of knowledge and rejection of essentialist understandings and realist theorisations of social life (Burr, 1995; Parker, 1998). It is concerned to stress that the experiences and lives of the women in my research are more than mere stories. Through exploring the power at play within their narratives I expose how my subjective reading relates to a specific socio-political and historical moment. Through the research process alternative readings of the gendered, classed and 'raced' lives of nursery workers becomes possible.

This account is concerned to expose the effects of power through and within discourse, and is informed by poststructuralist concerns to deconstruct and dismantle (see Derrida, 1972, 1976; Barthes, 1990). Foucault (1972, 1978, 1979, 1980, 1983, 1994) is of central importance since his various works provide a framework through which it is possible to demonstrate how certain taken-for-granted ideas come to be understood as reasonable, because they are formulated and reinstated through discourse. Foucault urges problematisation and presentation of alternative readings, and to seek to understand whose interests are served by creating and sustaining hegemonic discourses. In doing this it becomes possible to reach new understandings. This book questions widely held assumptions that nursery workers are persistently marginalised, pathologised and othered by virtue of their 'professional', classed, gendered and 'raced' identities. In challenging such constructions the potential for transformation and the exercise of personal agency is explored (Osgood, 2006a, 2006b). Through dismantling, unsettling and problematising societal constructions of what it means to be a woman engaged in work with young children, it is argued that the nursery worker can become constructed in alternative (and more positive) ways (Cannella, 1997), and so this book represents a project with feminist emancipatory, transformative potential to re-envision the nursery worker at this (social, political, economic) moment.

Book outline

The book is divided into eight chapters. This introduction is intended to set out the broad aims, objectives and theoretical positioning of the study. Through a review of relevant literature, Chapter 2 is devoted to mapping the context in which the study is located. Particular attention is drawn to studies that have informed and shaped this research. Key debates, policies and strategies designed to promote professionalism are introduced and outlined (e.g. the marketisation of childcare; the introduction of 'early years professional status'; the Tickell Review of the early years foundation stage curriculum). The chapter commentary provides a link across and between these debates, enabling readers to grasp how issues of professionalism within nurseries are addressed in popular/media debates and in policy and practice.

Chapter 3 provides the conceptual framework for the book. Readers are introduced to the theoretical tools that are employed in the book. The chapter contains separate sections which aim to develop critical understandings of the processes involved in identity construction. Attention is turned to concepts such as reflexivity, deconstruction, knowledge/'truth', discourse, power, subjectivity, agency and performativity. The chapter provides an account of the methodological approach taken in this study with early childhood practitioners.

Chapter 4 offers a critical deconstruction of government policy discourse. Through a problematisation and appraisal of official policy documents and related materials, the way in which 'the early years professional' has been constructed is exposed and attention paid to the myriad effects upon the ontological security of this group of workers.

Chapters 5, 6 and 7 draw directly upon the primary data gathered. Chapter 5 takes the social construction of childhood as its focus. The various discourses of childhood that are drawn upon, rejected, negotiated and created from personal experiences of being a child to professional encounters with children are explored. The specificity of this study, notably the political locatedness of nursery workers within a particular workforce reform agenda, is a key focus. The nursery workers' location within, and contribution to, a complex and contradictory discursive landscape is considered. By attending to a deconstruction and problematisation of the notion of childhood, the way in which practitioners wrestle with different discourses at different times and to what effect is demonstrated. Hegemonic constructions of childhood are named and the implications of such discourses for practitioners working in nurseries explored.

Chapter 6 is devoted to exploring the interconnections and tensions between maternalistic and professionalism discourses. Drawing on the autobiographical data provided by nursery workers, the classed, gendered and 'raced' assumptions surrounding motherhood and nursery work are exposed. I investigate the ways in which nursery workers become implicated in, and instrumental to, promoting maternalistic constructions. Congruence between maternalistic and authoritative ECEC discourses is identified; at first glance there appears to be considerable overlap and interplay. However, normalising middle-class discourses (about good/sensitive mothering; and about good/quality nursery provision) inflect and shape both maternalistic and authoritative ECEC discourse to provide a particular form of ECEC professionalism. It is argued that such professionalism permits a narrow, regulated and controlled form of 'other(ed)-motherliness'.

Chapter 7 focuses upon the construction of professional identities in nursery work. The argument offered in this chapter cumulatively builds upon the findings and discussions in earlier chapters. It summarises key debates within the academic field regarding identity construction. It explores the treatment of professionalism and the notable absence of debates around 'race'/ethnicity, gender and social class in research and practice. Specific attention is given to popular/dominant constructions of nursery workers, and these are contrasted with alternative, more critical, conceptualisations of professional identity and culture. The chapter questions what is meant by professionalism in the nursery. Illustrations are provided to help suggest ways that professionalism might be better understood as connected to autobiography, private aspects of the nursery workers' life, and subject to change. Issues of ethics and how to undertake autobiographical research are also discussed.

I critically debate the notion of professionalism in ECEC by drawing attention to policy discourses and the discursive constructions offered by the nursery workers. Considerable time is devoted to exploring the notions of emotional capital and emotional labour. Drawing together the various strands of argument offered throughout the book, I offer a theorisation of effective nursery work that places an emphasis and value on 'critically reflective emotional professionalism'.

The final chapter draws together themes and implications from throughout the book and makes suggestions and recommendations for future policy, research and practice. Conclusions and suggestions are made at a number of levels, including the conceptual, practical and strategic. Findings from previous chapters are synthesised and integrated to produce an analysis of the effects of the professionalisation agenda on nursery workers. For example, the idea that professionalism is gendered, classed and 'raced' and inherently linked to individual biography. The chapter also asks what lessons can be learnt and identifies transferable knowledge and implications for other practitioner groups engaged in work with children. Suggestions are made for nursery workers to critically appraise and reflect upon the importance of their biographies to their professional identities and practice.

Chapter 2

Policy context

The purpose of this chapter is to set out what has come before, map the salient themes that have informed the shape of the study and (in the Foucauldian tradition) to identify the unasked questions.

Setting the context

Early Childhood Education and Care (ECEC) services in England received unparalleled attention, resources and initiatives under the New Labour Government (1997–2010). During this period educational provision was massively expanded so that it became available to all three and four year olds. Since 1997 a raft of initiatives, developments and policies have come on stream and all share the principal objectives of expansion, affordability, quality and accessibility (although these terms have been variously deconstructed and problematised; for example, Dahlberg *et al.*, 1999). In effect, ECEC became an all-encompassing term, to occupy the concerns of 'joined-up' government as demonstrated by the authors of a key policy document, *Choice for Parents, the Best Start for Children: A Ten Year Strategy*, which included HM Treasury, Department for Education and Skills, Department for Work and Pensions and Department for Trade and Industry (HM Treasury *et al.*, 2004). This attention has continued under the Conservative–Liberal Democrat Government (2010–present) which, within its first year in office, commissioned a review of the Early Years Foundation Stage (Tickell, 2011). Despite appearing at a time of financial austerity, and under the uncertain politics of a coalition government, the review signals sustained support for early years, albeit in a pared-down form. The review indicates that the direction of policy in respect of the early years workforce remains broadly similar. This ongoing and intense attention denotes the central position that ECEC has come to occupy in education and social welfare policy developments.

However, inherent within these developments remains a conceptual division between 'education' and 'care' (Dahlberg *et al.*, 1999). While government policy emphasises the close relationship between education and care, administrative practice and policy formation continues to effectively compartmentalise the dual aspect of ECEC. This has important implications for the workforces that comprise ECEC services. The present system of staffing is highlighted by Moss (2006) as including a disparate mix of an elite body of teachers in nursery and reception classes and a much larger body of 'childcare workers' with generally lower levels of training and qualifications but who cover the entire early childhood range (0–5). In effect there is a two-tier system of ECEC in England. This distinction is important to understandings of how the childcare worker is constructed within/through public discourses and furthermore to understanding the subjective experiences of 'being a childcare worker'. The professional identities that childcare workers have of themselves are inflected and shaped by their everyday experiences within the setting that they work. But these identities are also shaped by and through wider discourses.

The local site within which the nursery worker is located was crucial to this research. A focus on different forms of nursery provision (i.e. statutory, voluntary and private sector) was important since this assured a degree of similarity in terms of work context, staff composition, pedagogical approaches and so on. However, by contrasting these three sectors, the opportunities to expose and explore arguments around the heterogeneous composition of the workforce (in terms of educational level, experience, and crucially sense of professionalism) and the differing structural inequalities became available. Furthermore, opportunities to explore the classed consumption of provision, i.e. who makes use of which provision, became available. So, for example, private sector nurseries are principally the preserve of relatively wealthy fee-paying middle-class parents, whilst voluntary nurseries tend to be located within the heart of diverse communities and often involve parent/mother volunteers. Meantime, statutory nurseries are widely constructed as the localised embodiment of national government policy, in that targeted and universal (fee paying and subsidised) places are available and highly qualified staff members tend to be appointed and rewarded with relatively preferable conditions of employment. The intersection of gendered, classed, 'raced' as well as professional identities provide a complex and important site of enquiry when the consumption of ECEC is analysed.

Drawing on recent literature, a number of important aspects of the ECEC workforce are highlighted. First, attention must be drawn to the highly gendered composition of the workforce. This aspect of ECEC has attracted much attention and is widely considered an important factor shaping the ways in which the occupation is viewed, the status which is attached to the work, and the nature of what happens in nurseries (in terms of pedagogical approaches and staff relations). I then turn to a growing body of literature that relates to research undertaken with parents who use childcare. The enormous growth in childcare is in part a consequence (and in part a cause) of increased labour market participation of working parents/mothers. Therefore the views, experiences and opinions of this group are important in considering how particular constructions of the childcare worker come to have currency in wider debates and act to shape public understandings.

Gender and the early years

Much research into the early years workforce has focused upon gender, and has found it to be a significant issue in terms of theory, policy and practice. What early years practitioners *do* with children, through the pedagogical approaches taken, has been widely debated and reconceptualised (Davies, 1989; Walkerdine, 1990; MacNaughton, 1998; Sumsion, 2005). As a consequence of this sustained attention, both theoretical and practical advancements have been made in the field of early childhood education and care. There is international evidence of gendered considerations of the early years curriculum, practices and activities (e.g. the international popularity of the Danish model of a 'gendered peda-gogy'; see Jensen, 1996). Poststructuralist commentators continue to trouble and unsettle this aspect of early childhood education and care so that greater reflexivity is exercised in the nursery (MacNaughton, 1998; Ryan, 2005), in training programmes (Goodfellow, 2004; Ryan and Grieshaber, 2005) and in policy formation (Cannella, 1997; Grieshaber, 2002; Sumsion, 2005). Whilst this considerable body of research is both important and influential, my specific concern is to focus upon the subjective identities of the early years practitioner. Clearly what practitioners do, and how they learn to do it, and the abilities/opportunities to reflect upon their pedagogical activities, is central to construct-ing and re-negotiating professional identities. However, the focus of this research was to understand the ways in which discourses outside the nursery intersect with practitioners' multiple understandings of themselves, for example as gendered, 'raced', classed subjects.

Therefore I turn to another, and related, gendered aspect of the nursery, the composition of the workforce, which is of more direct relevance to my research objectives. The 'feminised' nature of early childhood education and care has been the focus of much research, both nationally (Hilton, 1991; Elfer, 1994; Penn and McQuail, 1996; Mooney and Munton, 1997; Sataoen, 1998; Cameron *et al.*, 1999; Brannen and Moss, 2002) and internationally (Clyde, 1989; Cameron, 1997; Penn, 1997; Owen *et al.*, 1998; Dahlberg *et al.*, 1999). In most research about the gendered nature of ECEC the term 'feminised' is taken to have a dual meaning: first, it refers to the numerical predominance of women; and second, that the nature of the work is founded upon an essentialist understanding of 'femi-nine' characteristics (i.e. nurturance, care, emotion). A recent publication by the EOC (2006) reveals that childcare continues to be the most female dominated of all occupations in Great Britain, with 98 per cent of the workforce comprising women. Despite popular belief that Nordic countries have more gender equal soci-eties, Cameron *et al.* (1999) found the percentage of men working in childcare to remain nevertheless low (e.g. three per cent in Sweden, four per cent in Finland and five per cent in Denmark and Norway respectively). Whilst it does not necessarily follow that because the workforce is numerically dominated by women that the work undertaken will be 'feminine', those researching this issue tend to take this as a starting point; for example, Cameron *et al.* (1999) state:

our central proposition is that gender is, perhaps unwittingly, embedded within the being of childcare institutions and childcare work... [It] is widely understood to be, and is practiced as, women's work, something that women 'naturally' do...childcare work has been modelled on a particular concept of care – 'mother-care'.

(p. 8)

In taking this particular understanding of the gendered practice, composition and power relations within nursery settings, through their research Cameron and colleagues set out to explore what effect gender (i.e. a minority male presence in a predominantly female workforce) has upon institutional relations between staff, between staff and parents, and in working with pre-school children.

The study included 21 childcare workers (11 male, 10 female), who were drawn from ten institutions from the private sector (two day nurseries and a Montessori school); voluntary sector (two family centres and one worker's co-operative children's centre); and public sector (three day nurseries/combined centres, and one family centre). The study also involved interviews with 77 parents (52 mothers and 25 fathers) whose children attended one of the ten institutions. The principal focus of the research was to explore the experiences of male childcare workers; to understand their reasons for entering a female-dominated occupation; and to explore the relationships men have with female colleagues, children and parents in everyday work and practice. The authors, however, argue that the study was also concerned to understand 'gender in the workforce' by comparing the experiences and views of women and men working in ECEC. The authors intended that the study should 'make visible' their finding that work with young children is underpinned by gendered understandings of the job. They argue that the work of childcare

is not only gendered by virtue of the distribution in the workforce but ideas on which the work is based are also infused with gendered understandings of roles...the work is threaded with ideas about caring as substitute motherhood. This posed difficulties for men workers, whose role within childcare work is seen to be at odds with emulating motherhood

(p. 158)

The conclusions reached tend to emphasise a 'caring as substitute motherhood' discourse, which could be seen to rest upon binary gender divisions and essentialist conceptualisations. Where the authors identified alternative models of childcare they tended to rest upon the differences between men and women; for example

men were described as 'playful', 'spontaneous', and 'fun'. These kinds of attributes could be meshed with theories of workers as co-constructors to develop new models of workers' methods with young children that are less reliant on a model of nurturance derived from, and informed by, ideologies of motherhood...akin to the Norwegian debate on 'masculine caring'.

(p. 166)

I find the authors' position problematic for two reasons. First, that this 'alternative model' appears only available to men; because women were not described as playful, spontaneous or fun renders them excluded from the possibilities of 'masculine caring' (Nilsen and Manum, 1998). Second, nurturance, caring, emotion and so on are widely considered vital attributes to those working with young children (Katz, 1995; Friere, 1999; Moyles, 2001), but because they are constructed as 'feminine' characteristics they are denigrated in public discourse and have come to be equated with low status. However, I would argue that is not reason enough for them to be banished from the 'models' that workers adopt when working with young children. Elsewhere I have argued that early years practitioners should reclaim such a model as part of a process of resisting neo-liberal demands for performative practice (Osgood, 2006a). Furthermore, Cameron et al.'s (1999) offer of an alternative model based upon the premise of 'masculine caring' could act to deny men the option of performing what has come to be considered 'feminised' childcare practice. Through my study with nursery practitioners the discourse of 'childcare as substitute motherhood' was widely refuted; this is a theme I develop further in Chapter 6.

Cameron et al. (1999) extend their argument by recognising the limitations of (potentially) essentialist conclusions by referring to 'multiple gender identities, in order to lend complexity' (p. 158). I would argue that this aspect of the study could have been developed further to understand the differences between the female workers and between the male workers' experiences and views, as well as comparison between men and women. Whilst the principal focus of the study (to explore male workers' experiences) was satisfied, I would suggest that the secondary aim to make visible gender issues might have been expanded. The authors claim to explore 'the idea of *difference* and show how a tension exists for workers between being different from each other and being the same as each other' (p. 167). However, 'difference' appears to be limited to 'gender' difference, not other markers. Although reference is made to 'religious and cultural background', this was in relation to parents.

The absence of either a classed or 'raced' analysis represents a missed opportunity to explore the intersectionality of multiple identities (Anthias and Yuval-Davies, 1992; Phoenix, 1994) in childcare workers' understandings of themselves. The study was concerned with differences in terms of gender, but I would argue that to understand the subjective experiences of nursery workers requires consideration and analyses of the effects that other markers of difference, such as class background, 'race', age, sexuality and so on, have upon subjective experiences of being and doing childcare work. I would argue that exploring and seeking to understand the salience of differences between women (in nurseries) has the potential to challenge received wisdom and acceptance of the 'mother substitute' model of childcare. Consequently, instersectionality of multiple identities has come to shape the direction of my research with nursery workers, and analyses of the data reflect this concern.

Whilst Cameron *et al.*'s (1999) study explores (gendered) constructions of the (male) nursery worker, a range of other important groups play a significant role in identity construction, negotiation, acceptance/resistance of all nursery workers, not just male nursery workers. Therefore, I now turn to research that has principally gathered the views of parents who make use of childcare provision.

Parental understandings of the childcarer

There is a growing body of literature about parental experiences of using childcare (Brannen and Moss, 1991, 1998; Holloway, 1998; Crompton, 2001) and hence understandings of the ways in which the childcare worker is constructed by this 'user-group'. I am particularly interested to review the relationship between middle-class parents and childcare workers, as this is a powerful theme to emerge from the research undertaken with nursery workers in this study. The discursive positioning that participants experienced in respect of their relationships with middle-class parents was amongst some of the most emotive to appear in the data and will form the basis of discussions in later chapters.

Middle-class parents' relationship with their childcarers has been the focus of much research and commentary (e.g. Jordan *et al.*, 1994; Crompton, 2001), but I want to outline the findings from research undertaken by Carol Vincent and colleagues (Ball and Vincent, 1998; Vincent and Ball, 2001, 2006; Vincent *et al.*, 2003) as this particular study shares a number of similarities to my own, in that it was located in London, occurred within the same policy climate, addressed similar concerns around nursery provision (rather than exclusively childminding, which forms the primary focus of much research in this area, e.g. Uttal, 1996, 1997, 2002) and includes the views and experiences of nursery workers (albeit as a very small sub-sample of childcare providers).

Between 2001 and 2003 Vincent *et al.* undertook a study of predominantly white, middle-class families in two areas of London (Battersea and Stoke Newington) to explore how middle-class parents choose childcare for their pre-school children (aged 0–5 years) and how they interact with childcare providers. The study involved 109 qualitative semi-structured interviews with 71 parents (57 mothers, 14 fathers). Twenty-one childcare providers were also interviewed (the sample was selected from childcarers used directly by respondent families). The research found that childcare is 'saturated by emotions', with tensions arising from financial exchange and emotional dimensions of childcare. The authors found that childcare is highly gendered, 'with the main players in both supply and demand being women'. Furthermore, they found that mothers play a central role in childcare by changing their working practices, taking the 'choice' to work either full time, part time or to retract from their careers altogether whilst their children are very young (whereas fathers' careers remained unchanged by parenting responsibilities) and for choosing, then subsequently managing, relationships with childcarers.

Vincent and Ball (2006) published their research in a book entitled *Childcare, Choice and Class Practices*. Therein the authors attend to a specific focus upon the relationship between middle-class parents and their childcarer, and highlight the issues of power and control that shape such relationships. They contend that the childcare market is provider driven, in that parents (mothers) are resigned to take what is available rather than provision that satisfies their perceived needs. The authors identified antagonism between parents and their childcarer. Although this antagonism was rarely overt or directed at individuals, it was often class-inflected. Relationships were frequently characterised by opposing agendas: parents held strong (and often negative) opinions about childcarers and childcare providers held equally forceful opinions about motherhood; such opinions were said to be characterised by dissension and fracture. For example, a number of childcarers believed that mothers should renege on careers in order to assume full-time mothering responsibility. Meantime, many of the mothers raised doubts over the intellectual capacities and the professionalism of childcarers. Whilst such views were expressed to Vincent and her colleagues throughout the course of the research, they were not recounted within the working relationship between parent and childcarer; this led the authors to conclude that such relationships were characterised by absences and silences:

> Silence surrounds issues of power and control shaping carer–family relationships. There is a tendency for each party to see itself as vulnerable and reliant on the other: carers on the parents' behaviour as service users, their ultimate say in dictating the extent of the relationship with the child; and parents on carer's behaviour towards their children.
>
> (p. 134)

Uttal (2002: 110) refers to this situation as 'dual powerlessness' locating it as a result of 'the political economy of the childcare market which privatises care and devalues [childcare] labour'.

The body of research about middle-class parents (and Vincent and Ball's 2006 study in particular) is especially salient and useful as it provides valuable insights into the complex relationships that exist between childcare workers and the parents who make use of them. The issues of power and control are especially important as I contend that the ontological insecurity that nursery workers feel in relation to their sense of professionalism is shaped by and through hegemonic discourses. As such, it is important to locate my research, so that discourses of middle-class parent(s)/mother(s) are exposed as one of several important forces that come to shape subjective identity constructions of the nursery worker.

Having drawn attention to specific research studies that help to locate my own research I want now to turn to a more conceptual debate, drawing on a wider body of literature in an attempt to address the question: what/whose purpose(s) does childcare serve? By undertaking this exercise I aim to demonstrate the power borne by hegemonic discourses to discursively position nursery workers in certain ways. I draw attention to competing yet intersecting themes: 'the needs of the working mother' and 'the politicised nursery worker'. I trace how these themes are produced/underpinned by discourses (through research, popular culture and policy formation) and the potential effects that they might have upon the professional identities of childcare workers. This exercise in mapping the fabricated identities of the nursery worker acts to outline the underpinning rationale and direction of my study.

The fabricated identity of the nursery worker

'Fostering a generation of Vicky Pollards'[1] was the headline in an edition of The *Guardian* (2006a). The article described how the chair of the Professional Association of Teachers lambasted nursery workers for failing to meet minimum standards or present positive role models. She went on to state that a growing number of young (female) nursery staff dress inappropriately, with long nails and 'chunky' shoes, frequently complain about hangovers and are unable to articulate beyond 'yeah-but, no-but' or to spell beyond the limits of text-messaging. The work of Skeggs (1997, 2003) and Bourdieu (1986) usefully explore the interplay between class aesthetics and power. Tracing the origins of this postmodern class prejudice provides a useful starting place for mapping out the social construction of women who make up the nursery workforce.

The absence of a class analysis in the study by Cameron *et al.* (1999) leaves many unexplored and unanswered questions that are central to understanding how nursery workers come to conceive of themselves as professional (or not). The analogous reference above to Vicky Pollard demonstrates that classed understandings of the nursery worker are prevalent and hence potentially very damaging. Vincent and Ball in their analyses, however, address the very highly classed nature of the relationship that exists between a sample of middle-class mothers and (working-class) childcarers. As illustrated above, such relationships are fraught with emotion, tension, prejudice, silences and antagonism. Through their research and analysis Vincent and Ball have 'made visible' the classed dimension of the relationship between parent (mother) and childcarer. Whilst the sample of 109 parents in two localised areas of London could appear very focused, the massive expansion of childcare has resulted in such relationships becoming far more commonplace. With over 55 per cent of mothers currently working (EOC, 2006), the experiences that Vincent and Ball represent will have resonance more widely. Therefore concerns over the needs of working (middle-class) mothers have come to occupy space in both the public conscience and in policy formation. By drawing on a wide range of literature, and referring back to the studies by Cameron *et al.* (1999) and Vincent and Ball (2006), my intention is to trace the origins of this concern and demonstrate the power that it has in relation to the professional identity constructions of 'the nursery worker'.

Needs of the working mother

The provision of childcare has been historically constructed in feminist discourses as a means to achieve emancipation (David, 1980). In the 1960s and 1970s second-wave feminists were concerned with gaining full social and economic equality; as such, debates included the 'debilitating' issue of motherhood and the need for childcare, with the main thrust of the argument following the logic that if there was more affordable childcare then women would be facilitated to enter the labour market (Siann *et al.*, 2000). In overcoming the 'obstacle' of maternal childcare, it was assumed that women would then be in a position to concentrate on achieving material equality with men in a patriarchal society (Friedan, 1963). Obviously, this is a gross over-simplification, and not intended to undermine the feminist cause of that era. Rather, stating it in such terms allows for a critical examination of the silences that such an argument allows. It is important to ask precisely which women were emancipated and enabled to compete with men and by implication which women were denied such opportunities. Witz (1992) is amongst many feminist commentators to argue that the labour market is a site of complex and cross-cutting inequalities of class, 'race' and gender. The modernist grand narratives and binary conceptualisations of gendered difference in second-wave feminism were exposed as inadequate and led to feminist theorisations of differences *between* women, as well as of commonalities of women's positions in, and experiences of, paid work (Walby, 1990, 1997; Anthias and Yuval-Davies, 1992; Bradley, 1996).

Liberal feminism of the 1960s and 1970s was criticised and exposed as being dominated by white middle-class concerns, and hence principally meeting the needs of white middle-class women. The feminist bell hooks produced an influential body of work (hooks, 1981, 1984, 2000a, 2000b) which highlighted the serious short-comings of feminism in its failure to represent the voices/experiences of 'other' women. The silencing of those 'other' women was particularly problematic for a movement united upon a shared gendered identity but which failed to acknowledge other marks of difference such as 'race', class, sexuality, age and so on. For authors and activists representing those 'othered' groups, awareness of, and engagement with, 'difference' entered into the feminist arena, and the focus on intersectionality and the importance of multiple identities has come to occupy a central place in contemporary feminist theorising (Spivak, 1987; Anthias and Yuval-Davies, 1992; Brah, 1992; Bhavani and Phoenix, 1994; Reay, 1996; and more recently Reay, 2004; Francis and Archer, 2005).

Whilst endeavours to understand difference are prominent within academic poststructuralist feminism, the effects of achievement of liberal feminism's goals (i.e. the growth of women in middle-class occupations) continue to be mirrored by female marginalisation elsewhere in the labour market. In this respect, nurseries and nursery staff represent a stubborn challenge to the gains of second wave feminists. To facilitate the equalisation of some women/mothers (through social mobility) has (necessarily) meant that others are positioned in servitude.

Through their social positioning (low pay, poor status, long hours, poor working conditions; see CESI, 2006) nursery workers are relatively regulated, surveilled and controlled (Foucault, 1979; Novinger and O'Brien, 2003; Osgood, 2006a, 2006c; Fenech and Sumsion, 2007). It is my contention that liberal feminism has failed to fully engage in the differences between women, in particular the consequences of class difference and unequal power relations.

Therefore, it is crucial to understand the ways in which mothers *use* nursery workers and to unearth the nature of such relationships; to understand whether there is capacity for respectful relationships to emerge – relationships wherein difference is acknowledged but attempts to understand and accept difference are possible (Uttal, 2002). As reviewed, the recent research with middle-class parents by Vincent and Ball (2006) paints a largely bleak picture of the views and experiences held of early years staff. The nuanced class analysis that the authors undertake reveals that class prejudice and emotionality are key in shaping opinions. They illustrate, from the perspectives of middle-class mothers, the complexity of such relationships, and expose tensions and prejudices. Whilst Vincent and Ball (op. cit.) included a small sample of childcarers, these were spread across the range of sectors, and they draw heavily upon the experiences of home-based care where the emotional dimension of the relationship becomes further heightened. My research provides an opportunity to explore many of the same issues but from the perspective of a sample of nursery workers, and so builds upon Cameron *et al.*'s (1999) considerations for the occupational setting and impact of staff relations upon professional identities.

Differences between women: the working mother and the nursery worker

Although many members of the nursery workforce are themselves working mothers, discourses around 'work–life balance' have increasingly produced a dichotomy whereby consumers of childcare are typically middle-class professional working mothers, and nursery workers are not readily constructed as working mothers. Many commentators highlight that women working in (child)care do not enjoy recognition and respect for their labour market contribution in the ways that mothers working in professional careers can be understood to (Hochschild, 2003). A recent survey (CESI, 2006) found that nursery staff remain unrewarded for a critical contribution, earn only a fraction of the salary awarded to teachers, work long hours and have no guarantee of professional development and training activities. Furthermore, many practical tasks undertaken in the course of a day's work at nursery are precisely what 'working mothers' commit to escape by pursuing (professional middle-class) careers. The domesticated and emotional nature of much work in the nursery is negatively constructed as an extension of the practical skills involved in mothering (Oakley, 2005). In short, the toil of a nursery worker is constructed as hyper-feminine in public discourse and hence lacks much exchange value in the labour market (Skeggs, 2003), and the subsequent lack of status contributes to a cyclical scenario where the work is undervalued, underpaid and the preserve of working-class women (McKie *et al.*, 2001; Osgood, 2005).

Literature about mothers working in professional occupations (Nicolson, 2002) reveals that decisions *not* to embark on a full-time mothering role are related to a desire for self-esteem, a firm and valued identity, financial security and so on. Nicolson (1996, 2002) is supported by Walters (2005) in arguing that the realities of returning to work are complex; the psychological and social benefits that many working mothers anticipate come to intersect with the demands of motherhood in unexpected ways. The psychological costs of balancing careers and motherhood are well rehearsed. Nevertheless, recent figures issued by the Equal Opportunities Commission (2006) reveal there has been an increasing trend in Great Britain for the majority of mothers with dependent children (55 per cent) to attempt to combine both work and motherhood, by working either full time (42 per cent) or part time (58 per cent). Evidently, combining part-time employment with motherhood is the most prevalent arrangement currently for women living in Britain. This 'solution', although very 'popular', is problematic, and the inability to achieve a 'work–life balance' or to 'have it all' is widely researched and theorised (see Nicolson, 1996, 2002; Aveling, 2002; Walters, 2005). The challenge of combining motherhood and a career receives vast media coverage, perhaps precisely because many of the journalists, editors and novelists concerned are themselves 'working mums'. For example, the popular magazine *She* is written by and for busy (middle-class) working mothers, as are best-selling books such as Allison Pearson's (2003) *I Don't Know How She Does It* (which gave an autobiographical account of 'juggling' a professional career and the demands of motherhood) and Libby Purves' (2004) *How Not to be a Perfect Mother* (which again is an autobiographical tale of balancing the competing demands of domesticity – including how to manage nannies – and a successful career). Websites such as www.mothersatwork.co.uk have also grown in popularity and provide evidence of the ways in which working-mother discourses become embedded in understandings of organisations, law, policy, and family structures and behaviours.

Meantime, an equally large but alternative body of literature exists that indicates 'stay-at-home mums' feel devalued by society, and so the psychic 'costs' of reneging on a professional career in favour of full-time maternity are considerable (Hock *et al.*, 1980; Pungello and Kurtz-Costes, 1999, 2000; Seo, 2003). Whichever 'choice' parents (ergo mothers) opt for, the angst and turmoil that is experienced is considered to be serious and persistent (Hakin, 2001; Caproni, 2004; Smithson and Stokoe, 2005; Dilworth and Kingsbury, 2005; Vincent and Ball, 2006). Furthermore, like Runte and Mills (2004), I would argue that it is still a very serious and persistent *feminist* issue.

This situation should be of particular concern to feminists since it is an issue that touches all women's lives whether childfree, career mums or mums with careers. Whichever camp the middle-class mother sits in, she is negatively discursively positioned as either the 'boring stay-at-home mum' or as the 'heartless career-obsessed harridan' by wider gender discourses. The defence then becomes to either discursively battle against each other or to project the sense of anxiety/guilt at using childcare onto those females who provide the care. Whatever the case, women (mothers) are pitched against each other in apparently gender-neutral territory of achieving a work–life balance.

The predicament faced by middle-class mothers raised above resonates with those of second wave feminists, in that the experiences and relative oppression of women who do not experience the privileges that come with a middle-class existence are invisible from the debate, and in effect their experiences become silenced (Ehrenreich and Hochschild, 2003; Armstrong, 2006). Transferring the negative constructions about middle-class mothers who perform childcare full time provides some insight into the ways in which nursery workers are constructed in public discourse, i.e. feeling devalued, invisible, marginal (Osgood, 2005). Notwithstanding this similarity, though, it can be argued that middle-class, stay-at-home mothers occupy privileged positions when compared to the average nursery worker (who may also be a mother but often doesn't have the financial option to stay at home).

As Steedman (1986) recounts in her semi-autobiographical account of motherhood and work in the 1920s and 1950s, the demands to combine paid work and motherhood are by no means new to working-class women. The challenges of 'juggling' and 'balancing' have long been the preserve of working-class mothers, and this historicity may explain the marginalisation of working-class women's experiences from the current 'needs of the working mothers discourse' (Warren, 2000, 2003, 2004). Armstrong (2006) presents a convincing theorisation of class difference between middle-class and working-class mothers who combine paid employment and motherhood. She identifies a conceptual difference, with middle-class mothers approaching the competing demands as 'compromised individualism' whilst working-class mothers embody 'relational-pragmatic' dispositions, and women who have traversed class boundaries through processes of social mobility experiencing acute ambivalence. I draw upon and develop Armstrong's theorisations later in this chapter, under the heading of 'A genealogy of the "politicised nursery worker"', to illustrate how policy formation is both classed and gendered. In effect, the working-class/working mother/nursery worker is marginal to hegemonic 'working mother' discourses and family-friendly, work–life balance rhetoric that has come to shape current debates about women in employment.

Aside from an 'average' annual salary of £10,000 (DfES, 2003b), nursery workers do not have the same access to 'hot knowledge' (Ball and Vincent, 1998) or the necessary social and cultural capital to make visible their marginalisation and subjugation (Bourdieu, 2000). Therefore, their 'plight' is not made public in the way that the voices of articulate, media savvy middle-class mothers are (e.g. see http://ftmuk.wordpress.com). Such forums provide opportunities for full-time mothers to share experiences and gain access to information and guidance, but another element of the movement is to critique perceived inadequacies of nursery provision and nursery workers (http://www.daycaresdontcare.org). In many ways the populist messages generated within 'stay-at-home-mum' discourses resonate with damning comments made by the chair of the Professional Association of Teachers (outlined earlier).

With these considerations in mind I argue that a focus upon the differences *between* women is vital to the debate around the ways in which nursery workers are constructed through discourse. I have argued that many mothers (often middle-class professionals) who use childcare in effect fail to recognise the relative oppression experienced by many nursery workers, or worse, create/sustain hegemonic discourses based upon negative stereotypes (Uttal, 1996, 2002; Vincent and Ball, 2001, 2006).

The childcare 'market'

Increasingly, terms such as 'childcare market' are used to describe the occupational landscape of nursery provision (Vincent and Ball, 2001, 2006; Blackburn, 2004). The use of the term 'market' is resisted and widely critiqued in other areas of education (e.g. schools and universities: Bowe *et al.*, 1992; Hey, 1996; Avis, 2003; Ball, 2003b). This resistance is principally due to the connotations the term conjures of processes of rationalisation, commercialisation and the prevalence of economic concerns (see for example Mahony and Hextall, 2000; Ozga, 2000; Ball, 2003a). However, in the context of childcare, the concept of the 'market' appears more readily accepted, because of the significant and growing presence of the private sector and opportunities for private investors to profit from this demand-led industry (although criticism from within the academy is increasingly heard: Kilderry, 2006; Osgood, 2006c; Fenech and Sumsion, 2007).

The heterogeneity within early childhood education and care, outlined at the start of this chapter, further compounds the situation by limiting the possibilities for unified resistance (Osgood, 2004). Debates continue about precisely what ECEC (the term most widely accepted to describe this fragmented and diverse sector) encompasses. A lack of consensus prevails over precisely what age range is catered for; although 0–5 years is widely accepted, there nevertheless exist alternative distinctions and boundaries. As also rehearsed earlier, distinctions between education and care have damaging implications for secure professional identities to be fostered (Dahlberg *et al.*, 1999; Dahlberg and Moss, 2005).

The lack of clarity and certainty around the precise focus and remit of ECEC is in part a consequence of rapid development due to increased demand from working parents. As I demonstrate below (under the heading 'A genealogy of the "politicised nursery worker"'), a discussion about the role of policy formation and political discourses reveals that the ways in which ECEC is conceptualised are complex and in some respects part of an exercise in social engineering (Hammersley, 2000), and also the consequence of an evolutionary process in a capitalist, market-driven society (Du Gay, 1996). The effects of the market in childcare, though, act to position the nursery worker as the front-line service provider, who is accountable to the customer, the employer and ultimately society, and as such is positioned within a regulatory gaze (Foucault, 1979; Osgood, 2006a, 2006b, 2006c).

The increased formalisation of the financial exchange between 'customer' and 'service provider' in the childcare market can be argued to have had the effect of heightening expectations, and consequently the foundations of the nursery–parent relationship have shifted (Fuqua and Labensohn, 1986; Uttal, 2002; Vincent and Ball, 2006). Neo-liberal emphases upon choice, accountability, consumer rights and customer satisfaction are argued to have 'hardened' the relationship (Osgood, 2004; Kilderry, 2006; Fenech and Sumsion, 2007). Parents bring expectations of what nursery provision should encompass and anticipate that the fees paid will ensure these expectations are largely satisfied (Chaplin *et al.*, 1996).

Pressures for nursery providers to adopt more entrepreneurial and commercial approaches to their 'business' are foregrounded in government discourse (see Osgood, 2005). Whilst such reforms were implemented to 'safeguard financial viability and sustainability', the (unintended) impact upon the quality of relationships between nursery workers and parents has had an important influence upon social constructions of the nursery worker (Osgood, 2004).

An emotional market

Accompanying such developments is the question posed by Vincent and Ball (2001) in the title of their paper, 'A market in love?', which is indicative of the emotionality implicit within relationships between parents and the childcare provider. Similarly, Colley (2006) suggests that trainee nursery nurses in her research were 'learning to labour with feeling'. Hakin (2001) highlights the tensions between the emotional investments parents (mothers) make about childcare provision and the demands for rational decision making that financial decisions require. The construction of parent as customer/client/consumer and the nursery as service provider theoretically creates a 'business-like' encounter. However, the considerable fees that parents (ineligible for government subsidies) pay frequently attract the attention of media and are a cause for public outcry, yet, as discussed earlier, an average nursery worker salary accounts for only a fraction of the fees generated by many private sector nurseries. Nursery workers are feeling the 'terrors of performativity' (Ball, 2003a) from a neo-liberal climate shaped by demands for accountability, transparency, efficiency, performativity and so on but reap few rewards from the financial gains that are generated through commercialisation of nursery provision.

As outlined above, the 'choice' that ambitious, professional, middle-class women encounter can contribute to feelings of guilt (Walzer, 1997). For the majority of women who opt to return to work after the birth of their child(ren), assurances are sought that nursery provision is good quality and that the experience will be beneficial to their child, or at the very least not harmful (Hakin, 2001; Vincent and Ball, 2006). Margaret Nelson (1989, 1990) argues that working mothers have instrumental relationships with daycare providers. She claims that childcare is constructed as a commodity – a flexible, convenient and affordable commodity. But in constructing it this way working mothers come to define the relationship narrowly. Vincent and Ball (2006) challenge this claim and point instead to a raft of emotions that characterise the relationship. Amongst those emotions was guilt that many mothers feel at returning to paid employment. The class-inflected relationships that Vincent and Ball (op. cit.) point to demonstrate ways in which middle-class mothers construct their childcarer in deficit terms. 'Deficiencies' in terms of (working-class styles of) speech, dress and behaviour that (some of the) middle-class mothers (in Vincent and Ball's study) perceived can contribute to stereotypical understandings of Vicky Pollard-like nursery workers. The very public declarations of deficiency, such as those voiced by the chair of the Professional Association of Teachers, act to reinforce negative constructions of nursery workers.

Therefore, attacks upon the nursery workforce appear to stem from a complex web of objectification (Foucault, 1978). In effect, nursery workers become constructed within and through the 'needs of the working-mother discourse' as deficient but necessary: 'necessary' to meet societal and feminist pressures to work; and 'necessarily deficient' to comfort the working mothers' psycho-social well-being (Tuominen, 2003). As nursery provision becomes ever more commercialised, so there is a danger that neo-liberal rationalism and austerity will exacerbate this situation and contribute to sustain class prejudice (Reay, 1997).

As outlined above, the childcare 'market' comprises a complex tapestry of provision; however, nurseries are easier to define and principally comprise statutory, voluntary and private sector settings. Whilst there is considerable parity between the three sectors of nursery provision (Ofsted inspected, strict adult:worker ratios, similar staff structures and so on), the composition of the workforce varies. Research (Bertram, 2005) has shown that private sector nurseries typically have a younger staff group, with fewer qualifications and the most acute recruitment and retention issues. Yet private sector nurseries meet the needs of middle-class parents because long day care is extended, and they are located within easy reach of home/work and offer safe, clean, orderly environments (Hakin, 2001). So a paradox emerges wherein those who are paying the most for childcare arguably are not guaranteed to receive the highest quality. This results in a stereotypical construction of nursery workers as deficient. But what is often hidden from the parental view is the inadequate training available to permanent members of staff, poor salaries and long hours, which leads to low staff morale and high staff turnover (Strober *et al.*, 1995; CESI, 2006). This study aims to demonstrate the debilitating effects of such structural barriers *and* the damaging implications of the discursive positioning of nursery workers in hegemonic discourses (including those generated and perpetuated by dissatisfied parents).

The development of my argument around 'the needs of the working mother' acts to illustrate how the power of such themes can create subjects; Foucault (1978) identifies this as a working definition of discourse. I have thus demonstrated how a 'needs of the working mother' discourse is inflected by, and acts to inform other discourses through/within which nursery workers come to understand and accept/resist their professional identities. I have drawn attention to the differences between women, between different types of mother (the working mother, the part-time mother, the full-time mother). The effect social class can have upon approaches to work has also been presented, and demonstrates that the middle-class privilege of 'choice' can become emotional and traumatic, not only to the middle-class parent (mother) in reaching decisions about childcare, but also for the nursery worker who can become implicated and therefore constructed in certain (negative) ways. The absence of the nursery worker (as working mother) from 'the needs of the working mother' discourse is significant. The privileging of the middle-class experience in discourses around work–life balance and juggling acts around childcare/paid employment act to effectively obscure and silence the experiences of working-class mothers (nursery workers included) from the debate. Yet the nursery worker still occupies a central position in such debates, but she becomes narrowly defined in negatively stereotypical ways (as a means to an end).

I now turn to other hegemonic discourses through which nursery workers are constructed in particular ways. Foucault took institutions (law, medicine, government) within society to exercise power and create and sustain dominant discourses, but which draw upon existing discourses (Foucault, 1980, 1994). Extending the arguments presented in respect of 'the needs of the working mother' discourse, I intend to map the ways in which the nursery worker has been constructed as a politicised entity through government discourses.

A genealogy of the 'politicised nursery worker'

The role of government in relation to childcare has shifted significantly over the past 30 years. Under successive Conservative governments (1979–1992) policy was limited to regulation of childcare provision. Childcare providers received limited budgetary support and even less policy attention; as a result childcare was largely self-regulated, albeit with notable exceptions of concerns for the health, safety and well-being of children, as encompassed in *The Children Act* (Department of Health, 1989). Under the Act, local authorities were given the principal responsibility for co-ordinating and providing services for children in need. This responsibility typically fell to social services and teams of under-eights workers (McQuail and Pugh, 1995). Over this period the number of statutory nurseries fell and there was an expansion in childminding and private and voluntary sector nurseries. Randall (2000) presents this era in childcare as characterised by a laissez-faire approach by the state and limited resource allocation, allowing for neo-liberal market forces to shape the extent and nature of provision (Hammersley, 2000). Where government did intervene it was only with the intention of enhancing market forces and orchestrating further retraction of state investment. For example, under the administration of John Major (1992–1997), the government target was to reduce state provision and allow for expansion of the private and voluntary sectors; the introduction of childcare vouchers was considered the means by which such a restructuring could occur (Randall, 2000).

The election success of the New Labour Party in 1997 marked a significant tide change to the way in which childcare services were governed and constructed in political discourses. The Government set out ambitious plans for childcare in its *National Childcare Strategy* announced in 1998; expansion, co-ordination and regulatory mechanisms were outlined. Whereas childcare had assumed a marginal position under Conservative Party rule, by contrast New Labour placed it at the heart of its social inclusion agenda (Levitas, 1998).

Related to the discussion outlined in preceding sections of this chapter, the needs of working parents (mothers) were cited as paramount in government employment/social policy (DfES, 1997). Increased childcare places were believed to be the means to facilitate greater labour-market participation, and hence improve national economic prosperity (Randall, 2000).

The sustained focus upon citizenship through work and the need for childcare to meet the 'challenge' of expansion, quality, affordability and so on has come to normalise certain attitudes, or as Irwin (2004) states: 'Norms and their reshaping are important; [they] manifest in [a] routine expectation, across an expanding section of the population, that women with young children will engage in paid employment' (para. 1.9).

Irwin (2004) goes on to illustrate that norms are vitally important in shaping gendered work and care commitments, and she seeks to demonstrate how these 'mesh with social structural processes'. The attitudes of working parents/mothers, employers and nursery workers are shaped and inflected by the normalising technologies of the state (Foucault, 1994). Under New Labour, parents and the childcare workforce have been party to a sustained rhetoric that conflates 'worthy citizen' with 'employed parent/mother' (Hey, 1996; Levitas, 1998). Williams (1999) and Dean (2001) argue that social policy is misaligned to the preferences of many parents, especially mothers committed to caring for their children. The conflicting emphases upon increased female employment and continuities in ideologies of good mothering present a double burden, and generate new moral dilemmas and levels of guilt for many mothers (Dean, 2001; McKie *et al.*, 2001; Saugeres and Duncan, 2002). Hey and Bradford (2006) highlight a series of assumptions inherent within government policies about the working mother and point to the 'persistence of the ideology that paid work is the *best* (and *only*) way to ensure individual and social prosperity...this emphasis makes "unthinkable" alternative settlements...of the care of young children...within social and economic relations' (p. 4).

Related to the increasingly normalised aim to increase maternal employment rates amongst the middle classes was a commitment to early 'intervention' in (working-class) family life to address a range of societal ills (Levitas, 1998). The year 1999 saw the introduction of Sure Start local programmes, which were designed to meet the 'needs' of the poorest communities across the country. Within Sure Start policies, mothers with constrained 'choice' (about whether or not to participate in the labour market) were a key target group. For families living in high levels of deprivation (in inner city locations), nursery education (and related family support services) became constructed as the means to remedy inadequacies of poor family nurturing (Hey and Bradford, 2006). Hence the increasing proliferation of local Sure Start programmes, made provision for child-care, family support services and encouragement for maternal employment.

The overt commitment to increase maternal employment, of both middle-class professional and working-class mothers (Hey and Bradford, 2006), positions the early childhood workforce in contradictory ways. As outlined earlier, discourses around the '*needs* of the working mother' are founded upon a normalised mid-dle-class understanding of maternal employment. The hegemonic discourses that encompass the professional middle-class mother and her childcarer are inflected with power relations based upon an exchange of labour founded upon a classed relationship (Vincent and Ball, 2006). However, a shift of power takes place when the early childhood professional is located within the context of Sure Start, serv-ing the *needs* of disadvantaged communities (i.e. working-class mothers and their children). The nursery worker, although constructed in particular ways within policy discourses, has the potential to transform and traverse accepted concep-tualisations of her subject position depending upon the context within which she is located at any given time. In effect, her expert knowledge and professional wisdom becomes accepted/interpreted in different ways at different times (Sachs, 2001; Goodfellow, 2004). This tension is explored fully in the chapters that fol-low where an analysis of the narratives of the nursery workers in this study are drawn upon.

Many commentators have stressed the implications of placing the early child-hood workforce, and therefore the nursery worker, at the heart of government policy. For example, Jones *et al.* (2005) and Moss (2006) explore how such a discursive positioning acts to construct this occupational group as holding the promise of shaping future generations. In effect, the army of nursery workers becomes the means by which the Government can achieve many of the social pol-icy goals it has set: increased maternal employment and therefore greater national economic prosperity; and regulation of feckless working-class communities, thereby reducing crime, increasing respectful behaviour, boosting educational attainment and instilling a work ethic in future generations. As Dahlberg and Moss (2005: 15) state:

> Early childhood has come to occupy an increasingly high profile on policy agendas...one reason is that early childhood services are seen as necessary conditions for both competing economically in an increasingly globalised and marketised capitalism and for ameliorating its associated social disorders.

Whether or not the childcare workforce invited this attention or indeed welcome such repositioning remains uncertain. Although this research, and other stud-ies undertaken elsewhere, for example by Novinger and O'Brien (2003) in the USA, and in Australia (Goodfellow, 2004; Fenech and Sumsion, 2007; Kilderry,

2006), reveal increased steerage from the state and accompanying regulation, calls for accountability and competitive marketisation bring a raft of (unexpected) tensions and ambiguities to working with young children (and their families). I have argued elsewhere (Osgood, 2004, 2005, 2006a, 2006c) that early years practitioners have to wrestle with increased demands for accountability (Ofsted inspections), attainment targets (league tables), a prescriptive mode of delivering provision to children (Foundation Stage curriculum) and increasingly standardised approaches (QCA qualifications framework). All these mark a sharp movement towards centralised control and prescription, which can be argued to pose a threat to professional autonomy and morale (Mahony and Hextall, 2000).

This development can appear relatively recent, since it was not until 2005 that the early childhood workforce came to learn of its destiny through the *Ten Year Strategy* (HM Treasury *et al.*, 2004). But announcements within the strategy came after eight years of unprecedented change, with an emphasis squarely placed upon technicist competence and accountability (Maguire and Ball, 1994; Ozga, 1995, 2000). The intervening period between the *National Childcare Strategy* (DfES, 1997) and the *Ten Year Strategy* (HM Treasury *et al.*, 2004) was characterised by a sustained emphasis upon a certain version of 'the (professional) nursery worker'. This era has witnessed persistent attention to the childcare workforce, where particular government priorities have been foregrounded over others; for example, entrepreneurialism, competitiveness, credentialism, transparency and accountability have come to hold sway over the more traditional constructs associated with early years practitioners such as collaboration, autonomy and hands-on experience (Osgood, 2004, 2005). This shift in focus with regards to what practitioners should value in their work has been intentional. Through their work, Gee *et al.* (1996) and Sinclair (1996) describe the considerable energy that governments invest in establishing and instilling certain discursive truths through discourse.

Elsewhere (Osgood, 2005, 2006a, 2006c) I have argued for the prevalence of hegemonic government discourses that narrowly construct professionalism in the early years. I revisit this contention to expand my analysis that government professionalism discourses have the implicit intention to contain and control a workforce in flux, through seemingly reasonable demands for self-regulation, compliance, and concerns to demonstrate 'excellence' against a culture of performativity. Extending this theoretical understanding of postmodern times leads me to draw on the populist, voyeuristic TV programme *Big Brother*, with its objectifying practices, to illustrate the positioning of nursery workers through and within government policy discourse. In this scenario the nursery worker emerges as a contestant on an eviction night from *Big Brother*. After prolonged scrutiny, surveillance, appraisal and routine prejudicial judgements, from fellow (house) mates and the (*Big Brother*) production team, the evictee/nursery worker emerges shell-shocked but uncertain of their ontology (Ramazanoglu with Holland, 2002; Ball, 2003a). Throughout the ordeal of their stay in the house, instructions to undertake seemingly nonsensical tasks have been issued with little if any explanation, only the promise of reward or non-punitive action for compliance. All the time, though, they have been under the spotlight, catapulted from obscurity and caught between feeling seduced by the attention and the promise of what the future might hold, whilst realising that the experience in some ways is a subjective desecration.

It can be argued that such attention has strengthened with the recent (2005) introduction of the Children's Workforce Development Council. The creation of the council stemmed from a concern to reform the children's workforce in light of recommendations in the *Ten Year Strategy*. However, most notable to this study is the introduction of a 'new professional status' for (some, aspiring) nursery workers. It is interesting to note a specific and hence narrow definition is applied when referring to the 'early years professional'. This narrow construction of 'professionalism' as a discrete and separate label (which denotes and distinguishes an elite nursery worker from the rest) in many ways acts to reinforce Moss' (2006) contention of a two-tiered system. Through this book I endeavour to demonstrate that being 'professional' and understandings of 'professionalism' within the nursery rest upon much more than a set of credentials and satisfaction of prescribed standards. By undertaking an investigation into the effects of intersecting multiple identities of nursery workers, I endeavour to expose the complex interplay of performativity (in a Butlerian sense), subjecthood and the power of various discourses to locate and construct nursery workers in certain ways in different contexts.

This brief overview of the policy legacy and current climate within which my research is located is an important means of contextualisation. In the next chapter I perform an exercise in deconstructing texts using critical discourse analysis to further explore, expose and problematise the issues raised here (Foucault, 1978). By focusing upon the ways in which childcare, the family and employment are variously, and at times contradictorily, constructed in policy, I aim to tease out and wrestle with how nursery workers become constructed in particular ways through policy discourses. In doing this I draw attention to the silences and further explore my concern with nursery workers' positionality on the margins of central discourses that occupy space (and hence power) in government policy. I take as my focus for analysis the *National Childcare Strategy* (DfES, 1997) and the more recent *Ten Year Strategy* (HM Treasury *et al.*, 2004).

Summary

In this chapter, through a review of selected literature, I have demonstrated that nursery workers are often constructed in deficit terms through the discourses of particular groups, at particular times, for particular reasons. Furthermore I have highlighted that what is often obscured from view is the structural confines within which the workforce are located. In public/policy discourses scant attention is drawn to constantly shifting goal posts (of accountability, expectations, standards), limited educational/training opportunities, lack of continuing professional development and inadequate employment rights. Therefore in the remaining chapters of this book I turn attention to these structural factors. In doing this I expose the process of 'othering' that occurs where particular discourses act to position nursery workers (many of whom are also mums) as marginal. The fashionable policy notions of 'family-friendly' employment policies, characterised by flexibility and a 'work–life balance' (that hold great sway in public discourse), are exposed as exclusionary to this occupational group.

Drawing on the conceptualisations of Ian Stronach and colleagues (Stronach *et al.*, 2003), I attempt to offer (an) alternative construction(s) of professionalism within the nursery; one that takes into account social class, gender, 'race', age, maternal status and so on to offer alternative understandings of what it is to be a nursery worker and crucially to understand professionalism from the *insider* perspective. As I have outlined, this study is principally concerned to hear the narratives of nursery workers (rather than 'giving voice') and endeavouring to reach interpretations of what professionalism looks and feels like from their experiences and perspectives. Ultimately I seek to identify the positioning of this occupational group within and through discourse and whether, how, and in what ways, resistance is acted out or indeed whether it is possible.

Note

1 Vicky Pollard is a character from a cult BBC comedy programme: *Little Britain*. The character is an exaggerated stereotype of an inarticulate 'chav' from an inner city housing estate. 'Chav' is derogatory slang for a lower-class, uneducated and ignorant person (www.urbandictionary.com).

Chapter 3

Putting theory to work

This chapter aims to provide an overview of the main theoretical concepts to frame the study and which are critical to developing understandings of the processes involved in identity construction. Attention is turned to concepts such as reflexivity, deconstruction, knowledge/'truth', discourse, power, subjectivity, agency and performativity. The remainder of the chapter provides an account of the methodological approach.

Feminists theorising identity

A key concern for poststructural feminists is the process of interpellation or subjectification (Davies, 2000): the means by which individuals construct the self. MacNaughton (2001: 122) insightfully highlights the significance of the centrality of gender and its intersection with multiple other identities in processes of subjectification:

> In redefining identity as multiple, contradictory, and dynamic, feminist post-structuralists have politicised identity formation. They have argued that identity is constituted in and by social relations of gender, sexuality, class, and race, and that each of our 'classed' and 'raced' identities in and through the power relations that constitute our daily lives. Their beginning point is that individuals are inseparable from social institutions; they do not simply interact but are interdependent and mutually constituting. Individuals are born into already-existing social worlds consisting of social structures, social processes and social meanings. The individual does not and cannot exist outside of the social, nor can the social exist over and above the individual.

MacNaughton, like other poststructuralist feminists (Hollway, 1984; Davies 1989, 1993, 1994; Walkerdine, 1990; Francis, 2001, 2003; Robinson and Jones-Diaz, 2006) stresses the social and discursive construction of identities. This theory refutes any essentialist conception of identity as fixed in biology. Rather, identities are constituted in and through everyday social interactions and relations of power. Through this lens, identities are understood as being shifted,

negotiated, managed and reinvented across time and space. Feminist poststruc-
turalists perceive the subject as socially constructed; following Weedon (1987),
subjectivity is defined as encompassing the un/conscious thoughts and emotions
of the individual – a sense of self and relation to the world.

Processes of subjectification

Feminist poststructural perspectives argue that individual subjects are constantly
in a process of subjectification in which the self is formed through discourse. Like
other feminist poststructuralist theorists I understand knowledge as only ever
partial and 'truths' as interpretations held by individuals or groups, not objective
fact.

Michel Foucault developed a theory of *discourse* which offered a theoretical
framework of understanding the social world in terms of identity and power. In a
Foucauldian sense discourse refers to historically variable ways of speaking, writing and talking about, as well as practices around, an issue. They have outcomes
and identifiable effects which specify what is morally, socially and legally un/
acceptable at any given moment in a culture (Carabine, 2001). Furthermore,
discourses reflect particular ways of thinking, feeling, believing, valuing and acting (Gee, 1999) and determine the pervasiveness and persuasiveness of what
becomes accepted as legitimised ways of behaving and being. Foucault's works
are critical of the rationalising process of power/knowledge and the way in which
hegemonic (rationalising) discourses come to suppress counter-discourses (from
marginalised groups). Foucault maintains that power is not a possession but is
constituted through multiple and constantly shifting discourses. He describes
power as never

> localised here or there, never in anybody's hands, never appropriated
> as commodity or a piece of wealth. Power is exercised through a net-like
> organisation. And not only do individuals circulate between its threads; they
> are always in the position of simultaneously undergoing and exercising this
> power. They are not its inert or consenting target; they are always also the
> elements of its articulation.
>
> (1980: 98)

In theorising power and discourse in this way, Foucault's idea around discursive
(re)positioning through discourse is a useful means to understand how identities are constructed, resisted and (re)negotiated when prevailing hegemonic
discourses and less dominant (marginalised) counter-discourses intersect and are
exposed. By adopting a critical discourse approach it becomes possible to problematise, disentangle and expose the ways in which power is played out within
and through discourse and the implications this has for the early years practitioner and for ontological professional identities.

The convergences of feminism and Foucault have been influential in shaping the aims, scope and analysis of this study. Diamond and Quinby (1988) usefully illustrate the promise of each approach as they both theoretically centre on:

- identification of the body as the site of power: through which docility is accomplished and subjectivity constituted;
- local and intimate operations of power rather than an exclusive focus on the supreme power of the state;
- the crucial role of discourse in its capacity to produce and sustain hegemonic power and emphasise the challenges contained within marginalised discourses; and
- criticism of the ways in which Western humanism has privileged the experience of the masculine elite as it proclaims essentialised claims to truth, freedom and human nature.

However, the many tensions that exist between Foucauldian and poststructuralist feminist theory have been widely debated (see Ramazanoglu, 1994; Francis, 2001; Tamboukou and Ball, 2003), with feminists troubling the overly deterministic assumptions within earlier Foucauldian theorisations that see individual subjects reduced to 'docile bodies' with control residing in cultural discourses through processes of subjectification. However, McNay (2000) notes a shift in Foucault's thinking to a more substantive notion of subjectivity through 'technologies of the self' understood as 'the practices and techniques through which individuals actively fashion their own identities' (McNay, 2000: 8). *Agency* is an important concept that has been taken up and extended by poststructualist feminist theorists (Sawicki, 1991; Davies, 1994; Robinson and Jones-Diaz, 1999). Individual subjects become active agents in the construction of their subjectivity. By critically deconstructing the discourses that constitute an individual's life, it becomes possible to resist them in process. Or as Hall (2001: 127) stresses: 'We are subject to discourse, not simply subjects through discourse with ability to turn around, contemplate, and rework our subjectivity at will.'

With this theoretical underpinning in place, it becomes possible to undertake identification, deconstruction and critical analyses of the various discourses within which and through which my study is located. By adopting a poststructural-feminist/Foucauldian approach possibilities become available to dismantle existing, but previously unrecognised/unnamed, modes of domination, and to bring attention to disciplinary and normalising technologies that have gained credence over what constitutes 'professionalism in the nursery'. By problematising and unsettling taken-for-granted assumptions and exposing the effects of power through discourse, opportunities to understand professionalism in other ways were created.

Researcher subjectivity

For researchers working within these theoretical frameworks, reflexivity is crucial. Critical poststructuralism requires the research to constantly question and unsettle. The researcher becomes centrally implicated so that researcher subjectivity is acknowledged, celebrated and worked into all aspects of the research from establishing a set of objectives and methodological design, through to execution in the field, and ultimately the approaches taken to analyses and dissemination. The study reported in this book was politically motivated by my subjective life experiences, feminist politics and multiple/shifting identities. As a feminist academic from a white working-class background, some identities remain more constant than others, for example gender has remained fairly constant; however, aspects of my gendered identity (e.g. the conferment of a maternal identity) have had profound implications on my sense of self – and consequently my research interests. Reay (1997: 18) considers the ways in which 'the influences of the past and the present are interwoven but also the myriad ways in which they clash and collide'. Such clashes and collisions are vital to developing understandings of the self and offering an account of oneself (Butler, 2005). Working within a poststructuralist framework reminds the researcher to consider shifting identities (of both researched and researcher), their own actions and thinking as a researcher and to be alert to the contradictions, tensions and ambiguities (Gray, 2007). Further to this understanding of identity – as multiple and shifting – is the work of Judith Butler, which points to identity as performance. Butler (1990, 2004) stresses the self as discursively constituted. Although I find the notion of identity as performance helpful, like other poststructuralist feminists (Davies, 1992; Skeggs, 1997; Reay, 2001; Francis, 2002) I find the self is best theorised as positional, positioned and self–other positioning – which recognises the self as both discursively and structurally produced.

With this in mind the remainder of the chapter outlines the methods used to obtain data about the ways in which professional identities in early childhood education and care are constructed, re/negotiated, sustained and/or contested. The rationale underpinning the choice of research techniques and the ways in which they were applied is explored, and some of the challenges encountered are presented.

Methods

The approach taken was broadly ethnographic through the inclusion of various forms of qualitative interviewing, observation and documentary policy analysis. The study involved working with 30 professionals from different levels of ECEC, including six stakeholders, three nursery managers and 21 childcare practitioners. The main methods included: documentary policy analysis; stakeholder interviews; life history interviews; semi-structured interviews; focus group discussions with ECEC practitioners; and informal observation of day-to-day practices in the nurseries.

The study sought to address four key aims:

1   explore nursery worker constructions of 'being professional'/doing professionalism;
2   examine the ways in which nursery workers negotiate the intersection of a 'professional' identity with their classed, gendered, raced identities;
3   compare and contrast the ways in which public discourses position nursery workers;
4   examine the extent to which practitioners resist/draw upon these public discourses to (re)position themselves as more or less 'professional'.

The policy context: authoritative voices

In order to contextualise the research study and investigate the hegemony of certain discourses over others, in debates about professionalism in ECEC, key policy materials and the views of stakeholders were included. Through this exercise the grounds upon which to examine the interconnection between power, knowledge and discourse (Foucault, 1983) were established. From a Foucauldian perspective such an examination can be undertaken through genealogy; genealogy offers a lens through which to analyse discourse (Tamboukou and Ball, 2003). Through this approach discourses can be read as being inflected with power/knowledge and as such playing a vital role in producing power/knowledge networks (Hall, 2001). The inclusion of policy materials, for example Green and White Papers and legal Acts, from different historical periods enabled the variability of official discourses about the early years workforce over time to be identified and explored. Foucault takes some discourses to be more powerful than others and to have more authority (Rabinow, 1991). In effect, dominant discourses become the means by which discursive 'truths' are established which act as common sense, taken-for-granted normalisations. So through the inclusion of official policy materials and views of key stakeholders, it was intended that such dominant discourses could be identified (and deconstructed) in relation to the professionalisation agenda in the early years, at a specific historical moment and within a specific socio-political location and cultural context.

The key policy document *Choice for Parents, the Best Start for Children: A Ten Year Strategy for Childcare* (HM Treasury *et al.*, 2004) was included. In addition a series of related consultation documents were also subjected to discourse analysis. The strategy represented a significant text as it was within this 85-page document that the Government set down its views on, and plans for, the childcare workforce over the coming decade. The strategy was hailed as a prime example of 'joined-up' government planning and working (Sure Start Unit, 2005). It followed a tumultuous political period in children's services in the UK, emerging as it did from the tragic case of Victoria Climbié, who 'fell through the net' of various services that were insufficiently 'joined-up' to prevent her death. This set a highly emotional scene for the reform to childhood services and the Government's vision for how the childcare workforce should be reconfigured. Nursery staff were amongst others working directly with children and families to be hailed as ultimately responsible for the welfare of the nation's children, and hence the future workforce and therefore future economic prosperity (Burke *et al.*, 2002). With such high expectations of the children's workforce new forms of professionalism were conceived of and presented through text and discourse in the various policy documents. As a document, I intended that the strategy would provide insights into dominant constructions of professionalism in ECEC and could therefore be understood as conveying specific messages to achieve particular effects and outcomes. By identifying certain discourses that are drawn upon, it is also possible to simultaneously find evidence of new discourses being created in the text, so that new ways of conceptualising professionalism in the early years became possible.

To trace constructions of professionalism in ECEC over time, through government policy, the *National Childcare Strategy* (DfES, 1997) was a primary focus. This strategy is particularly key to the debate since, with the exception of the *Ten Year Strategy*, it arguably marks the most significant drive from central government to overhaul children's services in recent history. The then newly elected Labour Government outlined its vision, bold plans and intentions for childcare as part of a wider political programme of welfare, work and education reform.

The views, perspectives and experiences of a number of key stakeholders who played influential roles in childcare policy in the past 30 years were also sought. Senior personnel at a range of government, independent and charitable organisations at the forefront of childcare workforce reform were included. Interviews were conducted with two senior civil servants at the Department for Education and Skills, senior members of the Children's Workforce Development Council, the Day Care Trust and the National Day Nurseries Association, and the Head of Early Childhood Services in a chosen inner London local authority. These semi-structured interviews were conducted to further illuminate and extend the issues that emerged from the documentary analysis and identification of certain discourses. The diversity of stakeholders allowed other (counter) discourses to emerge and provide the opportunity for multiple, nuanced, yet still 'official' and dominant, constructions of 'professionalism' to materialise. Data from the stakeholder interviews are less visible than that generated from interviews with other respondents since the stakeholder interviews principally informed understandings of the policy context and facilitated the critical discourse analysis of policy presented in Chapter 4.

The local context: gathering narratives from the nursery

The second main stage of the study took place in a central London borough. There were over 40 nurseries in the inner city borough, from which three were selected to participate in the study. This assured a degree of anonymity to the nurseries and the individual participants. Census data indicated that, like other inner London boroughs, every ward in the case study authority was character- ised by pockets of affluence alongside areas of relative poverty. This resulted in stark polarisation in terms of social class and privilege; for example, some areas were among the top two per cent most deprived in England, whilst other areas nearby were defined as the wealthiest in the country. The rich cultural and socio- economic diversity of the local population was important in research concerned to explore class relations and professional identity.

Since the aim of the study was not to seek to make generalisations to larger populations but to identify competing discourses around professionalism in the early years, the 'representativeness' in the positivist sense of replicability and generalisability (Ramazanoglu with Holland, 2002) did not inform the research design. Therefore selecting a specific case study local authority was purposive and intentional (Bassey, 1999). The poststructural feminist aim of the study was to gather data and present findings that might have currency in other situations, and be of use to others engaged in theorising identity construction/negotiation and the interplay of power within and through discourse.

The nurseries included in this research were all located in the case study bor- ough, and have been given pseudonyms (Apple Tree, Mango Grove and Mulberry Bush). The nurseries were selected according to a set of criteria established to allow for similarities and differences amongst a sample of early years practition- ers. Previous research (Osgood and Stone, 2002; Osgood, 2003) highlighted that the sector within which nurseries are located has profound implications for how individuals feel about their 'professionalism' as well as the access they have to professional development activities and structures (Osgood, 2004). Therefore nurseries from the private, voluntary and statutory sectors were included. The nursery education sector is particularly interesting from a social justice perspective in the sense that private sector involvement in education and care has been the focus of much debate, particularly with regard to the de-professionalising effect it is claimed to have (Mahony and Hextall, 2000; Ball, 2003a; Osgood, 2004; Kilderry, 2006). Each of the nurseries included in the study offered full-day care; had approximately 50 children on roll; catered for children from birth to five years; had at least eight members of qualified staff; and was established in the 1990s.

Apple Tree Nursery was a statutory sector setting located in a converted Victorian town house in the heart of an affluent area of the borough; it was tucked away on a tree-lined street but there was a marked proportion of local authority housing interspersed with more affluent Victorian conversions. The manager, Debbie, was supported by approximately 20 members of staff. There was an eclectic mix of practitioners, ranging in age from early 20s to late 50s; there was one male member of the team, and a range of ethnicity was represented. Staff at this nursery were very enthused by the research and readily volunteered to participate.

Specificity: time and place

By contrast, the private sector presented particular challenges in terms of economic rational decision making and a widely held view that participating in
research was of limited value. The timing and focus of my study 'Professionalism
in the nursery' engendered a defensive response; and my role as 'investigator'
took on negative connotations. Fieldwork coincided with the airing of a controversial BBC documentary, which exposed private sector nursery staff behaving
less than professionally in their duty of care to children. The 'fly-on-the-wall'
documentary *Nurseries Undercover* was aired in August 2004 on the BBC. A
partial and negatively selective representation of nursery practice was given; early
years practitioners were pathologised as lacking in professionalism and morals.
Scant attention was drawn to attitudinal, cultural and structural factors (such as
low status, poor working conditions, inadequate pay, lack of support and professional development opportunities). The documentary hit the headlines in the
United Kingdom (Collins, 2004; *Daily Telegraph*, 2004; Taylor, 2004), thereby
creating something of a moral panic and raising questions about the professionalism amongst nursery practitioners in the private sector. This signals the important
effect of public and media discourses on professional ontological in/security in
private sector nurseries. After numerous failed attempts to negotiate access, a
bottom-up approach was taken whereby the nursery manager in one of a chain
of private day nurseries was convinced of the value of the study and therefore
negotiated with the directors/shareholders of the nurseries for the research to
proceed.

Mulberry Bush was a private sector nursery housed in an impressive period
property, which was converted for use as a nursery; an Ofsted report suggested
that it had previously been used as a schoolhouse. It had a uniformity and 'cor-
porate' identity that was not evident at Apple Tree. The nursery appeared well
resourced and concerned to present an aesthetically pleasing façade, for example
most fixtures and fittings appeared relatively new and colour co-ordinated, and
staff wore matching tabards with cartoon farmyard animals printed on them: a
type of uniform which was not in place at Apple Tree. The youthfulness of the
staff team was striking, with most aged between 18 and 25; it was an entirely
female staff, very mixed in terms of 'race' and nationality. The class difference
between the team and the manager was quite pronounced (with the majority of
staff embodying working-class identities and the manager middle class through
signifiers of speech, dress and mannerisms).

Mango Grove nursery (voluntary sector) was difficult to locate as it was
obscured from view by the many high-rise housing blocks that surround it. The
nursery was built in the 1980s and was ramshackle and seemingly neglected. The
staff group was managed by a self-assured, middle-aged black woman of Afro-
Caribbean descent. The team was diverse in terms of age and cultural/ethnic
background, which is reflected in the sample (see Table 3.3, below). The team
did not fit the white, working-class, school-leaver stereotype that is so readily

associated with nursery staff (Bertram, 2005); instead most of the women were aged between 25 and 45 and came from a diverse range of backgrounds. There was considerable enthusiasm for the research.

Nursery worker sample

Tables 3.1–3.3 outline details of the sample of participants included in the study. Diversity in the sample was sought at each nursery in terms of age, ethnicity, qualification level and length of experience. Approximately half (11) of the entire sample (24) had children of their own, although parental status was not a sampling requirement.

Data collection in the nurseries occurred over an 18-month period. The triangulation of life history interviews, semi-structured 'professionalism' interviews, the final group discussion and ongoing observation of day-to-day interactions in the nurseries generated a rich body of data; the methods used meant that the data generated were in effect cumulative and complementary. Whilst a number of issues were revisited, the different emphasis in each data collection method avoided duplication and repetition. The broadly ethnographic approach was in large part a consequence of the three interconnected and cumulative methods of data collection from the same participants in the three nurseries.

Critically analysing the data

Confronted with endless pages of text (in the form of interview transcripts, field notes, policy documents and reflective notes compiled at various points), how to transform them into interesting and meaningful research findings became a pressing concern. The process of transcription, reading, re-reading and general immersion in the issues that shaped the study produced an intimate familiarity with the discursive landscape. However, a rigorous and systematic approach was necessary in order that hegemonic, counter and unanticipated discourses could be unearthed and interrogated.

As many commentators have argued, the discourse analyst (unlike the content analyst) is concerned with nuance, contradiction, ambiguity and areas of vagueness (Parker, 1998; Carabine, 2001; Fairclough, 2001; Taylor, 2001). Part of the process of analysing discourse is inevitably and necessarily about a critical interrogation of how *I* make presuppositions and the techniques *I* use for making sense of the world. Analysis involves searching for patterns in the data (in terms of both commonalities and differences) as well as searching for the function and effect of what people say. My classed, 'raced', gendered (maternal) and professional subjectivity (having informed the shape of the research study, the research questions, the conduct of the fieldwork and so on) inevitably shaped my approach to the analysis of the data. This in turn forced me to question my interpretations of the data and therefore revisit the transcripts again and again to establish the precise reading I was making.

Table 3.1 Apple Tree Nursery (statutory): staff profile

Pseudonym	Position	Qualification	Gender	Age	Parental status	Ethnicity	Class origin[1]
Debbie	Manager	Studying ECS Degree	Female	41	Mother	White British	Working class
Toni	Senior Practitioner	Completed ECS Degree	Female	48	Mother	White British	Working class
Natalia	Teacher	Completed ECS Degree and Masters in EC	Female	31	Child-free	White Italian/Australian	Working class
Francelle	Educator	Completed NVQ3	Female	49	Mother	Black Jamaican	Working class (father experienced downward mobility following immigration; mother semi-skilled professional)
Terry	Educator	Pursuing NVQ3	Male	35	Child-free	White British	Working class
Iesha	Educator	Completed CACHE National Diploma	Female	36	Child-free	Mixed race (White British and Asian)	Working class
Gazala	Senior Practitioner	Completing ECS Degree	Female	38	Mother	Mixed race (White German and Pakistani)	Lower middle class (father experienced downward mobility following immigration; mother semi-skilled professional)
Bella	Trainee	Unqualified	Female	36	Child-free	Latin American	Upper middle class

Table 3.2 Mulberry Bush Nursery (private): staff profile

Pseudonym	Position	Qualification	Gender	Age	Parental status	Ethnicity	Class origin[1]
Delia	Manager	Completed ECS Degree	Female	25	Child-free	White British	Upper middle class
Nina	Senior Practitioner	Pursuing NVQ4	Female	32	Mother	Black British	Working class
Orla	Senior Practitioner	Pursuing NVQ4	Female	25	Child-free	Mixed race (White/Black British)	Lower middle class
Juanita	Educator	Completed Degree and Masters in Pedagogy	Female	30	Child-free	White Spanish	Middle class
Precious	Practitioner	Pursuing NVQ 3	Female	22	Mother	Black British	Working class
Radka	Educator	Completed Teaching Degree	Female	30	Child-free	White Bulgarian	Middle class
Ordina	Practitioner	Completed NVQ2	Female	18	Child-free	Black British	Working class
Batinah	Educator	Completed BTEC National Diploma	Female	21	Child-free	British Asian	Working class
Nyesha	Educator	Completed CACHE National Diploma	Female	19	Child-free	Black British	Working class

Table 3.3 Mango Grove Nursery (voluntary): staff profile

Pseudonym	Position	Qualification	Gender	Age	Parental status	Ethnicity	Class origin[1]
Bertrise	Manager	Completed NVQ4, started ECS Degree	Female	51	Mother	Black Jamaican	Lower middle class (experienced downward mobility as result of immigration and parental divorce)
Elspeth	Deputy Manager	Started ECS Degree	Female	40	Pregnant	White British	Working class
Ruth	Senior Practitioner	Completed NVQ4	Female	43	Mother	Black British	Working class
Shavarni	Educator	NNEB	Female	27	Mother	Bangladeshi	Working class
Ysabelle	Educator	Completed NVQ4	Female	32	Pregnant	White Italian	Middle class
Zanthe	Educator	Completed Psychology Degree	Female	23	Child-free	White British-Greek	Working class
Bhadra	Trainee	Pursuing ECS Degree	Female	32	Mother	Indian	Middle class

1 Class background of the nursery respondents was judged on parental occupation, although it is important to note that class is understood as a fluid concept that is constantly shifting and context specific. Furthermore, given the focus of this study upon the intersection of multiple identities (i.e. age, gender, parental status, ethnicity, etc.), it cannot be assumed that respondents experience their classed identity in uniform ways.

In writing this account of the research I was yet again challenged to present my analysis and conclusions in such a way as to enable the reader to assess how I interpreted the data. The numerous quotes and illustrative examples from the data presented throughout this book are intended to expose and document the reasoning process (from discursive data to conclusions), thereby affording the reader with the opportunity to evaluate and dis/agree. Potter and Wetherell (1992) highlight the difficulty in describing the 'method' used in discourse analysis. Analysing discourse has come to be understood as a broad theoretical framework concerning the nature of discourse and its role in social life. With this in mind, I now present a (Foucauldian) theorisation of discourse, which informed the approach taken to make sense of the data generated in this study. The following chapters present the 'findings' from this study, and an implicit invitation is offered to the reader to critically engage with 'truths' that are being offered to make sense of professionalism in early childhood education.

Chapter 4

Government policy and childcare workforce reform

A critical discourse analysis

In this chapter my aim is to explore the ways in which the nursery worker is constructed through government discourse. I do this by offering a deconstruction of key policy texts. In Chapter 2 (under the heading 'A genealogy of the "politicised nursery worker"') I offered an overview of the shifts that have occurred in relation to the political significance of ECEC within government policy over the past 20 or so years. The literature reviewed in Chapter 2 pointed to an evolving situation whereby ECEC services have been the subject of intense policy attention and hence reform. In order to embark upon a sustained programme of unprecedented reform, the Government began by setting out the (perceived) weaknesses of ECEC services, as they existed in the 1990s. In effect, the New Labour Government invested heavily in offering a particular discursive construction of ECEC services broadly, and by implication of those (women) who make up the workforce. The Government, through a plethora of policy documents, initially mapped the perceived inadequacies of nursery provision in England and consequently constructed a (seemingly) justifiable plan to overhaul the sector. The vision offered might stem from a commonsensical and objective appraisal of ECEC, yet I would contend that the Government cultivated and promoted a discursive 'crisis in childcare' in order that ECEC might be refashioned in particular ways. In this chapter I explore that discursive construction in order to understand how nursery workers have become fabricated through texts as more or less professional at particular political moments.

If, as I contend, governments are understood to invest in particular discourses to serve specific political agendas (Gee *et al.*, 1996; Dahlberg and Moss, 2005) then it is important to dismantle those discourses and assess their effects upon the subjective professional identities of those working within nurseries. My intention is to track how discourses change over time and the ways in which they are inflected by wider social and moral concerns that occupy space in government policy making and implementation (Carabine, 2001; Fairclough, 2001).

By naming the discourses promulgated within the *National Childcare Strategy* (DfES, 1997), it becomes possible to identify the neo-liberal vision set out by a then newly elected government. The strategy was launched as part of a wider raft of policies to explicitly promote a 'welfare to work' agenda (Levitas, 1998). Within the policy climate of that time, ECEC was constructed as the crucial means by which full employment (and importantly the employment of women/ mothers) could be facilitated (Rahilly and Johnston, 2002).

Following on from the strategy came a decade of sustained and high-profile policy attention. During this time the Government reiterated the 'need to radically reform' the children's workforce in order to improve the employability of parents and outcomes for children. The *Every Child Matters* Green Paper (HM Government, 2003) promoted the idea that integrated provision could tackle disadvantage, reduce social inequality and provide support to working parents. These ideas were further elaborated in subsequent policy pronouncements including *Choice for Parents, the Best Start for Children: A Ten Year Strategy* (HM Treasury *et al.*, 2004); which in turn led to the development of the *Children's Workforce Strategy* (DfES, 2005), which focused on the skills, qualifications, training and career needs within the sector. Following consultation the Government reiterated its commitment to improved career pathways, an integrated qualifications framework, development of new roles (including 'The Early Years Professional') and increased support for the training of existing staff as well as an expansion of the provision of services (DfES, 2006a, 2006b). These intentions were enshrined in the *Childcare Act* (2006) – the first of its kind in England. This overview of policy developments in ECEC maps a raft of reform that has been constructed as both necessary and commonsensical. In this chapter I illustrate the means by which the notion of quality and the professional identity of nursery workers become fabricated through text (Luke, 1995; MacLure, 2003). By deconstructing certain government texts I offer an alternative reading, which exposes the effects of discourse upon the identity construction of nursery workers.

ECEC as the saviour...of the economy, of children and of working mothers

When government policy is understood as both text and discourse, as argued by Bowe *et al.* (1992), it becomes possible to conceive of policy makers seeking to establish a 'correct reading' or the promotion of certain discursive truths. Within government policy it is possible to trace the ways in which the ECEC workforce has been constructed in contradictory ways: as the salvation of society *and* as shambolic/disordered. Drawing on the narratives offered by nursery workers, in subsequent chapters I demonstrate that such constructions are met with a combination of bewilderment, ambivalence and resentment. For working-class women occupied in caring work, elevation from obscurity in policy terms to a central position can have various effects. These effects are by no means unintended. Gee *et al.* (1996: 19–21) describe the investment government makes in establishing and seeking to instil a set of preferred discursive truths:

> The new capitalism puts a great deal of faith in creating goals, core values, a vision, a culture – whatever one wants to call it (we would call it creating a Discourse) and communicating it to workers... [It] is now quite open about the need to socialise people in 'communities of practice' that position people

to be certain kinds of people. They now realise that they are in the business of creating and sustaining Discourses.

Occupying a key position on the policy agenda has meant that the ECEC workforce has come to be constructed as the means by which the Government can achieve its vision for an economically successful nation state and the amelioration of many societal ills:

> Government has long recognised the collective interest in ensuring that children get a good start in life: it is in the nation's social and economic interests: children are the citizens, workers, parents and leaders of the future. It is in everyone's interests... Investment in children to ensure that they have opportunities and capabilities to contribute in positive ways throughout their lives is money well spent and it will reduce the costs of social failure.
>
> (HM Treasury *et al.*, 2004, section 2.11: 7)

Through policy discourses government orchestrates a particular discursive landscape, one that heralds ECEC as central to the economic prosperity of society. The nursery worker becomes constructed as the guardian of the nation's children, and her capacity to protect, nurture and educate them in *appropriate* ways becomes all-important in the government vision for the nation state:

> Investment in learning in the 21st century is the equivalent of investment in the machinery and technical innovation that was essential in the first great industrial revolution. Then it was physical capital; now it is human capital... We know that children who benefit from nursery education – especially from disadvantaged backgrounds – are more likely to succeed in primary school... Our aim is that all children should begin school with a head start in literacy, numeracy and behaviour, ready to learn and make the most of primary education.
>
> (DfEE, 1997: 14–16)

But the nursery worker's critical contribution to the realisation of the policy vision does not end there – she becomes the facilitatory means by which women can become full and active citizens through participation in the paid labour market (Hey and Bradford, 2006). In effect, a great deal rests upon her metaphorical shoulders – she can enable parents to work and thereby improve national economic prosperity and she can cultivate children to become the right sorts of citizens for the future to safeguard long-term economic well-being.

By elevating those working in ECEC as key to government policy, the nursery worker is in effect catapulted from the margins. She is charged with responsibility for meeting the needs of children who are variously constructed as relational to adults and 'particularly vulnerable' and 'in need of protection' (DfES, 1997: 15) and required to be made 'safe and healthy' (DfES, 1997: 17) and given 'the best start in life' through ECEC experiences (HM Treasury *et al.*, 2004:5). Furthermore she is charged with providing working mothers with the opportunity 'to exercise genuine choice whether to work'. In short, the nursery worker must rise to the 'childcare challenge' (DfES, 1997). It becomes possible to view the nursery worker as objectified through government discourse; she becomes dehumanised and takes on a mechanistic quality. ECEC broadly, and each nursery worker, becomes charged with the execution of government policy – the stakes are high for a workforce principally comprised of working-class women. The discursive positioning of the nursery worker effectively obscures from view the structural injustices (poor pay and working conditions) that are associated with working in ECEC. Furthermore this process of discursive positioning leaves little space for challenge or critique of the nature of the exigent reforms that appear foisted upon the workforce.

Throughout the various policy texts the workforce is presented as the *potential* means by which central government's vision for childcare can be achieved. For example, the *Children's Workforce Strategy* (DfES, 2005) states that 'the early years' workforce is critical to…giving children the best start in life'; further, 'the workforce plays a crucial role in determining the quality of provision'; and 'the better the quality of childcare and early education, the better it is for children's development' (pp. 24–25). However, this construction of the ECEC workforce (as capable of nurturing citizens for the future) is demonstrated as being principally dependent upon the success of an intense and sustained programme of top-down reform: 'The government vision includes a commitment to radical reform of the early years and childcare workforce through a new qualification and career structure…and a reformed regulatory framework and inspection regime' (HM Treasury *et al.*, 2004: 43).

The prevalent construction of the nursery worker in policy discourse implies that she is currently 'lacking' and in need of transformation through top-down measures including new qualifications and a process of professionalisation conceived by government. A concern to improve the image and status of working in ECEC is reiterated throughout the various policy texts. Government recognises the symbolic significance attached to working with children in the earliest years:

> We want to improve the overall image of the childcare and playwork sector… [It] has much to offer to the right people…lone parents are a key potential source of childcare and play workers…advice, guidance and support to help them care successfully for their own children and help them to build on their parenting skills so they can take up employment looking after other children.
> (DfES, 1997: 18)

So the 'right people' come to be readily understood as (working-class/single) mothers. Whilst the strategy highlights the importance of childcare to enable women (middle-class mothers) to re/enter the labour market and participate as active citizens (Vincent and Ball, 2006), the implicit message is conveyed that childcare is not 'real' work. It is constructed as a mechanism whereby working-class women enable others to participate in careers that are afforded status, prestige and relative wealth (McKie *et al.*, 2001; Lewis, 2003). Elsewhere (Osgood, 2005) I attend to the construction of a childcare utopia within government discourses that target 'the right people'. I previously argued that government discourse is laden with classed and gendered notions about who should enter the childcare workforce. Childcare careers are readily trivialised and positioned as 'default' careers available to those with spare time on their hands but lacking educational and social capital to gain 'real' employment (Skeggs, 1997, 2003). Interestingly the prevailing discourse that shapes the direction of the various policy texts – the needs of the working mother – fail to incorporate the needs of the nursery worker, who might also be a mother. Therefore, the raft of policies acts to normalise middle-classness through a needs of the *middle-class* working-mother discourse. Precisely how a nursery worker who is also a mother is to strike a 'work–life balance' and access affordable childcare for her own children, so that she can service the needs of other (middle-class) mothers, is left unaddressed in the government policy. Yet unemployed mothers are constructed as a reserve army of labour that can potentially fill the shortage of recruits in the ECEC workforce (Lewis, 2003; Rolfe, 2005).

It becomes evident that the ECEC workforce is positioned in the role of servitude to middle-class families; the demographic profile and the structural barriers encountered by working-class women working in a poorly paid employment sector are barely addressed. Within the various policy documents a clear message is conveyed that everyone (every mother) has a duty to contribute to the economy, but that it is the needs of the middle-class mother that are of greatest concern (Gewirtz, 2001). Further, it is the duty of working-class mothers to serve the needs of the middle-class mother by extending 'good quality' childcare. But childcare is only deemed 'good quality' if it can be assessed and measured against a middle-class norm. Suggestions for unemployed mothers to fill gaps within the ECEC workforce actively reinforce maternalistic discourses that are associated with the nature of the work (see Chapter 6 for a full discussion of the prevalence and resistance of maternalistic discourses in ECEC). Further, the 'advice, guidance and support to help them care successfully for their own children and help them to build on their parenting skills' (*National Childcare Strategy*; see above quote) signals the implicit aim to socialise working-class mothers to parent in accordance with normalised middle-class practices (Walkerdine and Lucey, 1989; Lawler, 2000). The effects of this are two-fold: first it is assumed that ECEC is like mothering, and second that ECEC practice *should* be like middle-class mothering. The complexities and challenges posed when maternalistic discourses and practices play out in nursery practice are fully rehearsed in subsequent chapters, but it is important to highlight the messages that are conveyed in government discourse and that act to reinforce gendered and classed assumptions associated with the nature of the work and who (should) comprise(s) the ECEC workforce.

With the above considerations in mind, the notion of 'professionalism' in ECEC becomes problematic because the work is highly gendered and classed. Policy discourses promote an understanding that the work is undertaken principally by working-class women who are encouraged into ECEC by default, and only as an alternative to a life claiming benefits. This raises questions about whether or not such individuals can construct themselves or be constructed as 'professional', since they are performing gendered roles of 'mothering' (albeit for other mothers' children) – for which the skills and capabilities come to be understood as stemming from biological determinism. The hegemonic construction of professionalism (which is explored in depth in Chapter 7) is shaped by middle-class discourses, which promote ideas of 'the professional' as a distinguished and learned individual with significant expertise (rather than someone who casually embarks upon a default career because they have a natural predisposition determined by gender and class). These tensions are fully explored in subsequent chapters, but by noting them here it becomes possible to understand the ways in which nursery workers are constructed in narrow, limiting and contradictory ways.

Individualisation discourses: failing to meet the childcare challenge

Further tension and ambiguity is detectable within the policy discourses; for example, the Government staunchly adheres to top-down reform for the sector but simultaneously attributes shortcomings to wavering individual responsibility:

> Our goal must be to make working with children an attractive, high status career, and to develop a more skilled, flexible workforce...improve the skills and effectiveness of the children's workforce...this will review rewards, incentives and relativities across children's practice with the aim of moving towards a framework that fairly rewards skills and responsibilities, and ensure effective incentives for good practitioners to stay on the front-line.
>
> (DfES, 2003a: 10)

Following individualisation theorists Beck (1992) and Bauman (2000), I note the extent to which the policy texts are littered with normative assumptions – assumptions that it is the responsibility of the individual to raise the profile and status of childcare through personal motivation and commitment. Placing the onus on individual early years workers effectively obscures structural explanations for poor status/image. Furthermore, placing an emphasis on the individual denies space for 'politics of professionalism' from within a workforce; instead the externally imposed version of professionalism becomes justified because the individual workers fail to collectively lay claim to an alternative version (Stronach et al., 2003) – see Chapter 7 for a full discussion. The competitive individualism, that comes to characterise neo-liberal policy, acts to separate individuals in their attempts to achieve targets and standards, and ultimately embodies an externally set vision of their profession (Rose, 1999).

For the ECEC workforce the 'childcare challenge' set by central government maps out a specific version of quality and hence professional standards in nursery provision – variation and deviation from that conveyed in government discourse becomes unthinkable because it is so persuasively presented as obvious and necessary (Davies, 2003). As Gee *et al.* (1996) stress, government is committed to creating and communicating particular discourses that act to silence alternative discourses that might pose a threat. Within the policy texts a vision of the 'childcare worker fit for the 21st century' (HM Treasury *et al.*, 2004: 3) emerges; she becomes 'the neo-liberal subject' (Walkerdine, 2003) who is so preoccupied with embodying the discursive construction passed onto her through policy discourse (Novinger and O'Brien, 2003) that inconsistencies, ambiguities and injustices remain unchallenged. The political significance of childcare, and the unprecedented funding to support the reform agenda, discursively position the nursery worker in an elevated but submissive position. The normalising technologies of reform policies are both seductive and all-consuming to the nursery worker who comes to understand herself as experiencing a form of rescue – from neglect, under-funding, lack of direction. Consequently, childcare workforce reform holds a significant degree of purchase as it offers the promise of improved status, heightened professionalism and so on. However, whether there is dissonance between what the nursery worker holds dear in her professional conduct and what the Government envisions and determines will be available (in the form of curriculum, standards, qualifications, training, career structures and so on) remains a central concern and is debated in subsequent chapters, most notably Chapter 7.

An example of the 'persuasive fictions' (Strathern, 1987) that are generated through policy discourses with great effect upon the professional subjectivities of the nursery worker can be found in the government preoccupation with 'quality'. Throughout the texts government sets out its intention for a particular form of quality and prescribes the means by which it should be achieved. For example, within the *National Childcare Strategy* (DfES, 1997), an entire chapter is devoted to 'Raising the Quality of Care'. Implicit within this aim, though, is the assumption that ECEC lacks quality. Having established that ECEC services are deficient, the need to 'raise quality' and the means by which this is to be achieved become entirely reasonable and based upon commonsense (Foucault, 1980). Normalising discourses around the notion of quality are cultivated and become embedded, so that it is possible to identify neo-liberal values within the text whereby good quality (via professional standards) is deemed 'attainable'. The acquisition of 'quality' becomes possible through the neo-liberal constructs of regulation, accountability, measurability, excellence/best practice, standardisation and symbolic value (i.e. improved image/status). Alternative constructions of quality become silenced, and the naturalness of neo-liberalism to ECEC practice and professionalism is established in the everyday practices and subjective professional identities of the nursery worker (see Chapter 7 for a full discussion).

Deficit discourses: the workforce as lacking

I would argue that the Government has a vested interest in constructing nurseries and nursery workers as 'failing' because through a deficit discourse demands for 'radical reform' through the imposition of top-down policy is presented as entirely justifiable and a reasonable remedy to the 'problem'.

> A National Childcare Strategy matters to children, parents and employers. For too long the UK has lagged behind in developing good quality, affordable and accessible childcare. The approach taken by previous Governments to the formal childcare sector has been to leave it almost exclusively to the market. But this simply hasn't worked.
>
> (DfES, 1997: 5)

Within this quote the ECEC workforce is absent from the list of stakeholders for whom the strategy matters. Furthermore, the ECEC workforce becomes constructed as an entity that has little or no autonomy; this excerpt constructs nursery provision as historically determined by 'the market'. In the case of ECEC, the Government considers market forces inappropriate to meet the economic needs of society (because citizens are unable to fully contribute to the economy where childcare is inadequate and/or insufficient). This historical construction lays ground for the justification of centralised steerage from the state. Or as Forrester (2000: 133) contends, education is 'steered through the simultaneous centralisation of content and direction, and the decentralisation and devolution of responsibility to individual institutions'. Where centralised control is the objective, it becomes possible to conceive of the heavy investment made by government in constructing ECEC services as inadequate:

> We have three key problems: the quality of care can be variable. There is no definition of standards of good quality care which is recognised and applied across all childcare settings. There are gaps and inconsistencies in the system of regulation. [The second problem is that] the cost of childcare is high and out of reach of many parents [and the third] that there are not enough childcare places and parents' access to them is hampered by poor information.
>
> (DfES, 1997: 5–7)

Throughout the strategy (DfES, 1997) the ECEC workforce is variously constructed as 'neglected' (p. 3); as 'lagging behind' (p. 10); 'failing to meet the needs of many children and parents as society has changed' (p. 10); 'under-qualified' (p. 11) and 'difficult to recruit people of the right calibre and retain them' (p. 11). The various policy documents centre around the reform of ECEC services and the workforce, yet the language used acts to foreground parental choice and economic rationalism, and presents a 'crisis in childcare' which simultaneously obscures the voices of the workforce. Each group that constitutes the

ECEC workforce, nursery workers included, is objectified (Foucault, 1980). ECEC takes on a monolithic quality and is constructed as a mechanism that requires significant redress to ensure the aims of government can be achieved. Hence those working in ECEC services become constructed as part of a facilitating mechanism for societal and economic national success: 'Government action is needed... Our economy will prosper if more skilled and capable people are able to take up job opportunities because they have access to good quality, affordable, and accessible childcare' (DfES, 1997: 7).

This analysis resonates with Foucauldian (1979) ideas around 'docile bodies that yield to the discourse'. In effect the workforce is persuasively constructed as 'lacking' and the entire sector in a state of crisis (Cameron *et al.*, 1999, 2002; Rolfe, 2005). Such a negative construction coupled with very tangible structural factors such as low pay and poor working conditions offers a 'persuasive fiction' aimed at a 'certain effect' (Strathern, 1987: 251). Located within this discursive landscape, where policy making and parental choice reign supreme, the subjective identity that the nursery worker fashions is inevitably inflected by these wider hegemonic discourses (which I demonstrate in depth in subsequent chapters). The *National Childcare Strategy* (DfES, 1997) set the discursive foundations for a decade of unprecedented policy reform designed to shape an employment sector in particular ways. The workforce is presented as 'the problem' – a political conundrum that must be harnessed and reworked to ensure that wider government objectives will be realised.

In summary, government policies outline a demonstrable intention to overhaul ECEC services to meet the economic and social needs of society. The policy documents are produced by and for the state to act as 'normalising technologies' where individuals are fixed in a web of objective codification (Foucault, 1980). I have argued elsewhere (Osgood, 2006a, 2006c) that a model of social engineering emerges that is characterised by regulation and control through a standards agenda and adherence to mechanistic reductionism – so that the power elite (government and its agencies) act as regulator of the behaviours of the subordinate (the ECEC workforce). The discursive construction of 'a crisis in ECEC' provides sufficient justification for regulation and control. As illustrated above, ECEC is variously constructed as failing to meet the needs of children and families, and therefore the rationale for regulation becomes legitimated and a regulatory gaze deemed expedient and necessary. The form that regulation and control takes is presented as entirely rational, reasonable and necessary. It can be argued that the persuasive fiction presented by government, through discourses of deficiency, have been taken up by a range of actors (including consumer parents exercising their right to choose) and those within the children's workforce more broadly (including local authorities charged with the responsibility of implementing policy at local level).

Therefore the form and nature of reformed ECEC services that are the subject of policy engineering takes on unquestionable primacy. Sinclair (1996: 232) illustrates the processes by which particular discourses are to be taken as 'normal' and others dismissed as lacking in authenticity:

People locate themselves in relation to certain discourses [which] reflect the socially sanctioned dominance of certain ideologies and subjugation of others. Because discourses vary in their authority at one particular time one discourse, such as managerialism or market approach seems 'natural' while another struggles to find expression.

So whether or not ECEC pre-1998 represented 'good quality' is no longer the issue; rather, the means by which to achieve 'good quality' as articulated in policy discourse becomes the principal concern. Consequently, the means by which to achieve quality, as set out by government, is socially sanctioned because it is deemed a necessary solution to the problem. The *National Childcare Strategy* (DfES, 1997) contends that quality can be attained through a 'more consistent regulatory regime' characterised by heightened accountability, standardisation and credentialism. The form and structure of this 'regime' becomes a secondary concern to the claim that a regime, any regime, is necessary to ensure quality.

In Chapter 7 I explore the effects of government discourses (around quality assurance, regulation and surveillance) upon nursery workers' sense of professionalism and professional conduct. There I argue that neo-liberal constructions of quality and professionalism (that rest upon public accountability, transparency and standardisation) hold a certain degree of appeal to practitioners since it is considered to provide a level of legitimation. Yet conversely, participants voiced concerns that inspection, regulation and standardisation lacked objectivity and furthermore that a neo-liberal regime designed to produce quality fails to contribute to professional authenticity. These protestations and concerns appear silenced in government discourses. Rather, the Government persistently maintains that quality is attainable through regulation, surveillance and the demonstration of technical competence.

Are policy reforms working? The persistence of a deficiency discourse

When questioned, the continued pursuance of a deficiency discourse within the government discourse becomes problematic and unsustainable. A subtle discursive shift is identifiable in more recent policy texts, which is probably attributable to the will to demonstrate effectiveness of the reform agenda and hence political success. The *Ten Year Strategy* (HM Treasury *et al.*, 2004, section 6), published seven years on from the *National Childcare Strategy*, continues to promote the dominance of neo-liberal mechanisms for ensuring quality (standardisation, accountability, measurability, regulation and so on). Furthermore, despite almost a decade of unprecedented reform, the workforce continues to be constructed in deficit terms, with claims that 'radical reform' of the workforce is still necessary (p. 45). The continued calls for 'radical reform' could be interpreted as a failure to deliver policy objectives – hence a weakness of government planning and strategy. By continuing to construct the (principally working-class) women that make up the workforce as lacking and failing to deliver the strategy in localised sites, two effects are achieved. First, attention to the inappropriateness of neo-liberal policy in education/care is diverted, and second, the 'failure' to achieve the government vision rests with the individuals that make up the workforce – not those who devised the policies.

Within the *Ten Year Strategy* (HM Treasury *et al.*, 2004), attention is drawn to a 'wealth of relevant knowledge and skills acquired through education, training, work and personal experience' (p. 45) within the ECEC workforce; however, this is readily dismissed as being the exception rather than the norm and therefore woefully inadequate. Many of the 'challenges' and 'solutions' remain the same over the course of the various policy texts that relate to workforce reform from 1998 to 2006. Yet the workforce continues to be constructed as consistently deficient and problematic, while acknowledgement of structural barriers is presented: 'The single biggest factor that determines the quality of childcare is the workforce...it [is] difficult to recruit staff...[there are] high levels of staff turnover...low levels of pay and [the] absence of clear career ladder' (HM Treasury *et al.*, 2004: 44).

Structural explanations become overshadowed by the discursive construction of the workforce as deficient and therefore requiring transformation to meet the government agenda. The government lays claim to significant progress and success, whilst simultaneously (and persistently) constructing the workforce as inadequate, consequently the strong grip upon workforce reform remains discursively justifiable. The Government standards agenda remains intact and the same preoccupation with regulation/inspection, 'good quality', affordability, consumer choice and so on is in evidence: 'Regulation and inspection...ensure minimum standards are met and that quality is objectively measured and assessed and reported transparently; parents...can use their market power to increase quality' (HM Treasury *et al.*, 2004: 25).

Workforce reform policies have maintained their intensity over the past decade. This study demonstrates that nursery workers continue to wrestle with the implementation of policy and reform in their daily pedagogical practices, the management of settings and in their daily interactions with colleagues, other professionals and parents. As subsequent chapters illustrate, the sustained rate and pace of policy-driven change to nursery work can, at times, feel overwhelming, and at others nonsensical. Yet the persuasiveness and pervasiveness of hegemonic government discourses, that promote neo-liberal technicist competence above other forms of professionalism, inflect nursery worker subjectivities.

At the time the fieldwork for this study was undertaken, the Children's Workforce Development Council (CWDC) was in its infancy as a quasi-non-governmental organisation charged with delivering the *Every Child Matters* programme of reform by supporting and guiding those working in the children's workforce – including nursery workers. The most significant development to have taken place in respect of the professionalisation of the early years workforce was the introduction of a discrete status that can be conferred upon graduate-level workers in the private, voluntary and independent sectors. 'The Early Years

Professional' was introduced in 2007 and was met with a great deal of controversy (*Nursery World*, 2008). Unfortunately, due to timing, it was not possible to canvass the views and experiences of the participants in this study in relation to this development. Nevertheless, I want to attend to a critical deconstruction of the discourses surrounding its introduction and its effects to the ECEC workforce as presented in textual form on the CWDC webpages (CWDC, 2007a, 2008a) and published materials (CWDC, 2007b, 2008b).

'The Early Years Professional'

The claim that 'radical reform' remains an imperative in ECEC policy (HM Treasury *et al.*, 2004; HM Government, 2003) implies a continued lack of professionalism. The introduction of the Early Years Professional Status (EYPS) is constructed as a key aspect of the reform agenda and means of addressing the (perceived) lack of professionalism amongst the current workforce:

> The Government recognises that access to high quality childcare is important for all parents and their children. The move to a graduate-led profession represents a transformation of the early years workforce. To drive this transformation, the Government have made it clear that their aim is to have an Early Years Professional (EYP) in every full day care setting by 2015 and one in every children's centre by 2010.
>
> (CWDC, 2008a)

This excerpt from the CWDC website illustrates the continued predominance of a standards agenda driven by centrally determined targets. Others (Mahony and Hextall, 2000; Avis, 2003; Ball, 2003a) have critiqued the limiting effects of target-driven policies, arguing that in a quest to meet targets organisations and individuals become immersed in a tick-box culture of performativity that obscures more opaque aspects of professionalism from view. By foregrounding the focus on meeting targets, questions about whether the policy intention is based upon ethical and appropriate foundations remain unasked/unanswered. The government aim of ensuring that 'a professional' is working in every setting within a predetermined timescale ensures that meeting the target becomes the overriding concern, rather than whether or not the concept (of a discrete individual as professional) represents professionalism more broadly. Through normalising discourses, the obvious and reasonable means of achieving professionalism is established and imposed:

> CWDC's vision is for the early years workforce to be led by well-skilled and highly motivated graduates. Early Years Professionals (EYPs) are these graduate leaders. Together with our partners we have developed Early Years Professional Status (EYPS) to recognise graduate practitioners with the skills to lead high quality practice.
>
> (CWDC, 2008a)

Within the vision stated above, the silences in what is articulated are significant (Silin, 2005). This research, and other studies considering the ECEC workforce (Burn and Holland, 2000; Warren, 2000, 2003, 2004), highlight the difficulties that many nursery workers encounter in balancing full-time, poorly paid and inflexible work with the additional demands of study. Of the 24 nursery staff included in this study, the ten participants educated to degree level were either in the throes of struggling to complete their studies or recounted enormous self-sacrifice and difficulty in attaining a degree. The low pay and poor working conditions associated with working in ECEC remain intact even where the individual holds a higher-level qualification. Further, as others have noted (Maguire, 1997; Mahony and Zmroczek, 1997; Reay, 2001; Archer *et al.*, 2002), the cultural and social capital attached to graduate status can work against working-class women where others (in this case colleagues) cast accusations of them being 'above their station' (Iesha, Apple Tree).

The situation described poses a significant psychosocial obstacle to those who must invest heavily of themselves to pursue degree courses to attain graduate status. The reference to 'well-skilled and highly motivated graduates' implies that those who have not graduated are neither well skilled nor highly motivated. The structural barriers that come to shape the professional and personal lives of nursery workers in effect become silenced in the debate. What is also implied in this statement is that those currently leading the early years workforce are deficient because they lack graduate status. Constructing the current workforce in this way runs the risk of creating divisions and hostilities within the workforce. The potential for this is perhaps most significant where graduates from outside the profession are invited to pursue the course. There are four possible routes to follow in order that 'professional status' is conferred upon the individual, or as set out on the CWDC website:

> Early Years Professional Status (EYPS) is a graduate level status. If you already have a full degree or equivalent qualification, depending on your previous experience, you will be eligible for either: the four month part-time validation programme; the short extended professional development (EPD) pathway which lasts for six months part-time; or the full training pathway which lasts for twelve months fulltime.
>
> (CWDC, 2008a)

Aside from masking the structural barriers related to combining work and study, which I outline above, further problems emerge when the notion of 'the Early Years Professional' as a graduate-level status is explored. The 'full training pathway' is open to *any* graduate with an interest in young children. Therefore it becomes possible to conceive of scenarios where individuals with no prior knowledge, experience or expertise in the field of ECEC take on leadership roles within nursery settings.

Early Years Professional Status (EYPS) is a central element of the strategy to professionalise the early years sector. Early Years Professionals (EYPs) are 'practice leaders'. They are not intended to manage settings but in some smaller settings they may also be the setting leader. Their role as a practice leader is, in practice, to develop, introduce, lead and supervise developmental work with children under the age of five. We could draw on the analogy of senior surgeons and nurses compared with hospital managers to understand the intended focus and contribution of EYPs.

(CWDC, 2008a)

I contest the concept of EYPS as fundamentally problematic. Whilst I concur that recognition of professionalism in ECEC is a valuable pursuit, and that support for graduates in Early Childhood Studies (and related specialist pedagogical degrees) should be welcomed, extending the possibilities of leadership to non-experts acts to devalue the expertise that currently exists within the ECEC workforce. Furthermore, there is a strong likelihood that, once in post, the Early Years Professional (full pathway) would be met with suspicion and hostility by colleagues.

The issue of authenticity also arises in this debate – how do different constructions of professionalism vary in authenticity? In Chapter 7 I explore participant constructions of professionalism and identify the dissonance between these and external (government) hegemonic discourses around what professionalism should constitute. The EYP, particularly where the individual is recruited on the basis of graduate status rather than expertise in the field, comes to represent an embodiment of government constructions of professionalism. The 'politics of professionalism' to which Stronach *et al.* (2003) refer signal the importance of communities of practice and 'insider' constructions that are shaped by personal and professional subjectivities and an in-depth immersion in a particular workforce and its daily practices.

The possible discord between constructions of professionalism as embodied by the EYP (as neo-liberal subject) and those generated from within established communities of early years practice is problematic. To become an 'Early Years Professional' as constructed by the CWDC, the graduate must follow a predetermined assessment procedure:

All candidates will go through the same assessment process. This process includes: a one-day review of skills to provide feedback to the candidates; five written assessment tasks based on experiences of early years practice; a one-day assessment visit in an early years setting, including a tour of the setting, a review of the written tasks, an interview with the candidate, and interviews with others who know the candidate's work.

(CWDC, 2008a)

The assessment process foregrounds an emphasis on the ability for candidates to meet a set of prescribed competencies (CWDC, 2008b). In effect, professionalism is constructed as objective because it is deemed measurable, quantifiable and standardised. Candidates are required to demonstrate that they are 'competent technicians' (Foucault, 1979).

Through these developments and the concomitant discourses that construct professionalism within early years settings in a particular way, alternative versions become marginalised and devalued. I attend to a thorough examination of the nursery worker constructions of professionalism in Chapter 7. It is important to note in the context of this debate that those 'insider' constructions are silenced in the hegemonic discourses presented by the CWDC and through government policy texts.

Evidence-based policy?

The CWDC follow the example set in other policy texts, by offering a supporting 'evidence base' to justify the creation and imposition of particular approaches to address discursively constructed problems in ECEC:

> Research tells us that one of the key indicators of the quality of childcare is the qualifications held by staff. Early Years Professional Status (EYPS) has been introduced in response to this evidence to develop high quality services that will support the wellbeing, learning and development of all children.
>
> (CWDC, 2008a)

The evidence-based movement in education policy and practice has been widely critiqued (Davies *et al.*, 2000; Ozga, 2000; Archer, 2002; Davies, 2003) and argued to be part of neo-liberal strategies to support political dogma. Hammersley (2001: 5) claims that neo-liberalism is based on the assumption that professional practice:

> Should take the form of specifying goals explicitly, selecting strategies for achieving them on the basis of objective evidence about their effectiveness and then measuring outcomes in order to assess their degree of success (thereby providing the knowledge required for improving future performance).

The selection of policy documents and the webpages from the CWDC presented in this discussion rely heavily upon references to 'research' and an 'evidence base'. In constructing policy formation as reliant upon sound, objective and unequivocal evidence, policies assume a more credible and unquestionable status. The proponents of the evidence-based movement propose an unproblematic relationship between policy, research and practice. The notion of evidence-based policy and practice appears desirable and therefore impossible to challenge. As Davies (2003: 179) asks: 'Who could argue against the idea that professional practice should be based on evidence?' Relying upon an 'evidence-base' is discursively constructed as the right and proper way to create policy and alter practice to achieve the best results. But another reading is available if the evidence-based movement is considered a product of neo-liberalism and a means of implementing neo-liberal agendas. By problematising the notion of an 'evidence base', it becomes possible to conceive of government and related instruments using, commissioning and promoting the findings of selected research and dismissing the relevance of other sources of 'evidence' that do not support its position.

Findings from the government-funded EPPE project (Sylva *et al.*, 2003) are frequently cited throughout the various documents. This large-scale, principally quantitative project is the type of research preferred by government (Blunkett, 2000) since such research is considered less prone to researcher bias and more authoritative because it relies upon objective scientific methods. Within the narratives offered in this study it was possible to identify the trust that professionals working in nurseries can place in 'research evidence'. The relationship of research to government policy was extensively debated during the focus group discussions conducted with the participants in each nursery. I was keen to establish the motivations for participating in the research; the sentiments in this quote from Precious were echoed by others and illustrate the faith that practitioners place in a direct relationship between research and policy and the objective nature of both activities:

> You hear on the radio or the telly that 'a research study has shown x, y, z' and people seem to take notice of it and then the government has to do something. So I guess I was hoping that through this study, you know, you would get the findings on the telly or whatever and then the government has to listen to what we've said because it is there is black and white, like 'findings from research show' la de la, so yeah that was what I was hoping I guess.
> (Mulberry Bush Focus Group)

Where policy is thought to be founded upon objective, scientific, well-resourced and large-scale research evidence it becomes credible and unchallengeable (Davies, 2003). In effect, the participants in this research were fed discursive truths about a 'crisis in childcare', the *need* for top-down reform and the precise nature that a 'process of professionalisation' should take. These truths were readily interpreted as credible and authoritative because the discourses created and sustained by government were said to be based on evidence.

Summary

This chapter has illustrated that policy discourses are cultivated and carefully crafted to have certain effects. They make political ambitions and goals for ECEC seem logical, necessary and founded upon sound research evidence. However, this chapter has demonstrated that government policy and the reforms proposed and implemented within ECEC are not founded upon objectivity but instead stem from particular political motivations. I argue that the ways in which the ECEC workforce is fabricated through text is both deliberate and intentional. The deficit discourse identified throughout each policy text, and which is detectable more broadly in public discourse, promotes particular discursive truths or persuasive fictions about the (lack of) professionalism amongst nursery workers and the urgent need to tackle the 'crisis'. The 'solution to the problem' offered is founded upon the assumption that ECEC really is in crisis and that government has the most appropriate method and means to address it.

What I endeavour to unearth in subsequent chapters, through an analysis of the narratives of those working on the frontline in nurseries, is the ways in which these discourses are variously taken up, rejected, challenged and questioned and to what effects. By positioning nursery workers as central to the delivery of government policy on ECEC (and wider concerns around women's employment and national economic prosperity), the sustained attention that this workforce has received is likely to continue unabated. The reasons that this is permitted are inextricably linked to the highly gendered and classed composition of the workforce. For primarily working-class women, the form that professionalism does and might take in their work is currently under intense scrutiny.

The model of professionalism promoted by government and related authoritative bodies values technical competence and narrowly defined focus upon neo-liberal values which can assure transparency, accountability and measurable outcomes (Rose, 1999). What this model obscures from view is that 'professionalism' in ECEC might exist for its own sake, allowing the space for nursery workers (and others in ECEC) to identify and refashion professionalism in their work – because it holds the key to subjective and altruistic recompense. An alternative reading of 'professionalism' in ECEC might expose intrinsic and collective benefits to individual staff members working in nurseries, which furthermore have wider effects upon the children and communities that they serve. This study provides the opportunity to offer an understanding of what makes nursery workers feel committed and enthused in their work. Given the space and opportunity to explore the highly politicised construct 'professionalism', nursery workers come to a critical understanding of the ways in which they are positioned within discourse. The contradictions that emerge from becoming 'competent technicians' are exposed and dismantled in subsequent chapters, but would seem to indicate an underlying resistance to narrowly defined constructions of the early years professional.

As subsequent chapters illustrate, the participants invested heavily in seeking to negotiate and wrestle with the implementation of policy reform in their professional lives. As I explore in Chapter 7, the top-down, technicist, outcomes-driven nature of neo-liberal policy reform jarred with the motivations and values of those working in the sector. Other commentators have noted the effects of neo-liberalism on professional subjectivities of workers (Rose, 1999; Mahony and Hextall, 2000; Ball, 2003a). This study has afforded an opportunity to explore whether, and in what ways, early years professionals are constructed as 'docile bodies that yield to the discourse' (Foucault, 1980). This chapter has demonstrated that implicit within government discourse is an assumption that the ECEC workforce will be seduced by the sustained policy attention designed to 'overhaul early years services'. Yet, as I have illustrated, despite placing the workforce at the centre of the reform programme, the individuals that make up the workforce become silenced through a process of objectification (Foucault, 1980). The way in which practitioners are constructed renders them invisible as individuals but, para-doxically, the work of individualisation theorists (Rose, 1999; Bauman, 2000) highlights through neo-liberal discourses that it is the individual who is hailed responsible for the failings of government policy. So, in effect, the individual early years workers are held responsible for the inability of policy objectives to meet the (discursively constructed) 'childcare challenge'.

A persistent deficit discourse secures the prominence of the workforce in government policy and acts to divert attention from continued structural dis-advantages associated with working in the sector. As Skeggs (1997) and Colley (2006) argue, working-class women engaged in caring occupations are readily being exploited. In a quest to attain approval in public discourse, working-class women invest in a construction of 'the caring self', and in doing this achieve a level of ontological security which would otherwise be denied on account of their classed and gendered identities. Furthermore, the rescue from 'neglect' that policy discourses promise can be seductive. For this group of workers, propulsion from obscurity to prominence in policy terms, coupled with the rate and pace of reform to working practices, might divert attention from (unwitting) conformity to a narrow version of professionalism. It is my intention to explore the effects of hegemonic policy discourses upon the professional identity constructions of members of the workforce and expose the ways in which class, 'race', gender and other subjective identities inflect understandings of themselves as more or less professional.

Chapter 5

Imagined childhood

Subjectivities and pedagogical practices

In this chapter my intention is to build upon the preceding chapter by teasing out further hegemonic constructions of childhood, ECEC practice and professionalism and to identify the implications of such discourses for practitioners working in nurseries. By attending to a deconstruction and problematisation of the notion of childhood (as a discursive construction), my aim is to demonstrate the power of various discourses and the ways in which ECEC practitioners draw on, negotiate and reject different discourses at different times and to what effect.

In the previous chapter, authoritative government discourses in recent history were explored to reveal how the construction, promotion and persistence of particular discourses of childhood are highly politicised and located within a specific economic, social and moral moment. Within recent government policy and related publications, 'the child' is constructed as vulnerable, unformed and always relational to, and dependent upon, adults for their 'needs' to be met and hence appropriate developmental progress assured. Such constructions are incredibly powerful in terms of the expectations placed upon the childcare workforce, but also in terms of what children are permitted/encouraged to do and to their identities as citizens. The common thread uniting perspectives on the child within policy discourse is the interrelationship between power and control.

Following Aries (1962), Cannella (1997) convincingly argues that in Western discourse children are constructed as a distinct group that must be controlled, protected, guided and encouraged. Furthermore, Robinson and Jones-Diaz (2006) highlight the tendency for dominant discourses of childhood to perpetuate white, Western and middle-class values that are historically linked to strong religious and moral discourses. Critical poststructural theorists and other commentators variously argue that childhood is a romanticised discursive construct (James and Prout, 1990; Rancière, 1991; Jenks, 1996; James *et al.*, 1998; Dahlberg and Moss, 2005; Rinaldi, 2006). Constructing childhood as a time of 'innocence' has been critical in justifying the way that adults separate children from the public domains of active citizenship. In essence, these authors argue that children are constructed as dependent, innocent and ultimately relational to adults. Building upon such theorisations it is possible to view ECEC as a site where 'objective' knowledge is dichotomous. The adult/child binary constructs the adult as knowing, mature and capable and the child as relatively ignorant, unformed and incapable (Rancière, 1991). These discursive constructions inflect and are embedded in hegemonic discourses which become further reinforced through the micro politics and practices of authoritative institutions that work directly with children (Dahlberg and Moss, 2005), such as nurseries.

From within the professional ECEC community a range of discourses about childhood abound, and like government discourses are more or less fashionable at any given moment. However, models founded upon developmental psychology (e.g. Piagetian theories) continue to hold a prominent position (in training programmes, professional development activities, curriculum development and planning, etc.). Theories of childhood and child development that promote a humanist understanding of the universal child – that there is an innate phase in human development that constitutes 'childhood' and is universally experienced by all children – are accepted as authoritative knowledge, or the prevailing scientific 'truth'. For example, the work of Bowlby (1978a, 1978b) and Winnicott (1965) remains entrenched in contemporary theorisations of child development. The following quote illustrates the essentialism inherent within humanist understandings of the child:

> The essential needs of the under-fives belong to the individuals concerned and the basic principles do not change. This truth is applicable to human beings of the past, present and future, anywhere in the world and in any culture.
>
> (Winnicott, 1965: 84)

The hegemony of 'scientific' claims to truth about children and childhood has been subjected to critique by feminist poststructuralist and other postmodernist commentators. For example, Davies (1989, 1993); Walkerdine (1990); Cannella (1997), MacNaughton (2000), Grieshaber (2001), Robinson (2002, 2005a, 2005b), Dahlberg and Moss (2005) and Jones *et al.* (2005) have been vociferous in their challenges to the modernist thinking that has come to dominate understandings of childhood and children's learning. These authors have endeavoured to unsettle and contest modernist humanist perspectives of the universal child; they advocate a view of childhood as a social construction – a social process in which understandings of childhood are formed within the cultural and historical discourses available. I endeavour to draw upon and contribute to this body of critical work. By deconstructing the narratives offered by the participants in this research, my aim is to expose the ways in which hegemonic essentialist discourses about childhood come to inflect understandings of the self and, further, inform nursery work and daily interactions with children.

The English context

In England, curriculum guidance continues to rely upon developmental theories, which promote modernist understandings of childhood, the child and children's learning. Whilst recent curriculum developments such as the *Birth to Three Matters Framework* (Sure Start, 2005) focus more squarely on the individual needs of the child, they nevertheless continue to contribute to discourses that produce the child as innocent/dependent. Whilst the framework claims to take as its focus the child, there is nonetheless a continued reliance upon viewing children at distinct developmental stages (Sheridan, 1997). Although the framework document states that 'growth and development are less predictable for some children than for others', engaging with difference remains an issue that is dealt with separately. Inherent within the framework is a focus on a common set of skills or competencies that *all* young children can be encouraged to demonstrate and that are observable/recordable by practitioners. From a poststructuralist perspective it can be argued that working within such professional (pedagogical) frameworks can contribute to normalised expectations and particular constructions of the child and of childhood.

Developmental theories of child development have been critiqued for their failure to recognise the importance of socio-cultural factors and other issues such as gender, ethnicity and historical contexts (James and Prout, 1990; Gittins, 1998; James *et al.*, 1998). In contributing further to this poststructural counter-narrative, Robinson and Jones-Diaz (2006: 6) contend:

> The child is born into society as an embodied being, who grows and physically matures over time, but the collective notion of childhood and understandings of what this constitutes are primarily socially, culturally and historically variable across ethnicity, class and gender.

Modernist models of child development which categorise children's behaviours within chronologies of age/stage act to reinforce normative understandings; these understandings act to normalise white, middle-class perspectives and denigrate alternative understandings to the category of 'other'. Such discursive constructions of childhood are problematic because they are developed around discourses of incompetence, innocence/need for protection and dependency on adults, and encompass myriad power relations, which ultimately result in inequalities between adults and children. Furthermore, the modernist paradigm promotes the oppositional adult/child binary. This oppositional binary logic underpins taken-for-granted, commonsensical understandings of childhood – both in wider society and within the nursery (Rancière, 1991).

My contention is that a discourse of childhood innocence, constructed by adults, can act to limit what practitioners will and can do with children. By investing in limiting constructions of childhood, critical social, political and economic events and issues that have an impact on children can, and often are, dismissed as developmentally inappropriate, and therefore ECEC practice can act to (unwittingly) reinforce hegemonic constructions of childhood and the child. Blaise (2005a, 2005b), Robinson and Jones-Diaz (2006) and earlier Alloway (1997) highlighted that such white, Westernised and middle-classed views of childhood act to effectively silence/marginalise socio-cultural groups that may have alternative ways of viewing and understanding children and childhood.

In this chapter I aim to explore these various tensions and contradictions. I argue that the nursery workers in my study are located within, and contribute to, this discursive landscape; the training that they participate in, the curricula that they implement and the professional code(s) of conduct within which they operate, not to mention their own subject position, all come to shape how they look at the world, make judgements and interact with others. Through narrativising their life histories, the nursery workers were afforded an opportunity to reflect on subjective experiences of childhood. In 'working-up' an identity (Strathern, 1987) as 'early years professional' the participants became active in retelling and reinterpreting subjective experiences of the past to understand a present self (Lawler, 2008). In offering constructions of their own childhood it was clear that although modernist discourses were prevalent the nursery workers nevertheless contested them and offered counter-discourses in attempts to understand childhood as socially constructed.

Personal narratives of 'childhood': practitioner self-constructions

> An individual's subjectivity is made possible through the discourses s/he has access to, through a life history of being in the world. It is possible for each of us as teachers and students to research the process of subjectification in order to see its effect on us and on the learning environments we collaboratively produce.
>
> (Davies, 1994: 3)

What Davies refers to as a 'process of subjectification' resonates with Althusser's conceptualisation of interpellation, wherein subjects come to terms with authority/voice of culture to constitute themselves as 'normal', socially functional individuals through the process of interpellation. The individual becomes subject – the agency through which this is effected is always external and prior; it is only through the act of acknowledging authority that the individual is constituted as an 'autonomous' subject (Althusser, 1971). So the subject positions taken up by the participants in my sample, the ways in which they are positioned within the various discourses (dominant, counter and marginalised) and the processes through which they take up, reject or mediate by negotiating their childhood/adult narratives have very significant consequences for understanding an 'insider' view of the child and the construction of a professional identity when engaged in work with children.

Imagined childhood: romanticised constructions

The pervasiveness of essentialist, humanist discourses about the child were palpable in the accounts offered. There was clear evidence of participants wrestling with subjective accounts of childhood that sat outside hegemonic discourses of innocence and dependence on adults. Contradictory and inconsistent stories were given that frequently encompassed both romanticised tales of unrestrained playfulness *and* accounts of pain, struggle and discomfort at having to take on adult-like responsibility and bear witness to 'inappropriate' events. The constructions of childhood offered by the nursery workers were complex and in places incongruous; the investments that were made in drawing upon hegemonic normalisations of childhood were often challenged by subjective experiences shaped by class, 'race' and gender which positioned them as pathological or lacking. Terry's account of his childhood was inconsistent and often contradictory; he constructed his boyhood as hyper-masculine through analogies to the adventures of fictional characters:

> I do remember a sense of freedom which might sound a bit clichéd and that but there was a sense of freedom, you could go down to the woods and play all day; very Tom Sawyer-ish, Huckleberry Finn and all the rest and yeah there was an absolute sense of freedom, it was the countryside and it was really nice.

Like others, Terry draws upon discourses of childhood innocence and adventure through his approximation to Tom Sawyer and Huckleberry Finn. Yet fictional characters and storylines in fairytales are typified by both innocence and evil. The adventures of Finn are by no means an exception; whilst Terry foregrounds the innocent aspects of the adventures, the original tale is framed by a friendship characterised by class difference, set against a desperate need to escape family violence and alcoholism (Hutchison, 1993). An alternative reading of Finn's 'adventures' can be interpreted as attempts at social and geographical mobility.

Later in the interview Terry made reference to the support of a loving and kind family, which he drew upon when he encountered sexual discrimination and prejudice in childhood, which ultimately led to his migration to London at 16:

> As I got older there was a bit of curtain twitching that went on. And for me as well I guess because I am gay I felt there was a bit more of that, although as a child I didn't have a sense of being gay and being gay in [rural county], but I started to feel that I was in a small, you know really intense community...because I was 16 when I left and I didn't know what I wanted then anyway but there was a definite pull to get out, get away you know.

It is possible to understand Terry's selective retelling (of both the adventures of Huckleberry Finn and his own childhood) as an example of the ways adults discursively construct childhood based upon partial 'caricaturisations'. Such representations can act to downplay or silence the darker, more negative aspects. Terry's denial of a sexualised subjectivity in childhood and his alternative investment in a hegemonic masculine subjectivity – of the 'outdoor adventurer' – draws upon discourses that promote heteronormativity (Robinson, 2005a) and childhood innocence; both are subjectivities and normalisations that he forcefully challenges elsewhere in his narrative. Many accounts of childhood offered by others in this study were similarly characterised by ambiguity and contradiction. Through wrestling with pathological childhood discursive positionings that sit outside normalised, hegemonic constructions, the nursery workers invested in reworking their accounts. Yet, through this process, they can be understood as unwittingly implicated in sustaining and perpetuating normalising discourses of childhood.

Delia referred to 'the great outdoors' when recounting her prevailing memories of growing up in South Africa in the late 1970s and early 1980s:

> There was an incredible sense of freedom, we spent the majority of our time roaming free and playing outside; there were no restrictions on us you know, we were just free to enjoy our time and explore and have fun as children.

Again, when the narrative is contextualised, personal history becomes mediated within a particular sociological framework. Delia later highlighted the danger and fear that came to characterise life in apartheid South Africa and ultimately led to emigration back to England. Throughout early childhood Delia became acutely aware of her cultural, social and 'raced' identity, as an affluent white citizen in South Africa in the 1980s. The context in which she spent her early childhood was by no means 'innocent', and the realisation and understanding developed in childhood (of racial segregation characterised by political, legal and economic discrimination) sits in stark contrast to the romanticised construction of childhood as a time of innocence and freedom.

Others drew on discourses that acted to position childhood in nostalgic ways. Here, children and childhood are located in a mythical time and place where children were safely ensconced from danger. Toni recounts her childhood as a young girl in central London in the early 1960s as

> a really happy time…very relaxed…back then you could, I'm talking about when I was eight or nine, you could sort of go around to my friend's house and it wasn't a worry for my mum, she knew where I was going, what time I'd be back and that sort of thing and you felt a little bit more secure, because as I say you knew people so that was sort of security. But now it seems that it is no longer like that, there is no way you could have an eight year old girl travelling about central London on her own but back in those days we didn't think anything about it, it was a safer place, you know.

Zanthe grew up in an area very close to Toni, albeit 20 years later. She recounted the cohesion of the neighbourhood and a perceived safety that characterised 1980s London:

> Childhood was just great. We used to go out in the alley with all the neighbours and friends and play for hours, it's not like it is now, children live quite enclosed childhoods now. Obviously bad things happen and to protect them children are more restricted now in what they can do and where they can go.

Iesha presented a similar version of childhood in the 1970s, in north-east England:

> Then you used to know everybody in your street, now I couldn't tell you who half my neighbours are, but then you knew everybody from the bottom of the street up. We lived at number 26 and I knew every child from number one all the way to the top and it was safe at that point to play out...all us kids used to play out on the common for hours on end. I remember when it was the Silver Jubilee and we had a massive street party and everybody knew everybody so it was like us kids were allowed to just wander off and do our own thing, but it's not like that anymore.

The nostalgic reference to safety, freedom and community is striking across the three accounts; the distinctive cultural, historical and geographical locatedness of the childhoods recounted become obscured by the prevalence of romanticised discourses of a bygone era. Toni, Iesha and Zanthe are seduced by discourses of childhood innocence through their promotion of 'a golden age' but also hegemonic discourses of childhood vulnerability and risk play out in their narratives (Beck, 1992; Cannella, 1997; Furedi, 2008). In discursively constructing their subjective experiences as qualitatively different from contemporary childhoods, these nursery workers are active in promoting and sustaining discourses that position children as 'other' to adult – as dependent and in need of protection/containment.

In succumbing to a discursive construction of childhood as a time of innocence, experiences that fall outside such normalisations inevitably come to be understood as in some way deficient or 'other' (Walkerdine and Lucey, 1989). Subjective narrativisations of childhood expose the ways in which these participants variously embraced, negotiated and/or rejected hegemonic constructions. Despite claims to innocence and freedom, the nursery worker narratives were littered with emotional tales of deficiency, rebellion and for some ultimate escape. Where childhood experience was felt to lack the requisite innocence that the discourse implies should be omnipresent, participants reported feeling saddened or regretful that they had been denied the opportunities to experience a 'normal' childhood. For example, Debbie strongly believed that her working-class upbringing in London in the 1960s was firmly positioned outside discourses of childhood innocence. In the following quote it becomes clear that her exposure to domestic violence was something that shaped her subjective view of childhood and has resulted in a life-long project of self-reflection. This project involved her need to first understand that she was not responsible for the volatile relationship between her parents, and second that other models of childhood exist. But what is apparent in Debbie's narrative is that she ardently believes that 'normality' is attainable, and furthermore she believes that discourses of childhood innocence have credibility and are therefore justifiably hegemonic:

> I am not ashamed of my childhood because I wasn't to blame for what went on; took me a while to realise that though... I don't want [my children] to have to witness what I did. I mean, my childhood wasn't normal, standing seeing my dad hit my mum and my mum hitting my dad with a saucepan, all that sort of thing ain't normal and kids shouldn't have to see that.

Whilst Debbie's experiences of witnessing, and falling victim to, domestic violence are repugnant, they are nonetheless a reality of many childhoods. Others (Elspeth, Orla, Bertrise) recounted similar experiences, and so what becomes apparent is that, regardless of how unacceptable childhoods characterised by violent and unhappy family relationships are, they nevertheless exist. In drawing upon, promoting and sustaining discourses around childhood innocence, nursery workers become implicated in a process of myth making. Many of the children in their care will experience turmoil and upheaval in their home lives, but in promoting and sustaining a discourse of innocence practitioners become instrumental in silencing these experiences and positioning them as marginal. Robinson and Jones-Diaz (2006) argue that in their refusal to engage with issues that are seen as taboo or as purely adult concerns nursery workers deny opportunities for children to develop understandings of the world around them (a world characterised by inequality, power and difference). As the authors (op. cit.) go on to explain:

> Many of the early childhood educators in our research were located within this discourse and presumed that children were 'too young' and 'too innocent' to comprehend or think critically about what they saw as 'adult issues' such as difference, power, 'race' and sexuality. Many issues are excluded in children's early education in the name of protecting their 'childhood innocence'; thus we have the development of an imagined 'world of the child' constructed by adults. Consequently, for many early childhood educators, critical social, political and economic events and issues that are impacting on the lives of children and their families are seen as irrelevant.
>
> (2006: 7)

Throughout this chapter I draw attention to the tensions and contradictions within the practitioners' narratives of their own childhoods and the implications of this for their engagement with children in the nursery setting. Like Robinson and Jones-Diaz (2006), I identify at best reluctance, and at worst a total rejection, of the relevance of personal childhood experiences (most of which sit outside hegemonic discourses) to the lives of the children in their care. Rather, practitioners become unwittingly implicated in sustaining and promoting the continued existence of a 'childhood as innocence' discourse despite first-hand experiences that challenge its existence and credibility. Consequently there is a risk that the pain and discomfort experienced at being constructed outside normalising discourses will continue to be felt (in silence) by generations of children that pass through the nurseries in which they work. Domestic violence is a contentious and uncomfortable example; however, numerous other examples of experiences that do not sit comfortably within the confines of hegemonic discourses of childhood are available in the data including racism, class prejudice and social ostracism on the basis of sexual orientation. To illustrate the ways in which this plays out in the nursery worker narratives, I offer a critical deconstruction of the discourses that are variously drawn upon and rejected.

Childhoods on the margins

By drawing attention to particular childhood experiences, I attempt to expose the ways in which, as children, the nursery workers came to negotiate, resist and accept seemingly unacceptable 'adult' constructions of childhood that were squarely located on the margins of a discursively imagined normative childhood. Furthermore I explore the effects of children's lived experiences in family lives and communities that are affected by normative discourses of whiteness and racialising practices. In undertaking this exercise my intention is to expose the pervasiveness and salience of particular discourses to position the nursery workers in certain ways at certain times in their personal histories and the implications of these lived experiences and discursive positionings on their professional identities and practices.

In relation to racialised identity construction, Bhabha (1994, 1998) and Spivak (1999) draw on the influential work of Stuart Hall (1992, 1996) in arguing that identity is not fixed but rather fluid and transformative, and always subject to the 'play of difference' (Hall, 1996). This 'play of difference' is socially constructed through social interaction in different contexts and at different times, and through this process people become variously situated and this influences and shapes their identity. Identity formation/negotiation is thus understood as relational and social. Through relationships to others, individuals (children included) experience their identity as multiple and often contradictory; hence particular groups become marginalised/othered in dominant discursive representations of 'difference'.

The nursery workers included in this study came from a wide range of backgrounds (see the tables in Chapter 3), and the effect of their classed, 'raced' and gendered identities is a central focus of this study. As outlined in the preceding section, nursery workers variously positioned themselves within hegemonic childhood discourses, which are constructed around normative assumptions about white, middle-class, dual-parented families. Yet, lived experiences came to be alternatively positioned on the margins of this discursive construction of family life and childhood. It becomes possible to identify the power of discourses to seduce, convince and persuade individuals that they are in some way deficient in the failure of their life history to resemble that encapsulated in hegemonic, normalising discourses.

In contrast to discourses of childhood innocence, the nursery workers presented a series of counter-narratives that constructed childhood as a time of responsibility, independence and resourcefulness. The contradictions and tensions encountered in the telling of their personal biographies were palpable, and frequently participants were apologetic for the perceived inadequacies of their childhood experiences. The discourses of responsibility, independence, self-sufficiency and resourcefulness in many ways led participants to conclude that inappropriate expectations were made of them to behave as 'miniature adults' (James and James, 2004). Tales of positioning within family life and communities were typically about denial (of innocence) or burden (of responsibility) and far removed from dominant constructions of the child (as dependent, innocent, to be nurtured and moulded).

By drawing on the nursery worker narratives, I explore the intersection of 'race', class, cultural identity, location and context and the implications of this for 'projects of the self' (Lawler, 2008). Such analyses provide a challenge to hegemonic expectations of childhood, family and early childhood education that are encompassed in dominant discourses that act to normalise certain ways of doing childhood, doing family and doing early education. The hegemony of certain discourses necessarily results in the subjugation of others; it is to these discursive practices that I turn.

Without exception the nursery workers recounted experiences of prejudice from their childhood, which they felt to be a consequence of their 'difference' (be that social class, gender, 'race', sexuality, religion, family formation, and/or their physical size). Gazala emphasised feelings of difference and lack of authenticity in her childhood. As a child of mixed race and cultural heritage (white, European, atheist mother and Pakistani, Muslim father), she was at pains to explain the 'confusion' that she felt came to characterise her early years. In relation to her earliest memories of school in south London in the 1970s, Gazala recounted a tale of isolation and conspicuousness:

Jayne: What do you remember from your early school days?
Gazala: I felt very different because there was only a handful of Asian children; in fact I don't remember anyone but myself in my class, and in the playground there was a couple of black girls or children but no, and mixed race children half black but no Asians, but predominantly white, umm, so I felt there was a lot of racism in that children wouldn't play with us, wouldn't be our friends, I mean my best friend was a mixed race boy, I played with him all the time; I suppose I found something in common

with him because he probably felt the same... I don't think the teachers dealt with it very well either. I remember in the playground standing around a lot and watching, I wasn't included in games... I'd be looking for my sister and we'd play together in the playground, but when she went to junior there was a fence in between and I do remember standing there at that fence for a long time looking for her and she would come and find me, but there was a fence in between so we couldn't play together any more, and I was sad that she was in junior and I was still in infants.

In promoting/accepting discourses that construct childhood as a time of innocence, adults deny subjective experiences of racism and other forms of prejudice that are often commonplace. Gazala's account effectively illustrates the implications of prejudice on childhood memories and consequently adult subjectivities. Gazala's account demonstrates that a childhood is littered with sites where processes of othering can/do occur. The school or early childhood institution offers various opportunities for processes of othering to play out, both within the formal environment of the classroom and less adult-regulated arenas such as the playground (Epstein, 1999; Renold, 2005). For Gazala, conspicuousness at her difference was also felt within her extended family. Following her parents' separation, Gazala (aged eight) and her sisters were sent to Pakistan. She reflected upon the distinct cultural constructions of childhood and the concomitant expectations, coupled with the feeling of 'difference' that followed her, signifying the importance of locatedness and cultural specificity:

Gazala: We were there five years...went to school there. My aunt did a lot in terms of educating us, teaching us the Quran and the religion side of things, which my dad had wanted... But we had no contact with our mum and our dad didn't come to see us, or no more than once a year... Our aunt was really firm with us because she wanted us to achieve so much and there was a lot of pressure on us as girls, because 'girls don't play they have to learn housework' so she taught us all that side of things... My dad sent money but it was so limited, it wasn't enough according to her that eventually they bought a fridge...they had to put all these things in for us because we were used to it...

Jayne: How were they about your mixed race?

Gazala: Well that was another thing because here we face racism because of the fact that we were half Pakistani, but when we got there it was the other way around. The family didn't blame us but we were looked down upon... My uncle... He and his wife would say nasty things about us because we were not pure Pakistani... My other aunt used to protect us a lot because she knew it wasn't our fault and she was fond of us. But I always got that feeling that she also looked down on us at times too.

Giroux (1992) argued that where people occupy multiple, contradictory and complex subject positions within different social, cultural and economic locations it is important to avoid constructing the individuals involved as multiply deprived/oppressed. Instead, Robinson and Jones-Diaz (2006) argue that it is more important to understand how the subjectivities and identities of these individuals are shaped against the discursive construction of identities through discourses of gender, sexuality, 'race' and class. Through Gazala's account it is possible to discern the emotional cost to her of negotiating various subject positions throughout her childhood. Elsewhere, she spoke of her ability 'to pass' as a white South Londoner, and in Pakistan as a 'good Muslim girl; I think I was just brown enough to pass', but ultimately she 'never fitted in'. The painful experiences of racism and abandonment, loneliness and alienation sit in contrast to hegemonic constructions of childhood as carefree and protected. The 'confusion' that came to characterise her account of early childhood can be attributed in part to the constant re/negotiation of an authentic (gendered, 'raced', familial) identity. Like others, Gazala wrestled with her subjective experiences, simultaneously blaming and excusing particular individuals (peers, relatives, teachers) as well as herself, whilst recognising the importance of the specificity of her experiences – the time, place and socio-cultural context in which they were located. Depending upon her locatedness at any given time, the expectations for Gazala to do gender, do 'race' and do childhood varied widely. She experienced her identity as shifting, multiple, contradictory and ultimately on the margins of normalised constructions.

Lawler (2008), following Ricoeur (1991), emphasises the perpetual renegotiation of identity that subjects engage with throughout a lifetime. The telling and re-telling of a life story provides space to re-envision and reconstruct. Humanist approaches to understanding the child and childhood deny children the opportunities to make sense of their world (Cannella, 1997). To construct children as passive actors in their own lives, where adults shape subjective understandings *for* children, is to prevent the exercise of agency. The childhood narratives recounted in the course of this study draw upon hegemonic discourses to promote ideas that children must be protected and kept safe and innocent, yet the palpable failure of most subjective experiences to embody such discourses reveals that children are exposed to, readily encounter and effectively negotiate negative aspects of life. To refute the existence and appropriateness for children to experience pain, discomfort, power and so on in everyday life, or to assume that children are incapable of engaging with such concepts and emotions, could be interpreted as misguided and discourteous. Later in this chapter I turn to analyses of the impact that negotiating subjective experiences of otherness in childhood has upon professional motivations, values and practices with children. First, though, I intend to explore how seemingly benign adult constructions of how best to guide/educate/regulate childhood are played out and to what effects.

Negotiating religious identity: 'good Catholic girls'

Like cultural and 'raced' identities, the capacity to embody particular religious identities was another theme to run through the data. Whilst none of the nursery workers identified themselves as devoutly religious in adulthood, the role it had played in childhood was significant. As Gazala's account above indicates, for her 'to pass' in an Islamic culture was crucially important at certain points in her childhood. Similarly, for Ysabelle and Bella, Catholicism was a significant discursive positioning in their childhoods. Both explored the ways in which a Catholic identity intersects with a gendered identity, so that it becomes a means of regulation and control over girls. Ysabelle reflected on her childhood in Italy, where Catholicism came to inflect most aspects of life, from family traditions, timetables, rituals and mealtimes, to her school experiences. For Bella, Catholicism was interpreted and applied in particular ways by her parents and teachers, as distinct from the more liberal approaches in the case of her four brothers.

Others (Bertrise, Bhadra, Batinah, Francelle, Iesha, Juanita, Orla, Shavarni, Toni and Zanthe) highlighted the presence of a religious faith in their childhoods. A wide range of religions were cited throughout the narratives, including Catholicism, Judaism and Islamism, and whilst the subjective experiences of negotiating/embracing/rejecting a religious identity varied widely, the narratives were united by an identification of the regulatory and containing effect it had upon pre-adolescent femininity. Orla was raised a Roman Catholic; her family attended church infrequently but she attended a convent school:

> They never really allowed you to have a personality, you couldn't be loud or be seen to have too much fun, you couldn't really express yourself in any way really, through your clothes or whatever. If you were seen to have a personality then you were branded disruptive or a distraction… I mean it wasn't until I was thirteen that I realised I was a girl [laughs] no, you know what I mean [laughs] got more girly and feminine, it was something you were definitely steered away from.

It is possible to trace how childhood subjectivities become shaped against the discursive construction of identities through prevailing hegemonic discourses. The significance of religious discourses and practices in the everyday lives of these girls is apparent, yet it is possible to identify the tussle that occurs when encountering competing discourses of femininity and sexuality. It also became evident that certain religions (those associated with whiteness, with Englishness, with the middle-class establishment) played out differently in childhood subjectivities and into adulthood. There was a degree of kudos associated with embracing a 'good Catholic girl' identity, as a marker of social/moral superiority in childhood, and part of a shared collective gendered identity:

Zanthe: We were not like them. They were known as 'the tarts'. There were rumours going round that they would do anything to anyone. You know that they were giving blow jobs and we were like 'Urghh! What's that?!' This was when we didn't even know about kissing, you know eleven or twelve... Most of them have got babies now, single parents, really quite sad.

However, rebelling against a religious identity or set of practices also held a degree of cachet for some of the girls. Displaying wild and reckless forms of femininity was considered liberating, yet the regulatory practices learnt were apparently inculcated:

Ysabelle: I tried to be bad, you know, like I might not go to a lesson or something but then I would spend time in secret catching up, so I would be bad but could never really be that bad.

Religion came to be produced as both fluid and shifting throughout childhood. For example, Shavarni variously embraced and rejected the visible display of her faith at different points throughout her childhood. She described her Muslim parents as 'quite liberal' through their encouragement for her to 'be like my friends, up to a point'. Like Gazala, in early childhood Shavarni experienced racism and hostility from both peers and teachers; consequently, in attempts to 'fit in', Shavarni shunned her Muslim identity and endeavoured to avoid the critical white/Western gaze (Hall, 1996, 2001). Later, though, she embraced her cultural/religious identity only to encounter a sense of fraudulence and discomfort:

They [parents] said I didn't have to cover my head if I didn't want to, at 12, 13 I didn't, nobody else at school wore one [*hijab*] and I would've stood out like a sore thumb. But it's funny my dad said to me recently 'Why don't you cover your head?' and I just walked away, because he should have taught me to cover my head when I was a girl, so now I just feel embarrassed... I've tried wearing it and I just felt uncomfortable, it just doesn't feel like me, it doesn't feel right.

At the time of interview Shavarni had recently married through family arrangement and was concerned to foreground a religious identity as a discursive means of relaying particular messages to her husband (and her in-laws). Yet she also reflected upon her encounters with discursive constructions of British-Muslims through Islamaphobic discourses:

You have to be careful though, I think that to be *too* Muslim, you know to wear the veil like at work, on the bus or whatever then you are going to stand out... That's probably what my parents were trying to do when we were small, you know, make sure that we were like blended in, or not standing out you know.

Around the time I carried out the interview with Shavarni, the English media was consumed by the story of a Muslim teaching assistant, Aishah Azmi, who was contesting her suspension from work on the grounds that she should refrain from wearing the *hijab* in class (*Daily Telegraph*, 2006; *Guardian*, 2006b). Shavarni has negotiated her cultural and religious identity in various ways during and since her childhood; what is made visible in this analysis, though, is that the social and political importance attached to 'raced' identity is dependent upon wider public discourses that discursively convey particular (and often negative) messages that are picked up by adults and children alike.

The analysis offered above, of the ways in which children (girls) encounter particular subjectivities, signals the indelibility of early childhood experiences and the sophisticated appraisals and reappraisals that young people engage in. The narratives presented here unearth the impossibility and inappropriateness of protecting childhood from 'adult concerns'. I would contend that the world is not neatly carved into adult experiences and child experiences; rather, the arbitrary categorisations of adult/child merely act to mask the synergy of shared experiences. What is clear from the narratives offered in the course of this research is that participants constructed their childhood selves as perceptive, insightful and constantly engaged in negotiating a complex discursive landscape to make sense of their world. Furthermore, into late childhood, adolescence and adulthood, subjects come to constantly revisit and renegotiate those understandings in a project of the self (Lawler, 2008). The analyses presented here demonstrate that, in offering partial, authoritarian or abridged adult versions of the world, children are not protected from adult concerns; in essence childhood innocence cannot be safeguarded since it is a mythical construct.

Challenging relational constructions: childhood responsibility

I want to trouble the dominant understanding of children as dependent, as the responsibility of, and relational to, adults. This discursive truth has been perpetuated in public discourse in Anglo-American cultures since Victorian times (James and James, 2004) and still holds sway today. Whilst many of the participants in this study alluded to a tacit belief that children should be the responsibility of adults (parents, nursery workers and others in positions of legitimate authority in children's services), in recounting their own childhood experiences numerous examples were offered to contest this. Shavarni, Debbie, Gazala, Elspeth and Ruth variously described situations in their childhoods when they had assumed adult-like responsibilities. They were charged with responsibility for particular tasks around the home, and for their own safety and well-being when travelling to/from school, the homes of friends/family and when running errands. The expectation that as children they would embody adult-like independence was tacitly implied in family structures and practices. It was typical to take responsibility for siblings, or older siblings to take responsibility for their well-being and safety:

Debbie: I was one of five children, one girl four brothers, umm the boys were always in trouble, by the time they were teenagers the police were at our house for one or other of them... I grew up wise, I suppose I ended up being fairly tough because I had to be you know? When I was younger I felt quite responsible, my parents had a very volatile, very violent relationship so I had to take on responsibility – for myself and for my brothers; the way my family was I didn't really have much choice.

Despite the frequency with which adult-like responsibility in childhood was recounted in the narratives, it was always constructed as unusual, or pathological in some way. In a sense the women constructed a responsibility-laden childhood as an unhealthy and inappropriate discursive positioning. By assembling subjectivities as sitting outside a mythical childhood norm, the women unwittingly invest in reinforcing normalising discourses that promote the child as dependent. Gazala refers to her eight-year-old self as 'surrogate mother' to her younger (two-year-old) sister for whom she took principal responsibility. Within the narratives a sense of loss is conveyed at taking on responsibility at a young age, though this is frequently mitigated by fatalistic pragmatism; for example, Ruth recognised the impossibility for her working mother to take care of seven children:

Jayne: Did your older siblings look after you younger ones?
Ruth: Yeah, they were kind of like in charge of us but we were all very independent, I was always responsible for getting myself up and ready for school, my mum used to do my hair for school the night before and then tie it in a scarf...but beyond that...you know...I suppose we knew what was needed of us and we just got on with it.

The childhood experiences of these women are classed, 'raced' and gendered. Hegemonic white, Western, middle-class constructions of the child and family were conspicuous by their absence in the accounts offered. The women wrestled with their subjective experiences and the mythical norm:

Jayne: What was your relationship like with your siblings when you were growing up?
Shavarni: Good, I think I took charge because I was the oldest, well I wasn't the oldest but I thought I was. I was quite responsible as well, I don't know, I think we have been brought up where you take responsibility for your siblings, you know? All I can remember was being responsible for my brothers and sister...there were times when I wondered if I was missing out on something, but it was what you did.

Debbie's lack of choice, Ruth's resignation to necessity and Shavarni's sense of 'missing out' can be interpreted as subjective analyses of childhoods that are lacking or othered in relation to the white middle-class model (Walkerdine and

Lucey, 1989). The innocent, carefree middle-class model of childhood represents an unattainable myth. But the insidious effects of trying to measure up to such imagined constructs can become all-consuming, as the narratives offered in this study bear testament.

Several women in the research were separated from their families for extended periods in early childhood, mainly due to immigration and/or family breakdown. Like many children from the Caribbean in the 1960s, Bertrise and Francelle were separated from their families due to relocation to England (Barrow, 1996). Yet they relayed the anguish and emotional distress they encountered at being separated for a number of years. Both Bertrise and Francelle were aware of the acute racism and hostility experienced by their parents in the quest to find employment and housing; consequently they endeavoured to mask their unhappiness and feelings of abandonment. For Bertrise the situation was further compounded because she was not staying with relatives in Jamaica but had been 'boarded out' to family friends; she also reflected that being an only child furthered her sense of isolation:

Jayne: What happened then, when did you come to England?
Bertrise: I came to England when I was 11.
Jayne: How did that come about?
Bertrise: Mum came to England herself in 1962, I think and then I followed on, if it wasn't '62 it was '61 and I followed on four years later which was '65.
Jayne: So what about that intervening period? Those four years when you were still in Jamaica and your mum was here…
Bertrise: I was unhappy.
Jayne: Were you living with grandparents or relatives?
Bertrise: No, I was living with umm…they call it boarding out [laughs] so I wasn't actually living with family, mum chose not to because she was afraid they would spoil me too much or so, you know, it was a friend of my godmother, my mum then sent money and paid for them to look after me for them three years… I missed my mum and wanted to come and be with my mum because I was becoming increasingly unhappy as I got older…but that said I understood my mum's reasons and so I accepted it, focused on the good things, friends, school, you know…
Jayne: How was school?
Bertrise: It was great because I was very much into learning, I was an inquisitive child in terms of education, I was always a bright child so I went to pre-school, then infants, then juniors. I was very bright and articulate; I took my eleven plus when I was ten…

In the next chapter I explore the mother–daughter relationship and the impossibility of 'getting it right'. It is not my intention to deconstruct Bertrise's relationship with her mother; rather, I use this excerpt from her story as a means to illustrate the ways in which children can be positioned as 'other' on account of experiences that sit outside of the (white, Western, middle-class) norm. Although living away from parents/family was relatively common for young Jamaicans in the 1960s, and many recounted painful memories (Barrow, 1996), the connotations associated with 'boarding out' or being 'left behind' construct the experience as pathological – as a consequence of parenting that falls short of normalised expectations. The uncomfortable laughter and extended pauses throughout Bertrise's account signal her awareness of her childhood as 'other', yet she presents her childhood self as resilient, academic and confident. Her narrative highlights the capacity for children to encounter, negotiate and make sense of their worlds. In childhood, Bertrise and Francelle were required to devise coping strategies and form identities that could protect them from the sense of otherness that was conferred upon them and from the pain experienced at being separated from their parents. This construction of a child as resilient and stoic sits in contrast to the hegemonic understandings of the child as dependent, weak, innocent and so on. The narratives offered throughout this study are peppered with examples of childhood experiences that defy essentialist understandings of the child. Nevertheless, the often apologetic ways in which the nursery workers qualify their stories still reflect and (unwittingly) reinforce essentialist discourses.

In this chapter I have endeavoured to illustrate the ways in which nursery workers construct childhood subjectivities. Through this process the intention has been to unsettle and trouble taken-for-granted, commonsensical understandings of the child and childhoods, so that alternative understandings – the child as active agent in the social world – might be considered. The implications of this exercise though are far reaching when transposed onto the professional conduct and behaviours of nursery workers in their daily encounters with children. The remainder of this chapter is devoted to exploring whether, and in what ways, nursery workers negotiate subjective experiences of childhood and the often competing hegemonic humanist understandings of the child. I argue that the implications of this for early years practice are significant. I identify the extent to which prevailing discourses act to limit and regulate practitioners and the ways in which resistance is played out in the nursery.

As a key professional group working with young children, nursery workers are crucial agents involved in (re)producing and legitimising particular discourses of childhood. In this chapter I have attempted to demonstrate that the way in which nursery workers construct childhood works against subjective experience and is further informed by investments in hegemonic discourses that promote childhood as a time of innocence, where children should be protected from risk and where the adult knows best.

Despite a professional proximity to child-centred pedagogies, the practitioners' narratives reveal contradictions and tensions in their constructions of childhood. Subjective experiences of 'childhoods on the margins' (of discursively constructed white middle-class childhood) reveal the complexities involved in doing childhood and creating/sustaining an 'appropriate' child identity. Yet pathologised discursive positionings become mitigated by hegemonic discourses of imagined, normalised constructions of childhood. In the next section, I explore the nursery workers' narratives to provide understandings of the ways in which this plays out in their work; how nursery workers do child-centred pedagogy and the extent to which the unwitting promotion and legitimation of certain discourses can act to limit and constrain childhood experiences.

Hegemonic childhood discourses and professional practice

Within the study, all participants were asked about their motivations for wanting to work with very young children. For many, the subjective experiences of childhood, as illustrated above, acted as the catalyst to embark on a career in nursery education and care. Many cited serving children's needs, through assuming a key professional role in an authoritative framework, as a life-long ambition. Further, becoming part of ECEC services was constructed as a form of cathartic reconciliation for the perceived shortcomings of their own childhoods.

Debbie:　I always knew that I was going to work with children. For me it was about something I never had…at home, but school as well, it's all about respect or lack of respect…um…do you know what I'm saying? Like, well…I suppose for me the main reason, why I went into working with children was that I didn't want children to have the same experiences I had, being shouted at to the point of wetting myself, you know total humiliation, you know how can you abuse your position of power and do that to people?… And I don't think children are seen as people in their own right, they are just seen as these little beings that run around to be shouted at by you because you're the adult. There is a big issue of power and how we as adults abuse it, definitely…yeah…

Yet this therapeutic construction – of a career in ECEC as serving subjective psychic needs, layered upon altruistic goals towards young children – becomes further complicated by the prevalence of normative discourses that extol childhood as a time of innocence and dependence on adults. In effect, a number of the nursery workers constructed themselves as pivotal in *protecting* children and preserving an imagined innocence – despite and perhaps precisely because of their subjective experiences of marginalized childhoods. A complex picture emerges; through the retelling of subjective experience there is acknowledgement that childhood innocence is mythical, yet attempts are nevertheless made to promote/safeguard that innocence through professional ECEC practices designed to protect children from 'adult concerns'.

Reclaiming some purchase on childhood innocence was considered possible by the vicarious positioning of nursery worker to child. For example, Radka drew heavily on hegemonic constructions of the normative child and normative childhood, yet her narrative also included reference to political asylum and persecution. For her, a career working with children was in part constructed as means of accessing an imagined childhood:

> It is all to do with my childhood I think... I just really, really...maybe the best time of my life was when I was here [London] and I just quite often think, reflect back and think what do I want to do? What will make me happy? When was I happiest? Why don't I try working with children? So it all has to do with me and that is how come I work with children... It [working in a nursery] makes me happy in the way that you pass your knowledge on to little children because they pick up on things really easily and it is great to see them progress when you have put into them. I suppose I just think that I am worth something to them.

Whilst altruistic motivations were frequently cited, it becomes apparent through an analysis of the data that the participants were not acting in entirely selfless ways when entering careers in ECEC. Working with young children is widely accepted as challenging on multiple levels: physical, psychological and emotional, but a vocation/rescue discourse for adults that take on that role emerges from the data. In effect, the nursery workers come to construct themselves as instrumental in providing philanthropic opportunities to children *and* as the beneficiaries in terms of 'the pleasure to be gained from giving something back' (Gazala).

The pervasiveness of hegemonic discourses in practitioners' self-understandings (as 'other') can be traced through from subjective experiences of childhoods on the margins to a persistent desire to access or facilitate normative childhoods through their work. The promise of capturing an imagined childhood, and thereby mitigating the effects of pathological childhood subjectivities, was powerfully felt. Although this was a project viewed as both incongruous and problematic, offering empathy as motivation for entering ECEC appeared to lessen concerns at appearing narcissistic. Whilst Debbie, Radka and Gazala began by describing the cathartic benefits attached to working with children, they quickly qualified this by promoting the empathic nature of their career-making decisions. Perhaps such qualifications were made because viewing a career in ECEC as therapeutic sits uncomfortably with widely held understandings of nursery work as a vocation/a selfless calling to care for others. Elspeth reflects on the interplay between what a career in ECEC can offer her, and what she can offer on the basis of subjective experiences of a pathologised childhood:

> I think I am quite good with the children because I've come from quite a difficult background and they said I had behavioural problems when I didn't; put me in the remedial class when I shouldn't have been there. And then all that stuff I was telling you about my dad and his drink problem, the police and that, so I think I have got a bit of empathy with them and I don't really

judge people; parents or the children and the way they're behaving. To me everyone has got their own difficult backgrounds, you know if we had parents who are drug addicts, or alcoholics or whatever I wouldn't think any the less of them for the problems they've got... In the end I'd like to get into something related, but something different, something that I might find more rewarding.

Commitments to empathic approaches to professional practice were common throughout the narratives, and many proclaimed dedication to approaching children (and their families) in socially just ways. However, practices in this respect varied widely across and within nurseries, often contributing to the reinforcement of hegemonic constructions of the child (and through a process of 'othering', the unwitting pathologisation of groups of children and their families). For example, the commonplace practice of referring to particular families as having 'social services children' because the children were on the 'at risk' register and so under the jurisdiction of social workers and related authoritative frameworks. Whilst nursery staff spoke at length about treating these children as they would any other child at the nursery, the use of the label and the ways in which they were constructed (as problematic and multiply deprived) marked them as 'other'. By denying difference, the nursery workers became implicated in sustaining discourses that construct particular families in negative ways (Cannella and Grieshaber, 2001). Empathy alone is not sufficient as a means to unsettle and challenge normative assumptions that are deeply embedded in everyday practices. All the time that discourses of innocence play out in the nurseries engaging meaningfully with the ways in which families can become unwittingly pathologised, and the ways that children become subject to processes of othering, remains unchallenged. Through an analysis of the data I illustrate the ways in which practitioners sustain discourses of childhood innocence:

Shavarni: I do really love this job. It's a cliché, but it is the children that keep you going... I think that I am kind towards them, I don't want to force them to do things, I find it so interesting to see how they develop, do you know what I mean? They are incredible and I see it as my job, me and the others here, well everyone who works in nurseries I suppose, it is our responsibility to protect their world, do you know what I'm trying to say? I mean, it sounds silly but children are only little for a short time and we can, I, urm, we have to protect them, before you know it children aren't children any more, you know once they've got mobile phones, TV gets into their brains...peer pressure and all that...

Others echoed the sentiments expressed above by Shavarni. Most participants stressed a 'love of children' and a 'love of the job' as vital to nursery work at some point throughout the study. Impassioned pleas to safeguard childhood were frequently articulated as a justification for having chosen ECEC as a career:

Batinah: Here we have to be very responsible, very professional. We have to take care of the child's every need. The nursery is a safe haven for them when they are away from their parents. It is our responsibility to create a world where they can have fun and feel secure, protected you know? Through our training and our practice we know how to protect the child in lots of different ways, you know from food hygiene to equal opportunities – recognising everyone is different but they all have rights, following the code of conduct, obeying the rules and regulations. But at the end of the day it is our job to make sure that they are safe, protected and that nothing bad can happen to them. That's what the rules are for innit?

However, tension between the imagined worlds of the child (Robinson and Jones-Diaz, 2006) at home and at nursery represents a challenge to many of the participants. Like Vincent and Ball (2006), I highlight the challenges that stem from class-inflected relationships between parent and caregiver. Whilst policies and procedures (towards equal opportunities, respecting diversity and so on) are intended to ensure children are protected from the effects of marginalisation on account of perceived differences, how this plays out in practice is often problematic. Brooker (2005) highlights how well-intentioned attempts to respect difference (by treating 'everyone the same') can have unfortunate consequences. She reported on normative assumptions that are embedded within early years practices and cultures that can act to unwittingly marginalise children from diverse class and cultural backgrounds. This excerpt from Toni's interview illustrates that, within the wider professional context in which nursery workers are located, overt prejudice exists:

Toni: Sometimes I'm really surprised at other people's opinions, when I started doing the foundation degree in Early Childhood Studies there were other people there who were managers of nurseries and had a lot more experience than me and we got asked questions about how we feel about parents with problems, alcohol, gay parents, things like that, and a lot of people were saying things like they should have their children taken off them and things like that and I was outraged, I find that really quite difficult. If you are in an occupation where you are looking after children then you have to speak to their parents and how can you do that if you are looking down at them, if you are seeing them as something less than yourself just because they have problems or a different lifestyle to yours, and I found their reactions really shocking.

Such views were not articulated by any of the participants in this study. Rather, a consensus emerged that nurseries occupy an important position in promoting multi-culturalism and the celebration of diversity. However, these commitments rest upon principles of affirmation and acceptance. Festivals such as Eid, Ramadan, Yom Kippur, Hanukkah and Diwali become constructed as opportunities to enrich childhood and celebrate 'the other'. But what becomes obscured from view are the darker, painful aspects of childhood subjectivities where sameness is prized (Francis, 1999). Commentators have warned that where 'difference' is celebrated it can take on a carnivalesque quality and further reinforce processes of othering (Hall, 1992; Spivak, 1999). Rhedding-Jones (2008) focuses attention on Muslim pre-schools to offer an examination of the normalised practices and discourses that shape early childhood practices and the ways that practitioners, policies and organisational cultures contribute, promote and ultimately sustain them. She encourages a problematisation of diversity; she argues that merely showing respect, tolerance and compassion is insufficient and condescending. 'Dealing with difficult difference' has been widely debated by a range of critical theorists (Hall, 1996; Reay, 1996; Rhedding-Jones, 2005b) and highlights the complexity and seeming intractability of the hegemony of whiteness/Western discourses and practices. She argues that nurseries must find ways to avoid (albeit well-intentioned) tokenistic gestures at 'respecting the other'. Celebrating the difference/diversity that the 'social services child' represents is unlikely to ever find expression in nurseries, and so confronting the embedded normalised assumptions around the 'imagined' world of the child, shaped by innocence and protection, offers a starting point to move beyond empathy with the pathologised child.

Dealing with (difficult) differences

My intention here is to explore the ways in which hegemonic discourses come to inflect everyday practice in nurseries and to expose the challenges that nursery workers face in negotiating various discourses. I explore the decision-making processes that occur when nursery workers reject/promote counter-narratives and to what effects.

Heteronormativity in the nursery

First, I turn to the case of Terry, the only male nursery worker in this study. His inclusion in the study highlighted the normative assumptions that abound in ECEC in relation to a mixed gender workforce. The principal assumption is that men working in childcare must be gay, and further that they will have ill-intentioned motivations for entering a career involving work with children (Cameron et al., 1999). All the participants in this research were aware of the public discourses that construct male nursery staff in pathological ways and as worthy of suspicion based upon the potential risk that they might pose in nurseries. Sexuality was widely discounted as 'irrelevant', and many shared the belief that ECEC was a principally meritocratic sector where professional competence was assessed on an individualised basis and therefore 'sexual orientation shouldn't make a jot of difference' (Francelle). The narratives and observations gathered in this study, though, offer a more complex interpretation of the significance of sexuality and gender in the nursery. I distinguish sexuality and gender as separate (but related) concerns. Like other adults, the nursery workers actively constructed children as innocent and worthy of protection; implicit within this construction is the notion that children are asexual beings. This adult construction cast upon children is limiting and unhelpful in that it denies the possibility that children are constantly and enduringly subjected to discursive constructions of sexuality through their everyday lives (Casper *et al.*, 1998). Yet there is clear evidence that the participants in this study accept and reinforce the discursive positioning of children as asexual (and therefore in need of protection from notions of sexuality).

I draw attention to Terry, since the way in which his homosexual identity was 'managed' in the work context reveals how nursery workers come to be governed and regulated by hegemonic discourses (despite heavy investments in counter-narratives). Subjective experiences of 'childhoods on the margins' and the consequent commitment to empathic conduct in nurseries theoretically provide the foundations for an employment sector accepting of difference and prepared to challenge all forms of discrimination. Whilst the nurseries were overtly committed to equal opportunities and anti-discriminatory policies, the everyday practices and strategies employed to discursively construct this male, homosexual nursery worker in normative and hence acceptable ways is indicative of the hegemony of heteronormative discourses:

Terry: Because I would never sit and say to the kids 'oh I'm gay' just like I wouldn't expect anybody to sit there and say 'oh I'm going to get married' you know, unless it's relevant. And children have asked me, children have said you know, not often but you know, 'who do you live with?' and you know and I'll say 'oh a friend of mine' not because I don't want to say it but because it's making it relevant and you know, and I've had parents ask me before 'oh, do you have kids of your own?'

Jayne: So there are heterosexual assumptions?

Terry: Yeah… But I have said to parents before, you know they've asked me about 'your girlfriend' and that and I've said 'well actually you know I have a boyfriend'. But you do have to be careful sometimes, I still find it a little bit, sometimes when dads walk in and ask me about, because you know you build up a relationship, it's always a professional relationship, but you know if somebody says something about umm, because you know, sometimes I might say 'my partner' and then they'll ask you 'your girlfriend' and sometimes I choose not to answer, I don't know why, but you know. It's nothing to do with parents first of all, it's going over that professional boundary, but sometimes I do say something, when children have asked me if I have a girlfriend then I say 'I've got lots of girlfriends, lots of friends who are girls and lots of friends who are boys' so *putting it in context for children*… [emphasis added]

Terry told me that, at a previous nursery, he was subjected to false accusations based on his sexual orientation, which may in part explain his reluctance to forcefully challenge homophobia or the prevalence of heteronormative discourses. However, by concealing his sexuality – or not drawing attention to his 'difference' – in the interests of protecting children from adult concerns and protecting himself from the heteronormative gaze (Boldt, 1997), he becomes implicated in myth-making. As a consequence of these practices, children are offered only a partial view into the world around them – as asexual or heterosexual (Blaise and Andrew, 2005). In raising questions about his romantic relationship and household configuration, the children reveal a level of inquisitiveness and awareness of the world around them. Terry's guarded responses signal his position within the institutionalised heterosexual matrix (Butler, 1990). He is positioned so that he is constrained and silenced, and consequently narrow and normative representations of the adult world become reinforced.

The nursery workers in this study generally held the view that children are 'too young' to deal with sexuality issues. Yet from the observational work undertaken in each nursery there was clear evidence of heteronormativity in everyday practices; for example, the incorporation and encouragement of particular games and activities in the home corner (such as mummies and daddies, wedding ceremonies and so on) and kissing games and girlfriends/boyfriends were commonplace. Such activities were rarely questioned but can act to normalise the construction of heterosexual desire and the inscription of heteronormative gendered identities (Epstein, 1994). So sexuality is implicit and embedded in the everyday practices in nurseries but remains unquestioned and unproblematised, providing normative heterosexual discourses are being drawn upon and played out.

As Epstein (1994) demonstrates, adults frequently assume that issues of sexuality do not feature in imagined childhoods or as part of children's everyday conversations and practices with each other. Yet, Robinson and Jones-Diaz (2006) stress that children are constantly negotiating discourses associated with homosexuality that are spoken/enacted by their families, peers, teachers, media and other popular cultural contexts – often in derogatory ways (Chasnoff and Cohen, 1997; Renold, 2005). The silences that exist (because of a desire to protect children from taboo subjects or perceived 'irrelevancies') are as powerful as what *is* said (Silin, 2005) in terms of what individual subjects take up as 'truth' (Foucault, 1978). The nursery is a site where, through daily interactions, children are afforded opportunities to take up, embody and speak the discursive 'truths' transmitted by/through popular culture and social institutions. Dealing with difficult differences is an issue that has been addressed by a range of critical theorists and feminist scholars (Reay, 1996; Francis and Archer, 2005), and one that should occupy space in reflections on ECEC practice.

Brown Snowmen and *Baa Baa Green Sheep*: dissonance between subjective experience and professional practice

Many of the participants in this study described subjective experiences of prejudice and racism throughout their lives starting in early childhood. Earlier in this chapter, through an analysis of selected life histories, I demonstrated experiences as being positioned as 'other' via racist discourses. Each nursery in this study made overt policy commitments to 'multi-culturalism' and to 'respecting ethnic and cultural diversity'. However, the translation of such policies into practice varied across the settings and were informed and inflected by the subjectivities of the individual nursery workers. My intention is to explore the ways in which public declarations (through equal opportunities policies, professional training and so on) to multi-culturalism can be considered tokenistic. In attempts to appreciate/tolerate diversity, particular identities (based upon 'race', gender, language, culture, disability and sexuality) become unwittingly homogenised and fixed (Anthias and Yuval-Davies, 1992; Luke and Luke, 1999). Such homogenisation acts to obscure structural inequalities and marginalisation (Rhedding-Jones, 2005a). Addressing multi-culturalism becomes a distinct activity, a conscious exercise where the subjective childhood experiences of the nursery workers become eclipsed by dominant authoritative normalising discourses. I endeavour to illustrate examples of the ways in which nursery workers struggle to connect subjective experiences of racism in childhood to their pedagogical practices with children in the nurseries.

Whilst observing a session at Mulberry Bush Nursery, I noted a conversation between Ruth and Shavarni. They were recounting a training session attended on the previous day about ways to be culturally sensitive in curriculum planning and delivery. Both women were laughing at the suggestion that they should include Brown as well as White Snowmen in their artwork for display in the nursery. At Apple Tree Nursery, Iesha was similarly dismissive of suggestions to improve the cultural sensitivity in her ECEC practices:

Jayne: You said you think that ECE has changed in the political sense, how do you mean?

Iesha: When I worked for [London Borough] in the Early Years Centre it was just like little things like being politically correct, I mean, another story I had heard of but I can't confirm this, but I heard in a nursery in [London] you weren't allowed to sing *Baa Baa Black Sheep* it had to be *Baa Baa Green Sheep* and I remember laughing about it at the time, how ridiculous it's a nursery rhyme! Things like do you remember Golly Wogs, I used to have a Golly Wog, I didn't think anything of it, it was a cuddly soft rag doll type of toy to me, you know with the Robertson's jam and you used to save up for the little men, I remember I was quite young, you used to save up the tokens and you used to get little mini ones, ceramic ones and one would be playing the drums, one would be playing the trumpet you know *I just think sometimes adults put these thoughts into other adults and children*. I mean to me *Baa Baa Black Sheep* is a nursery rhyme I didn't think of it being racist or anything like that, you know you weren't allowed to say things like blackboard it had to be chalkboard, now when I was growing up it was a blackboard, and I remember when I said something about a handyman, like we have [X] who comes here once or twice a week to sort out jobs it is not handyman it is a handyperson, it is not a fireman or firewomen it is a firefighter and stuff like that. When I talk about things like that I mean I think you can take things a bit too far.

Jayne: So there is a heightened awareness of potential...

Iesha: Yes a lot of it *just comes from the adults* some of them are just ridiculous, you know *children don't think of these things* whilst they are singing a nursery rhyme. You know other things like Noddy being gay and one of the Telly Tubbies, like where do they get this from? You know *are you telling me two or three year olds are going to pick up on something like that?* [emphasis added]

These participants are unconvinced that discursive constructions and prevailing discourses in popular culture and media can/do inflect child (and adult) views of the world (Palmer, 2006). For Iesha, suggestions to make small modifications to her practice with young children are considered to stem from unfettered political correctness. For these women, addressing prejudice and discrimination in this way does not relate to subjective experiences of racism. Despite first-hand experience of racism perpetrated upon them in childhood by other children (as well as significant adults in positions of authority), there is a persistent investment in the 'childhood innocence' discourse that views children as incapable of witting racism. Or as Toni stated: 'It's just not on their radar at that age'. And Zanthe shared her view of children's awareness of cultural and ethnic difference:

> They are aware of different races and cultures and that, partly through the activities that we put on for them, and we have different food, you know Monday Caribbean, Tuesday Turkish, Wednesday is Chinese or whatever. And we put up displays when there is a festival on. And they know, from being with each other, playing with each other that there are different colours and cultures but it is not a big issue, it's never a problem. So they have awareness but is not something that's bad or anything, it is a good thing, the nursery makes it a good thing, you know?

Zanthe's construction of the children as accepting or indifferent to cultural diversity signals a belief that racism, intentional or otherwise, is not a feature of young children's lives. Yet, there is dissonance between personal narratives of childhood juxtaposed the professional views of children's capabilities (i.e. childhood capacities to be hurtful, prejudicial, etc.). Further, I would argue that hegemonic discourses (around childhood innocence) act to silence subjective experience. Children are constructed in limiting ways, as unable to engage with issues of cultural and 'racial' difference, particularly when that difference is performed in derogatory or hurtful ways (Troyna and Carrington, 1988; Troyna and Hatcher, 1992; Troyna, 1993). Rather, sensitivity to multi-cultural education is constructed as unproblematic, simplistic respect for/acknowledgement of diversity rather than an engagement with issues such as abuse of power and processes of 'othering' (Robinson and Jones-Diaz, 2006).

For these nursery workers, addressing issues of 'race' cannot be achieved through measures that amount to little more than tokenistic political correctness. However, the assumption that young children lack the capacity and insightfulness to engage with (and participate in) racialising practices is problematic. Through these examples, and that offered above in relation to the predominance of asexual/heteronormative discourses within nurseries, it becomes evident that hegemonic constructions of children as ignorant/fragile/innocent are actively reinforced by the reluctance of practitioners to engage children in 'adult concerns' deemed irrelevant/inappropriate (Yelland and Kilderry, 2005). Through their practices, nursery workers are actively reinforcing discourses of childhood innocence by denying the significance of issues such as sexuality and racism –sites of power and inequality – where white western heteronormative discourses prevail.

Summary

When tolerance and acceptance of difference are emphasised at the expense of critiquing the relationship between difference, power and inequity, our capacity to work towards a pedagogical agenda that addresses various social inequities based on 'difference' is limited.

(Robinson and Jones-Diaz, 2006: 71)

It is my contention that nursery workers have a moral and professional duty to acknowledge that young children are routinely subjected to, witness and contribute to all forms of discrimination throughout their daily lives (Troyna and Hatcher, 1992; Epstein, 1994, 2001; Epstein *et al.*, 1997; Renold, 2005). Following on from recognition that childhood innocence is a mythical construct comes the need for nursery workers to seek to understand how forms of discrimination implicitly and discursively impact on children in their everyday lives. The current positioning of nursery workers in frameworks of authority, their discursive positioning as 'professional' and the duty afforded to them as transmitters of government policy to future generations act to disconnect subjective experience from professional practice.

As I argue in Chapter 4 and revisit in Chapter 7, nursery workers are contained and regulated through policy discourses. In the context of this discussion, policies that espouse certain approaches to dealing with diversity and difference can lack a sense of authenticity, as witnessed in the derision toward *Baa Baa Green*

Sheep and Brown Snowmen. In effect, the nursery workers in this study described a sense of professional disillusionment brought about by performing political correctness through minor alterations to their practice or by obscuring 'adult concerns' from view. Space to challenge embedded normative expectations of nursery practice (where the child is constructed as the unknowing in need of protection and the adult as the protector and governor of childhood innocence) is denied, and so issues of social justice remain largely unchallenged.

The analyses offered in this chapter signal significant dissonance between nursery workers' subjective experiences of childhood and their professional practice with children. To question and challenge hegemonic discourses (of childhood and pedagogical practice) could afford vital opportunities to form interconnections between subjective experiences and professional practice. Practitioners' claims to empathic approaches to their work offer the foundation upon which more in-depth conceptual work could be undertaken to address this fissure.

Chapter 6

Maternal discourses and the formation of 'professional' identities

Ailwood (2008) discusses some of the ways in which discourses of maternalism, and what it means to be a good mother/nursery worker, have been embedded in discourses of ECEC. She states:

> ECEC teachers continue to have their skills and knowledge regularly and enduringly attributed to a natural mothering instinct. These links between nature, maternalism and the work of the ECEC teacher are difficult and contradictory. It needs to be acknowledged that many women in ECEC take pride and pleasure in their work and identity as teacher/mother. However, others have attempted to refuse this discourse, pointing out their years of university education and the need for early childhood teachers to be recognised as professionals. For these women, the naturalisation of their work undermines their struggle for professional status.
>
> (p. 162)

As outlined in Chapter 3, motherhood is a central and recurring theme, which emerges in debates about ECEC practice, practitioners and professional identities. Cameron *et al.* (1999: 8) refer to pervasive maternalistic discourses through which ECEC practice becomes widely accepted as a form of 'mother-care'. Furthermore, the work of Carol Vincent and colleagues (Vincent and Ball, 2006) highlights the tensions that can emerge between mothers in a childcare market (the authors paid particular attention to the relationship between providers and consumers of childcare).

It is perhaps precisely because the discursive landscape of nursery work is so inflected with, and shaped by, motherhood discourses that the women in this study invested heavily in narrativising tales of motherhood. The data are saturated with reference to motherhood, be that personal experiences of being mothered, rejecting motherhood or as taking up the role of mother. The stories recounted were typically highly emotional and characterised by a combination of anxiety, respect and resentment. The women in this study were vociferous about the importance of maternal guidance – either because they had been in receipt of that guidance or because they perceived it to have been lacking. They drew heavily upon normalising discourses which promote and extol the virtues of 'sensitive' mothering. Feminist scholars,

Walkerdine and Lucey (1989), Lawler (2000) and Walkerdine *et al.* (2001) focus on mother–daughter relationships and contemporary constructions of 'sensitive' mothering and expose them as being highly classed and 'raced' so that 'good/sensitive' mothering is understood as a white, middle-class model characterised by liberalism and self-regulation. Given the demographic profile of the women in this study, it is interesting to note the pernicious effects of such normalising discourses to a group of women that fall outside hegemonic maternal constructions in multiple ways.

In this chapter I want to focus attention upon those effects, especially in relation to identity formation. Lawler (2000: 77), in her study with mother–daughters, drew attention to:

> the ways in which women's knowledges of, and investments in, specific forms of regulation and specific models of self are likely to inflect both the ways in which they understand their own and their daughters' selves, and the way in which they mother.

My intention is to borrow from Lawler, and extend her ideas about 'projects of the self', to map the salience and effects of maternalism upon the formation of *professional* identity (amongst nursery workers) in addition to classed, 'raced', gendered and maternal understandings of the self.

I endeavour to relate understandings of the self, as a professional nursery worker, to the ways in which these women variously reject, invest and promote maternalistic discourses in relation to their work. I do this by reflecting upon the discursive retelling of the mother–daughter relationship and the ways this is drawn upon to make sense of memories and present selves. Then I move on to consider public constructions of motherhood and the ways in which the working-mother discourse plays out amongst nursery workers. By drawing on the nursery workers' stories I turn to a critical analysis of the classed, gendered and 'raced' relationship between childcare consumer (mothers) and childcare provider (nursery worker). From the stories presented throughout this study, I challenge a series of discursive 'truths' about nursery workers which act to create particular identities – identities which can act to reinforce limiting maternalistic discourses in nursery work and which are made up within relations of power/knowledge (which manifest in 'technologies of the self') (Foucault, 1980). As a result of this discursive positioning and through a process of interpellation (Butler, 1990 and 2004), I argue that nursery workers come to understand their (professional) self in particular (and sometimes contradictory) ways.

The discursive retelling of the mother–daughter relationship

> Whether it is read as 'democratic', as 'sensitive', or as 'natural', the type of mothering associated with white, middle-class women is marked as 'normal', with any deviation from this 'norm' constructed as pathological.
>
> (Woollett and Phoenix, 1991: 22)

The women in this research narrativised their lives through a spiral of interpretation and reinterpretation. Through this process the interplay and tensions of multiple identities – classed, 'raced', gendered selves – became a site where normalising discourses pathologise particular experiences of motherhood. Through the telling of their life histories, and through a specific and enduring focus on the mother–daughter relationship, identity formation is part of a 'project of the self'. For these women, this enduring project was one often characterised by pain, contradiction, confusion, guilt and regret when set against normalising discourses, which I illustrate throughout this chapter.

Being mothered

The mothers of the women in this research were typically described as 'housewife' or 'stay-at-home mums', but such descriptions obscure the pivotal role in maintaining family cohesion and instilling order within the home that they performed. Vincent and Ball (2006) point to the naturalisation and normalisation of a mother being the full-time carer of her own children. However, they point to the risks associated with that particular maternal status (for middle-class mothers): the risk of loss of self and identity. The mothers of the women in this study were almost exclusively working class, and the identity of 'stay-at-home' mum carries different connotations when a classed and 'raced' analysis is applied. As Steedman (1986) highlighted, working-class mothers who take principal responsibility for the upbringing of their children are confined to the domestic sphere of necessity, rather than choice, and, furthermore, such women frequently combine motherhood with casualised paid labour. Such dual roles were described in this study; for example, Zanthe's mother worked in 'the rag trade' as a machinist at home, Toni's mother 'did a bit of babysitting for neighbours' and Debbie's mother 'looked after some old people in the area'. The informality and casual nature of their employment acted to obscure the heavy investment these women made as secondary breadwinners in their homes. They become discursively constructed as full-time mothers, when, in fact, competing demands were made on their time, and hence their capacity to commit *all* of their time to mothering was compromised.

Lawler (2000) argues that black and white working-class mothers are subject to a construction of their mothering as inadequate, insensitive or authoritarian. The power of such discursive constructions was evident in the narratives; the women recounted the matriarchal role that their mothers adopted in their family life. When asked to describe their mothers, the women constructed them as authoritarian boundary-setters and most often the enforcers of discipline. Despite awareness of the discursive constructions of authoritarian mothering as lacking or 'other', the women in this research were at pains to defend their mothers; their accounts were inflected with pride and awe at what they considered stoic and pragmatic mothering. For example, Bertrise described her mother's refusal to prepare her for the racism she would likely encounter upon being brought to England from Jamaica in the 1960s:

I guess in those days they didn't forewarn us, it was just a case of you had to learn...she wasn't, Mum was just not the type, never has been, that I could sit down and have a heart to heart with, it was just a case of 'I've sent for you now so we are just going to have to get on with it' you know? So when I did go home and tell her about it [racism] she would just tell me to take no notice and be proud of where you come from, just move on... I guess she had her reasons for dealing with it that way, but they were her reasons and I had to respect it.

Unquestioning respect and deference was a recurring theme in the narratives when recounting ways that mothers exerted authority and made decisions about their children's lives. However, the matriarchal constructions sat in tension with others that were presented. Like many of the other women in this study, Shavarni constructed her mother as the authoritarian force within the family, describing her as 'kind but strict, but not very strict; sort of modern strict'. Yet Shavarni offers alternative versions of her mother, and highlights a vulnerable, isolated and scared woman who was routinely 'othered' on account of her multiple differences (non-English speaking, immigrant, mother of four). Shavarni constructs her mother as strong and worthy of reverence whilst simultaneously as weak and marginalised. Shavarni felt ambivalence as a child and into her teenage years about her cultural identity and the role of women in society, which becomes evident in the context of her relationship with her mother and the hegemonic understandings of childhood, mother–child relationships and motherhood:

Shavarni: Yeah, my mum was the disciplinarian, harsher than my dad...Mum looked after us full time. I think that was because that was what was expected of her and also because she couldn't really integrate when we moved here because she didn't speak English, she's been here 30 years and still doesn't. So I guess she must have been really lonely sometimes. I think to start with she found it quite hard, but she had my dad, but she didn't really socialise outside apart from going to relatives. Which was quite often but she didn't socialise with any of the community... When I was growing up I was really aware that mum is Muslim, although Dad is too he didn't show it so much... They were quite conservative and they wanted girls to be brought up a certain way and boys to be brought up a certain way, in Bangladesh the girls and boys are separated and so they brought that view over as well. So I think their thinking was that if I went near boys I'd be up to no good. So I ended up being separated from the only other Bengalis I knew: my brothers and their friends, so spent most of my time around people not from my culture – which I didn't mind then. But as I grew up I was really aware that I didn't speak Bengali and looking at it now I would have liked to learn more Bengali but there weren't that many Bengali schools that you could go to, and there weren't any Islamic Centres...

Mum and my dad taught us at home but they couldn't do it basically because it didn't go into our heads [laughs]... I think my mum had quite high hopes for me she would like me to do a degree...she still has those high hopes for me. So I was kind of brought up with Bengali culture, values but then my mum had these sort of Western hopes for me, to have a career and be independent, but also wanted me married off, and to be a mum. So there were sort of two sets of goals for me; you know, expectations or whatever that I had to deal with and I was never quite sure.

Three of the women in this study described the death of their fathers in childhood and others recounted tales of divorce and separation. Mothers in these situations were constructed as unwaveringly stoic. Toni told of her 'strong, quiet' mother who 'just picked herself and got on with it' after the death of her 45-year-old husband. Similarly, Orla's mother was constructed as resilient and practical in her ability to escape a situation of domestic violence: 'She just got us out of there, we moved to the other end of the country and she just got on with it.' 'Just getting on with it' was a phrase to reappear throughout the data in reference to mothering styles and reactions to challenging situations. What is apparent from these accounts is the classed interpretation: the meanings that are placed on particular behaviours (Walkerdine and Lucey, 1989; Lawler, 2000). Whereas normalising discourses of sensitive, middle-class mothering would position the behaviours of these mothers as pathological or lacking, the women in this study provide an alternative reading. In place of 'insensitive, authoritarian', the mothers are offered as 'protective, practical', but whichever construction is offered, it falls outside the dominant discourse of the sensitive, democratic (white, middle-class) mother.

Steedman (1982, 1986), Walkerdine (1990, 1997) and Skeggs (1997, 2003) all highlight the ways in which working-class women, and especially mothers, become marked as 'other' when observed from a middle-class perspective. As women working in childcare, the women in this study are particularly susceptible to dominant authoritative discourses about children's 'needs' and the relational discourses about 'good enough' mothering that abound in developmental psychology which informs ECEC practice. In effect, they occupy competing subjectivities, as women with childhood experiences outside the normalised middle-class, white model, and as professionals located within the authoritative framework that promotes and facilitates that norm. This may account for the contradictions and tensions that emerge from an analysis of their narratives. For example, Debbie constructed her mother as resilient, proud, practical and caring. However, in recounting childhood experiences, Debbie draws upon dominant discourses that position her childhood outside normalised constructions and extols the virtues of a middle-class identity for her adult self and for her maternal self:

I want steady, I want reliable, I want honesty, I want normality. My child-hood wasn't normal... I am not ashamed of what happened because it happened and it's not my fault, it's what went on, I've always strived for better for my kids. I don't want them to see what I had to; they need nor-mality... I moved away from where I used to live, into a new area. I've got a nice new life; I mean stressful but whose isn't? You know, mortgage, nice home, nice area, I've got a husband with the same morals and values that I have, you know a commitment to family life.

To talk of shame, blame and distancing herself both physically and emotionally from her working-class background indicates the pain and vulnerability Debbie felt at being positioned as 'other'. Yet, elsewhere she hangs onto her working-class identity as an accolade of where 'she has come from'. Gazala spoke about a lack of authenticity, in terms of her 'raced' identity, and, like the other women in this study, she placed a significant importance upon the mother-daughter rela-tionship. She reflected upon a tumultuous childhood characterised by divorce, emigration, mixed race parentage and an arranged marriage at 15. For Gazala, the mother–daughter relationship was 'faulty', in that the mothering she received deviated from the dominant sensitive, selfless hegemonic model:

There was a lot of conflict, Mum was not a Muslim, he [father] was Muslim, he was brought up in a Muslim society and my mum was not prepared to take that on...whereas dad would say one thing, mum would do another. So behind his back she would feed us pork, things like that...I used to get smacked by my mum with a wooden spoon because I would tell... My mum used to, she was quite ignorant, quite negligent, she would leave us at home on our own when we were eight or nine – old enough to look after ourselves but not old enough to look after our baby sister. She had emotional issues, in the end she just left a note and left us for good.

The small acts of rebellion (feeding her children pork) that her mother performed and the ultimate desertion of the family were located within maternalistic dis-courses that position Gazala's mother in particular ways. She is constructed as pathological and deficient, or in Gazala's words as 'ignorant' and 'negligent', when understood in a maternal subject position. At a later point in the interview Gazala constructed her mother in alternative ways when considering her child-hood subjectivity:

There had been a lot of traumatic situations for her, in her own childhood; she was obviously a bit of a lost child. Her mum had her when she was a teenager so she was left with her gran for a mother, and then she [the gran] ran off and found somebody else and had another family, and my mum was brought up by her other grandma, and she had never met her dad because he died in the war, so she had a lot of loss in her childhood.

Despite passing critical judgement on their mothers' perceived inadequacies and inability to embody 'sensitive/good' mothering, the women were staunchly defensive of their mothers but often remained apologetic about the inability of their families to resemble the mythical norm. Debbie and Gazala, like others in this study, described the pain and anguish they felt at the failure of their families to 'get it right' or to pass as respectable/acceptable (Skeggs, 1997, 2003), as Walkerdine argues:

> In a number of domains, middle classness has become synonymous with nor-mality and working classness has been viewed as a deviant pathology, to be corrected if possible by correctional strategies that will make working-class subjects more like their middle-class counterparts.
>
> (Walkerdine, 1997: 29)

Throughout this chapter I draw on an analysis of the effects of class difference/ mobility and its implications for the discursive positioning of nursery workers, since it is central to understanding the myriad ways these women make sense of themselves and reject/invest in particular discourses.

The myth of 'sensitive' mothering

The mother–daughter relationship has long been considered complex and inflected with high emotion. Various psychoanalytic and psychosocial explana-tions and theorisations of the mother–daughter relationship have been offered (starting with Freud, in the 1930s) and, furthermore, feminist scholars have engaged with such theorisations and consequently offered critiques (perhaps the most notable is Chodorow's 1978 work *The Reproduction of Mothering*). Following on were a series of counter-theorisations (e.g. Eichenbaum and Orbach, 1982; Segal, 1987). It is not my intention to review them here, but it is important to highlight the significance of the mother–daughter relationship in terms of identity formation and discursive positioning of female subjects.

The legacy of such theorisations, though, is to expose a set of normalising dis-courses that herald the 'sensitive' mother as the hegemonic norm. Contemporary hegemonic discourses stemming from developmental psychology promote 'sen-sitive' mothering (Bowlby, 1978a, 1978b; Riley, 1983; Bradley, 1989; Singer, 1992). Those engaged in 'good' mothering must be sensitive; and to that end exercise empathy, interpretation, and prompt and appropriate responsiveness (Winnicott, 1965; Ainsworth, 1969; Ainsworth and Bell, 1974). Given this, it is unsurprising that so many mothers are found wanting. Yet, as I have attempted to demonstrate, when differences of class and 'race' come into play, the 'good mother' norm becomes further complicated.

Hays (1996) highlights the need for women to construct a morally adequate account of themselves as mother, and to do this she argues that mothers of *all* classes are required to prioritise their children's needs above all else. Therefore it becomes possible to conceive of times when middle-class mothers fall short of the 'sensitive' norm. An example of this can be found in this study. Radka moved to London from Bulgaria in the 1980s. Her mother left a professional career in Bulgaria to (reluctantly) assume a full-time, stay-at-home mothering role:

Jayne: What did your mum do when you came to England?
Radka: She was just a housewife, I suppose she had lots of time for us, which was great, but for her, you know, she felt left alone on her own during the day which was frustrating because she had been used to working, she missed her old life, and her friends... She didn't [speak English] but she coped okay, could get by, you know she could just about get around London if she needed to, but she was different here, not the mum we'd had back home.

From Radka's account it is possible to discern that her middle-class mother encountered a loss of self and a loss of her former identity (Gatrell, 2005). From being a mother with a professional career to a mother confined to the domestic sphere she faced the task of negotiating a new identity. Her reluctance to embrace a full-time maternal role was compounded by her dislocation from a familiar cultural identity. Radka reflected on her mother's consequential sense of isolation and loneliness – which could be interpreted as introspection, and which in turn acts to construct Radka's mother as lacking, as falling short of the hegemonic form of maternalism. Rather than a mother prioritising her child's needs above all else, like Gazala's mother, Radka's was preoccupied with her own needs and so comes to represent 'othered' mothering. Radka refers to her mother as '*just* a housewife' and intonates that her mother was in some way inferior to the working mother she'd known in Bulgaria. Radka is clearly drawing on hegemonic discourses that construct 'the worthy citizen' as the skilled, valued worker, contributing to the economy and achieving professional fulfilment (Rose, 1999). What is also detectable in her account, though, are competing maternalist discourses; discourses that celebrate a woman's natural propensity to mother, and a mother's vital role in prioritising and assuring her child's happiness and well-being.

On becoming mother

Following Foucault (1983) and his ideas around techniques of subjectification, it becomes possible to understand mothers as subjects, who become subjected to the norms of maternity. Expert discourses about motherhood are more than mere representations; they become interventions into family life and mother–child relationships (Fraser, 1989; Foucault, 1994). Lawler (2000) contends that hegemonic understandings of the mother–child relationship inform maternal behaviours, and consequently mothers become constructed in certain ways. However, as social actors, mothers have opportunities to resist the conditions of their subjugation through subversion, negotiation and refusal of the identities and positionings that are produced for them. As Lawler states (2000: 168): 'Even those who make very heavy investments in maternal discourses – do not whole-heartedly or straightforwardly embrace the maternal positionings which would construct them only in terms of child-centred responsiveness.'

As outlined earlier in this chapter, the mothers of the women in this study are constructed in a myriad of ways. Their daughters (the participants in this study) vari-ously draw upon and reject hegemonic discourses available to understand mothering and the 'good/sensitive' mother. In doing this, they consequently become implicit in techniques of subjectification that operate upon *their* mothers (and mothers more broadly). However, as women located perilously close to dominant maternalistic discourses (through their gendered biological identities as 'potential mother' and through their professional identities as 'other-mothers'), the women in this study invested heavily in seeking to understand their own subject position. To deconstruct the narratives by problematising notions of motherhood and maternal subjectivities it is hoped that purchase on new ways of understanding nursery work can be had. I do this by reflecting upon the process and effects of interpellation (Althusser, 1971) – of taking up a subject position (of mother) – and the ways in which this is played out and/or resisted (Butler, 1990). My intention is to offer an understanding of the ways in which nursery worker identities are formed.

Fear and risks of be/coming mother

Rich (1977) offered a conceptualisation of 'matrophobia': a fear of becoming like one's mother, something she claimed was characteristic of many mother–daughter relationships. She argued that this fear becomes compounded by an over-identification with the mother, so much so that the daughter comes to hate her mother. Lawler (2000) contends that matrophobia takes place around a particular configuration of class. So that where a daughter occupies a different (higher) class position to that of her mother, she 'knows' that her working-class mother is discursively constructed as lacking, and her fear is centred around becoming like her working-class mother and hence becoming positioned as pathological or 'other'.

The concept of matrophobia is helpful in the context of understanding the narratives offered in this research. As I have attempted to illustrate, several women in this study felt ambivalence towards their mothers. The seemingly con-tradictory, apologetic and often defensive ways in which the women constructed their mothers signalled a tension and dissonance between hegemonic notions and alternative constructions offered by their mothers' subjectivities. When this is taken alongside the dominant constructions of nursery work (as 'mother-care' or 'other-mothering') which systematically act to devalue the work undertaken and naturalise it as a gendered activity, then a complex picture emerges of a group of women simultaneously resisting and embracing maternalistic discourses which shape their identities as nursery workers.

A number of the younger women in this research were vociferous in condemning be/coming a mother as beneath their talents and aspirations. These women tended to construct be/coming a mother as pitiful and pathetic; a 'non-choice' for women of their generation. Again, the pervasiveness of the normalising (middle-class) motherhood discourse was palpable in the narratives; in essence the logic was offered that *if* women have children then it should exist as a secondary priority to a professional career (one that can be maintained throughout, or resumed shortly after, early motherhood). For example, Orla, a 25-year-old senior practitioner with aspirations to become a teacher, expressed her views about be/coming a mother:

> Even though my mum had us young, well young by today's standards, we were never brought up to believe that having children should be an ambition. I see people my age with children and I actually think it is quite pathetic. If that is all you aspire to be is a mother…making it your life's ambition to breed is just sad.

Like Orla, others described the role their mothers played in encouraging them to defer becoming mothers, and instead to prioritise a career in the public sphere. For example, Zanthe described the pivotal role her mother played in her educational trajectory:

> It's very important to succeed, because my mum's education got cut short because of her upbringing in Greece and then she came here when she was sixteen…she's always wanted me and my sister to succeed, to go onto university and make something of our lives rather than just get married and have babies which is the norm…at the age of 21 my mum was married with a child, whereas me at 21 – I was moving out to go to uni.

Several of the women in this research, who were mothers themselves, had taken on that status at a young age. Reflecting upon their early entry into motherhood, these women were very self-critical. Again, the pernicious effects of the hegemonic discourses around 'good' mothering were visible.

Jayne: So did you plan to have the baby?
Precious: No! [laughs] I did not plan to have the baby! I was 18, no, not at all. I wasn't too happy, you know at 18 to have my own baby, but I thought I can't get rid of it; I'd never do that. My mum was really shocked and then not at all happy about it because she wanted me to carry on [with education], she thinks I can do better – nursing is what she wanted for me…she helps out though, if I can't be there then she will pick her [daughter] up [from nursery].

Gazala became a mother at 16 as a result of consummating her arranged marriage; she was very critical of what she considered to be her naivety and reflected on how traumatic the experiences of pregnancy, childbirth and ultimately motherhood had been for her:

> It [pregnancy] was not something I wanted to share, I didn't feel excited by it or anything like that, I just felt this is part of my life and I have to get on with it and this is a different culture. They [white friends] will never understand, so I hid it for as long as I could, then dropped out of school... I remember sitting in the hospital after she was born and I felt so alone, but then I pulled myself together, thought 'come on, that's life, move on' I told myself I had to just think positively and move on. So I went home and got on with it... I look back now though and see that I could have done x, y, z with my children but I didn't because I didn't know how, it could have been better but it wasn't that bad if you know what I mean.

These women criticised themselves for being too young, too preoccupied to do mothering the 'right' way, and considered themselves to lack the correct knowledge to nurture their children appropriately. In effect, the failure to embody the middle-class normative model of 'sensitive/good enough' mothering was felt by these women on multiple levels. As teenage mothers they become constructed in particularly negative ways in public discourse – discourses which they and their parents, and their mothers especially, drew upon. In addition to the harsh personal judgements these women cast upon themselves (for becoming mothers 'too soon', and not 'getting it right'), they received strong reactions from their parents, ranging from condemnation and hostility to disbelief and disappointment (most often the latter were expressed by their mothers). Maternal disapproval and/or disappointment invoked strong emotional responses in the women when recounting particular aspects of their lives. Both mothers and daughters drew heavily upon discourses that act to position them as certain kinds of gendered and classed subjects – in this instance 'the feckless working-class teenage mum'. An example of this is available in Ruth's story; she became unexpectedly pregnant at 18:

> I was just too young to be a mum and I didn't want the responsibility. My mum was in total shock and my dad refused to speak to me, which was hard because I was living at home. I remember this one time I wanted to go to the funfair with my friends and Mum wouldn't look after the baby, just because my dad didn't want her to, so I had one of those things [baby harness] and I just strapped the baby in and went to the fair anyway, just to be spiteful... I was a horrible teenager, I came home really late and she was standing on the doorstep telling me to give her the baby... I suppose I knew Mum would always be there and she was always going to look out for the baby.

Hey and Bradford (2006), like others (Steedman, 1986; Skeggs, 1997, 2003), argue that working-class mothers are blamed for societal ills. As teenage mothers, the women in this study became effectively 'written off' as the hopes that their mothers held for their escape and betterment were suspended whilst they took on the role and duties of motherhood.

For the women in this research a fear of becoming like their own working-class mothers – and their mothers' fear that their daughters would not traverse class boundaries to enjoy better life chances than they had experienced – was variously expressed. This sits in contrast to Walkerdine and Lucey's (1989) proposition that working-class mothers regulate their daughters in particular ways to prepare them for an adult life of gendered and classed oppression. The women from working-class families in this study frequently referred to their mothers' aspirations that they should 'do better' than they had done. Debbie described her mother as wilful, strong and a source of inspiration to 'get on in life', as she explained:

> Mum didn't share Dad's views… Mum was of the view that, you know if you worked hard enough you could do whatever you wanted to do in life…she always said, she always instilled that in us that we could achieve, and I must admit that's what I have done with my children, I've said to them you know you can be whatever you want to be if you work hard enough… I've probably inherited some of that, her spirit, her determination to move forward, I think I have taken on some of Mum's qualities, everybody hones in on it actually.

Rather than rejecting her mother's stoic, classed identity as something to despise, Debbie takes on aspects of her mother's subjectivity in a project of self-improvement, as part of her project of the self to move on and 'do better'. For other women in this study, though, displays of disapproval and negative judgements from their mothers (when they failed to 'do better') were commonplace. For example, Ordina's childminding mother actively dissuaded her from entering a career in childcare:

> I love working with children, it's what I want to do, but she [mother] doesn't think it is the best thing for me because she doesn't think it has been the best thing for her. She wanted me to do something else, something more, but in the end she does support me.

Tales of aspirational mothering emerged repeatedly in the course of the research, particularly among women who had left their mothers' class position. It appears that the mothers of these women shared the matrophobia conceptualised by Rich (1977) and Lawler (2000) – but for the mothers the fear was that their daughters should avoid replicating the lives they had lived. For these women (and their mothers), paid employment represented a form of social mobility, from casualised, informal employment and confinement in the domestic sphere to a career and accompanying respectability (Skeggs, 1997). Yet, the ambitions and aspirations of these women become constructed in different ways when considered through normalising middle-class discourses. For many working-class mothers the public construction of childcare and nursery work failed to equate to social mobility or achieving betterment, and so many actively discouraged their daughters from pursuing careers in nurseries and instead urged them towards medical or legal roles with higher status.

Doing motherhood – being mum

It is interesting to focus upon the reflections of 'doing mothering' amongst the women in this study who were mothers in addition to being 'other-mothers' in their professional roles in nurseries. As I illustrate later in this chapter, and as highlighted by Ailwood (2008), women working in ECEC invest heavily in a mother-like identity in their work whilst others refute the similarities and endeavour to demarcate their private identity as 'mum' from their professional identity as nursery worker. Here, though, I want to explore the mothering styles taken up by the women in this research and map the legacies of their own experiences of being mothered onto their maternal subjectivities.

Upward social mobility for many of the women in this research came at a hefty cost. A lack of authenticity at assuming a middle-class lifestyle and identity in their adult lives was palpable in many of the women's accounts. Class has come to be understood as relational, where middle-classness is the norm and working-classness a 'negative reference point' (Bourdieu, 1986). An important way in which class operates is through the marking of identities and selves as right or wrong, normal or pathological. Lawler (2000) explored the effects of social mobility on the women in her research and argued that they came to narrativise middle-class cultural capital into the self, so that the self becomes a project to be worked on, and in which the 'true self' can be brought to life through this project. The ability to 'pass' (as middle-class mothers) becomes a preoccupation, but there remains a constant reminder that the legitimate cultural capital owned is a relatively new acquisition; in effect, class is embedded in personal history.

In this chapter I demonstrate the ways in which particular maternal identities can be constructed on the basis of classed differences. For the women from working-class families, the 'project of the self' involved a process of sifting, sorting, adopting and rejecting aspects of their experiences of being mothered from their own maternal identity of doing mothering. This process was by no means straightforward or painless. I draw attention to Debbie, who described her commitment to emulating a middle-class approach in mothering her children. She was well versed in what Lawler (2008) refers to as 'psy discourses'. She drew heavily upon psychotherapeutic discourses; throughout her interviews Debbie variously referred to 'quality time', 'positive reinforcement', 'self-improvement', 'critical awareness' and so on when talking about her relationship with her daughter. She was also acutely aware that aesthetics become markers of class, and aspects of her lifestyle and her possessions signified an indication to the authenticity of her classed identity and hence that of her daughter:

> My daughter wants to be either a doctor or a lawyer, she's got really high aspirations which I am really pleased about, she's going to university, she's known that for a long time that's what she wants to do... You know, it's like she does double bass lessons, she sings in a gospel choir...it's all these extra things that make her a rounded person... It's important for my daughters to have the best we can give them: nice house, nice rooms, you know like I think it is important for them to have music lessons, to be taken out, those sorts of things and for us to spend quality time together, things like reading stories with them, going to the park, swimming, cooking, those sorts of things are really important to family life.

Debbie later reflects on her capabilities as a mother in respect of nurturing the self of her daughter (Lawler, 2000). In dominant maternalist discourses good mothering practice is defined as a mother's capacity to nurture an autonomous child. Furthermore, the 'good enough' mother will naturally care for her child in such a way that the child's 'real self' (autonomous and self-directed) can develop (Winnicott, 1965).

> I would say I overdid it with my eldest daughter, I mean for the first five years of her life it was just the two of us, I never left her and wouldn't leave her – with anyone, I just didn't feel I could trust anybody to look after her. So I probably suffocated her to be honest, it hasn't done her any favours, she lacks confidence now and says things like she's ugly, she's fat...but my second one is much more confident, independent, assertive, you can see that quite clearly and that's because I let her make her own mistakes and I am not so in her face as I was with [eldest daughter].

In this quote we can see that Debbie's reference to 'suffocating' her daughter through her maternal practices is used to judge her mothering as inappropriate and pathological because it stifled an autonomous self to emerge in her daughter. Elsewhere in her narrative Debbie infers that when mothering her eldest daughter she occupied a working-class position, as an unemployed single mother. Yet with her second daughter, Debbie had 'moved on' in marital, geographical as well as class terms. As we see in her account, the newly middle-class Debbie felt more capable of performing normative (middle-class) mothering – by letting her youngest daughter make her own mistakes, she was able to nurture the self of her daughter to become autonomous and hence self-regulatory (Foucault, 1979).

Through Gazala's narrative it is possible to identify the interplay and tensions between various maternalistic discourses. Earlier in this chapter Gazala's mother is constructed as pathological in her failure to embody hegemonic mothering. In turn, when located in dominant maternalistic discourses, Gazala's own mothering becomes pathologised. At 16 she fell outside what is culturally and socially accepted as the 'right' age to become a mother, and her related inexperience and a lack of financial resources available to sufficiently meet the perceived 'needs' of her children compounds this construction further. Consequently, Gazala has a particularly negative identity conferred upon her. Yet she defends her maternalism for the effective reconciliatory function it served her with her past:

> With my own children, I have four children of my own and I felt I gave them what I didn't get in my childhood. You know you hear people say that it is usual for the abused to become the abuser, or if you've suffered then you inflict suffering, but I have not felt like that. I wanted to give my children what was missing for me… I look at my children now and they have been protected, they haven't got a clue about so many things, I had to, I had experiences that I shouldn't have had. I may not have been the best mother, at 16 I was too young and I realise now, having studied early childhood and worked with children professionally, that there are things I could have done with them that I didn't but I know that they haven't suffered, they have had balance, although they didn't have enough of some things it wasn't bad for them, if you know what I mean.

The influence of dominant authoritative ECEC discourses on maternal subjectivity is identifiable in this quote. Whilst nursery work becomes readily constructed through maternalistic discourses, so the authoritative discourses of ECEC practices come to inflect maternal practices and subjectivities. Other mothers, for example Bhadra, referred to the impact working in a nursery and studying an early childhood degree had upon her mothering style; she considered herself more 'insightful and reflective' about her son's behaviour and development and able to exercise greater empathy. This signals congruence between aspects of dominant maternalistic discourses and authoritative ECEC discourses, something I explore more extensively later in this chapter.

Like the studies undertaken by Walkerdine and Lucey (1989) and Lawler (2000), this study exposes authoritarian approaches to mothering as persistent in the women's narratives about their own mothering styles, although qualifications are made to suggest that mothering was also performed in sensitive, empathic and nurturing ways as well as the more widely accepted regulatory and authoritarian (working-class) approaches. The mothers in this study, perhaps precisely because they are located across a discursive landscape that encompasses knowledge and access to authoritative discourses about 'good mothering', come to exercise acute self-reflexivity about their own practices (as mother and as nursery worker). The mothers here tended to judge their maternal self in relation to various normalisations about how to mother and how to best define, then meet, children's needs. The locatedness within, and access to, hegemonic discourses have shaped the mothers' subjective understandings of their maternal (and professional) selves. What is also evident, though, is a resistance to particular identities being conferred upon these women.

Aspiring to be/come the other-mother

Throughout this study the women were invited to reflect upon their decisions to enter careers in nursery work. Although some stated lifelong impassioned commitments to working with children, for others, decisions to work with children were shaped and directed by influential actors, such as teachers and careers advisers. For the women who entered careers in childcare later, it tended to stem from their maternal status; in effect taking up a maternal subjectivity was seen to indicate a level of wisdom and experience necessary to work with children in a formal setting.

Nursery work is both highly gendered and classed (see Osgood, 2005) since it remains predominantly female (EOC, 2006) and predominantly the career 'choice' of working-class girls (Osgood *et al.*, 2006). As such it is a career laden with negative connotations in symbolic terms – that is, lack of status, prestige (Skeggs, 2003). Furthermore, in practice, careers in ECEC continue to be relatively poorly paid, offering unfavourable working conditions and generally limited career prospects. In previous research (Osgood *et al.*, 2006) I highlighted the ways in which working-class girls are channelled into working-class careers throughout their schooling and vocational experiences, which is further supported by this study. The routine devaluing of caring professions generally (Skeggs, 1997), and nursery work specifically in relation to this argument, results in social mobility that lacks validity for these women. Despite attempts to traverse class boundaries through education and employment, the women have failed in their quest to mark themselves as significantly different/superior to their mothers.

The professional identity of a nursery worker is discursively constructed in ways that act to limit the exchange value of highly gendered and classed work (Skeggs, 2003). For the younger women in this study, the high cost of living in central London, combined with the low salaries associated with nursery work, meant that it was typical to remain in the family home whilst in employment. This was a situation felt to further compound the effects of matrophobia; these women were effectively living a subsidised existence in the working-class home of their childhood where the prospect of achieving even spatial distance from their mothers was denied. Precious expressed her views on living with her mother into her 20s:

> I can't even afford to buy my own place, or rent for that matter at the moment. I mean I have a really good relationship with my mum and everything but still being there at this age is not ideal you know, it's not where I thought I'd be at this point in my life, and having Mum looking in on what I'm doing, or not doing [laughs] can be a bit intense sometimes.

I would suggest that the women in this study were fearful that their adult selves should avoid resembling their mothers too closely. This concern was transposed onto constructing a professional identity as nursery worker that was sufficiently distinct/superior to the maternal roles performed by their mothers, and for those who were mothers, distinct from their own maternal practices. When questioned about public constructions of nursery work and its location within maternalistic discourses, there was overwhelming protest that nursery work was distinct and markedly different from mothering. I pay particular attention to the prevalence and effects of maternalistic discourses on the formation of hegemonic professional identities later in this chapter and again in the next chapter. However, what remains is an acknowledgement among the women in this study that a career in ECEC, day-to-day work in a nursery setting, is publicly constructed in negative ways. Yet despite the negative constructions conferred on nursery work(ers) (through various authoritative discourses), these women remain committed and impassioned about the work that they do – even though the work is widely considered to resemble 'mother-care' and is not associated with the degree of social mobility that they (and their aspirational working-class mothers) had hoped for.

Remaining with the theme of mothering relationships, I next want to turn to a close examination of the relationships between nursery workers (as 'other-mothers' and potential/actual biological mothers) and the working mothers who make use of them. I endeavour to dismantle these relationships and the assumptions upon which they are based to expose the insidious effects of classed and 'raced' identities on a highly gendered relationship hinged upon an exchange of emotional labour – in the pursuit of caring for young children.

Making up the middle-class nursery worker

The classed relationship between childcarer and mother has been the focus of recent research (Vincent and Ball, 2006), but this study offers an opportunity to focus more intently on the views, experiences and perspectives of the nursery worker. I will demonstrate that the classed configuration of the relationship is significantly altered depending upon the type of childcare provision under consideration. I argue that nursery workers occupy particular subjectivities dependent upon their location in classed/'raced'/gendered relationships with parents and other professionals working with young children. As outlined in Chapter 3, my reasons for including a private for-profit nursery as well as nurseries from the statutory and voluntary sectors was so that the complex classed dimension of the relationship between nursery worker and mother could be explored.

Having previously undertaken extensive research in nurseries (from different sectors), I was unsurprised to find that the private nursery tended to have relatively high levels of staff turnover, a presence of temporary staff, generally low salaries, and minimally qualified staff. In this study, Mulberry Bush Nursery took exclusively fee-paying, predominantly white, middle-class children from three months to three years old. This provided a site for highly classed and 'raced' relationships between nursery worker and mother, where the nursery worker is positioned in an inferior position of servitude to the professional middle-class mother. Meantime, Apple Tree (statutory) provided provision to a more even mix of children from a range of class and minority ethnic backgrounds. The demographic profile of children at Mango Grove (voluntary) principally reflected the immediate urban working-class community it served; as such, it was ethnically diverse and included immigrant children with specific language and literacy needs. Furthermore, a number of the children in the statutory and voluntary sector nurseries were 'statemented' with special educational needs/behavioural difficulties, and others were referred from social services because they were considered 'at risk' in their home environment. Compared with the private nursery, workers in these settings were more readily constructed as 'experts' in child development and the classed relationship became inverted – where the nursery worker assumed a more middle-class, professional role which became increasingly pronounced in relationships with parents constructed as 'lacking' or pathological in public discourse (i.e. families referred by social services).

The various positionings of the nursery worker, as more or less professional/ more or less middle class, become dependent upon where she is located at any given moment. The fluid and constant shifts in identity were significant in terms of the subjective experiences of 'being professional' (Helsby, 1995) or doing professionalism authentically. This signals the importance of middle-class discourses that position particular subjects (nursery workers) in particular ways, and the process of interpellation that occurs – where the nursery worker takes up that subject position and comes to understand the self in certain ways. In drawing on the narratives from the women located in different sectors, I seek to demonstrate how this plays out in relation to the naming, formation and negotiation of a professional identity in nursery work.

As a statutory sector nursery, Apple Tree attracted a broadly mixed demographic profile to include children from inner city housing estates (predominantly occupied by benefit claimants and characterised by high levels of unemployment) to professional middle-class families (for whom their child's attendance at a state-run nursery was part of a broader moral-political commitment to leftist liberal values). In general, the staff felt valued and respected by the parents of the children in the nursery. Many constructed the relationship with parents as one founded upon mutual respect, partnership and shared goals/values, which was facilitated and maintained through good lines of communication. The nursery workers presented as confident in their professional role and stressed the responsibility they had to educate parents about the importance of their work:

Francelle: What we have got to remember as practitioners is that children are within our care five days a week and at the end the parents are in charge; sometimes we can tend to forget that. We [practitioners] can think that we know best because we are the professional but if we work well with parents, communicate well with them then they can see the benefits of what we are doing above and beyond what they do with their child at home and they come to respect us. It is our responsibility to help them to understand what we do.

Uttal (1996: 305) proposes that relations between parents and the childcare provider can be 'co-ordinated' when the relationship is characterised by 'synchronising philosophies, values and practices'. Evidence of working towards 'co-ordinated' relations was available in both the statutory and voluntary sector nurseries. Open days and parents' evenings were common practices at Apple Tree to engage and educate parents about the role, scope and underpinning philosophy of the nursery. At such events parents were invited to experience, first hand, the activities that their children engaged in on a daily basis and the rationale and theoretical justifications for the activities. Parents were also involved in 'an open dialogue' in respect of the strategic direction of the nursery; parents were regularly consulted and canvassed for their opinions on decisions around the management and direction of the nursery. Such activities were felt to foster strong lines of communication and had the inadvertent benefit of raising the status and profile of the nursery staff.

This is not to suggest that the staff at Apple Tree Nursery were entirely satisfied or free of criticism about the public constructions of nursery work and nursery workers. However, unlike the private sector nursery, there were no references to 'disrespectful' parents at either Apple Tree (statutory) or Mango Grove (voluntary). The power relations between parents and staff at these nurseries were distinct from those described at Mulberry Bush. Hence the ways in which nursery workers are constructed is through the lens of parental expectations and experiences. Although different groups of parents were deemed to have varying expectations of their child's nursery experience, this bore no relation to the ways in which the staff were constructed. As Iesha explained:

> There are those at one end of the spectrum that think it is *just* play and then at the other end you have parents who want their children reading and writing, you know that think we are in the business of cultivating little Einsteins ready for *real* school. But once we have educated them about what it is we are doing then they take it on board and accept that we know what we are doing and I think you can feel that they are mostly appreciative of our knowledge, our expertise you know?

In similar ways the staff at Mango Grove considered parental constructions of them as 'professional' to be generally positive. Again, through a range of partnership activities, relationships were considered to develop from a base of 'mutual respect' and 'genuine partnership'.

The demographic profile of the children at Mango Grove was more socioeconomically homogeneous than at Apple Tree; the intake was almost exclusively drawn from the immediate urban working-class community. Like Apple Tree, though, there was a strong emphasis placed on the active involvement of parents in the running of the nursery (as a voluntary sector nursery this was achieved through a committee structure with elected representatives from the local community shaping the strategic direction of the setting). Again, insights into the complexities of managing, running and doing nursery work were heightened amongst the parents using the nursery, which led to discursive constructions of the staff as esteemed experts:

Bertrise: Through the classes we run for parents, they are starting to recognise that we have the expertise in the area of child development. So through training and experience [of using the nursery] they come to rely on us for expert, professional knowledge, so we have become classed as professional in their eyes and that wasn't how it was before; we now have professional status and standing.

The nursery staff invested heavily and promulgated the construction of 'professional expert'. The women from Mango Grove described the crucial role they played in a professional capacity to provide children with opportunities to access/ acquire cultural capital from their nursery experiences. In effect, the nursery workers represent the means through which middle-class experiences became within reach of 'disadvantaged/vulnerable' urban working-class children:

Ruth: We take them to the theatre, to museums, to galleries; they have access to a whole lot of cultural artsy stuff, so their horizons are being broadened if you like. It is unlikely that anyone living round here would think to do those things with their children; it's just not on their radar, not an interest. It's outside their world basically.

Just as negative constructions of the nursery worker can become created and embedded through the social milieu within which they are located, so too can positive constructions. But it appears that positive constructions are less stable, transferable or sustainable when taken out of a specific time and space. For example, the voluntary sector nursery workers referred to the much less favourable constructions offered by colleagues in the statutory sector and/or by related professionals working with children (such as health visitors, social workers and child psychologists). Although the nursery worker forms part of the authoritative framework designed to support 'vulnerable' families, their relational (and inferior) discursive positioning became evident. What is exposed through the parental constructions of the nursery workers at both Apple Tree and Mango Grove is the very fragile nature of the discursive positionings offered. The 'expert, respected professional' and the 'transmitter/facilitator of cultural enrichment' become entirely dependent upon the social and cultural location, and the wider discourses that are drawn upon in constructing such identities. The career trajectories and qualifications held by the staff interviewed at Mulberry Bush were not significantly marked from those of the women at Apple Tree and Mango Grove, yet the ways in which the nursery worker is positioned as more or less expert, more or less professional and more or less middle class is shaped and determined by the discourses in which she is located at any given moment.

The classed subject: the nursery worker as working-class other(ed) mother

> They [mothers] acknowledge the degree to which other people are caring for and influencing their children's social and moral development...they perceive themselves as sharing mothering with their childcare providers.'
>
> (Uttal, 1996: 303)

This quote from Uttal reflects, perhaps more accurately, the situation at Apple Tree and Mango Grove (described above) than the case in the private sector nursery. I would argue that, while middle-class professional mothers at Mulberry Bush might acknowledge the influence the nursery workers have in their child's life, they are far from ready to 'share mothering' with them.

When asked to comment on the relationships with parents/mothers, the staff at Mulberry Bush devoted a disproportionate time in each of the three interviews specifically to this topic. The data are saturated with highly emotional accounts (expressed through a combination of anger, frustration, offence and injustice) when describing encounters with parents in their day-to-day work at the nursery. Through the interactions with middle-class mothers the nursery workers described a painful process of pathologisation. For example, Nyesha:

> It makes you question why you do this. The only reason I stay is the children, but it is the nursery and the parents that it attracts that are the issue here. The nursery is only interested in making money and the parents see us as part of the nursery – like the tables and chairs, we are just here. But come on, we have souls, we are human, we suffer and they sit there thinking that it is okay for us, well it's not. I think this is why so many people are leaving: no respect, why would they stay on? I think a lot of these girls have more courage than I do, but they are going, which is good for them and it sends a message, I respect what they do, I think go for it and if wasn't for my key children then I would probably go too.

This study exposes an acute class distinction between the professional working mother and nursery worker in the commercially driven private sector. Vincent and Ball (2006) suggest that parents have a more diffuse and distant relationship with the carers in nurseries than those who offer home-based care because the focus is centred on the ethos and character of the nursery rather than the individual workers. The quote from Nyesha's transcript (in particular, her reference to be being treated as part of the furniture) would seem to support this proposition. However, I would argue that the implications of a diffused/distant relationship are far reaching for the ontological security and professional identity of the nursery worker. Vincent and Ball (2006: 116) argue that the 'power in the care relationship lies with the provider and the parent has to take or leave what is on offer'. I would suggest the care relationship and the nexus of power is significantly more complex than this. It appears that workers in (private sector) nurseries become dehumanised and obscured from parental view where nursery provision is 'marketed' to parents as a 'service'. It is quite typical for nurseries from all sectors to set out aims, mission statements and institutional philosophies in marketing material. However, what marked Mulberry Bush as distinct from the other nurseries in this study was that the 'public face' of the nursery philosophy was embodied in the manager. I turn to my fieldnotes to convey my initial impressions of Delia juxtaposed the main staff body:

> I briefly met Delia before going in to chat to the rest of the team, she was much younger than I had thought she would be (perhaps mid-20s), quite tomboyish in her dress and manner, she appeared to be middle/upper class – I would hazard a guess that she was public school educated and probably very outdoorsy. She was very well spoken and direct almost to the point of abruptness, she struck me as extremely confident. I was whisked into the largest room in the nursery and shown to my seat, whereupon Delia left the room. The youthfulness of the group was striking, Delia (like most other nursery managers I have known) referred to her team as 'the girls', it seemed particularly apt at Mulberry Bush – I would estimate the average age was 20. The class distinction between Delia and 'the girls' was palpable. The team appeared very urban, very working class, bold, in-your-face, presenting a brash/distinctive version of femininity – one that attaches importance to teenage fashion and popular culture, no-nonsense, straight-talking working-class youthful femininity and seemingly brimming with confidence (not unlike Skeggs 'becoming respectable' girls' – Skeggs, 1997).

The data indicate that many middle-class mothers judged the working-class identities of the girls in pathological terms. Vincent and Ball (2006) exposed the class prejudice and emotionality that are central to shaping (negative) parental opinions about childcare workers. Hence, it appears that at Mulberry Bush there was a deliberate strategy in place to conceal or minimise the direct interaction between 'the girls' and the mothers; instead, the character of the nursery as a 'home from home', i.e. middle-class environment, was achieved through aesthetic resources and the middle-class identity of the manager. So middle-class mothers come to construct the nursery as 'acceptable' based upon an artificially constructed middle-class character and ethos. Of course, all parties – mothers, nursery workers, manager and ultimately children – were embedded within this artificiality. The classed and 'raced' interactions between 'the girls' and the mothers were obscured through formal practices (some parents preferred to liaise directly, and wherever possible, exclusively, with the manager rather than with the key worker assigned to their child). Furthermore, the daily interactions between the nursery worker and the white, middle-class children in her care were ubiquitously classed and 'raced', but this was a fact apparently and conveniently overlooked by the mothers. The lack of (positive) interaction between the (working-class) nursery worker and (middle-class) parent acted to position the women in this study in particularly damaging ways:

Ordina: Some parents think that I am lower than them because I am looking after their child, they think that maybe I am not clever...some just take liberties all the time; you know turning up late, or handing their child over with a dirty nappy, it's like they are almost thinking 'well what does it matter, she doesn't have a life, have feelings, she is there to look after my child and that's then end of the story' you know? They can really talk down to us you know, like we are so much lower in terms of worth, they just talk down to you the whole time.

Working-class feminists (Walkerdine and Lucey, 1989; Hey, 1997; Reay, 1997; Skeggs, 1997, 2003) have highlighted the ways in which working-class women are pathologised as bad, insensitive, repulsive and so on through a process of othering from middle-class normativity. The relationships and interactions between the working-class 'girls' and the middle-class mothers at Mulberry Bush illustrate this process of pathologisation. The coping mechanism for the mothers at handing the care of their child to working-class carers – the primary strategy employed – was to avoid engaging with the pathological nursery worker wherever possible, but failing that, some mothers overtly exerted power/control over the staff through derogatory and disrespectful behaviour:

Radka: I think some parents have no respect for us, you know for some parents it is a case of 'she's here to look after my child beyond that I don't care about her, I am paying for it, that is what she is paid to do and that is an end to it'. I find that very rude... I find it very hard to communicate with some, I try my best but it is difficult when you are made to feel worthless and yet our role in their child's life is so important.

As outlined in the literature review, there is a wealth of commentary and research which explores the psychic and emotional costs of returning to work for professional middle-class mothers. As I argued in Chapter 2, the sense of anxiety/ guilt that comes from using childcare is often projected onto the women who look after the working mothers' children. The analysis offered here supports this proposition and illustrates the theorisations offered by Armstrong (2006) of class difference between mothers who combine employment and motherhood, so that most of the middle-class mothers using Mulberry Bush Nursery experience 'compromised individualism' and the consequential sense of guilt and unease at leaving their children in the care of other women. This accounts for the antagonistic relationships between the mothers and the nursery workers in this setting. Meanwhile, the working-class mothers (which in this study comprise a proportion of the mothers using the Apple Tree and Mango Grove nurseries *and* some of the nursery workers who are also mothers) feel 'relational pragmatism'

– a 'needs must' approach to placing their children in nursery whilst they work. Armstrong also identifies acute ambivalence amongst mothers who have traversed class boundaries when reflecting on combining work and motherhood (again this includes a number of the nursery workers – particularly those in senior positions – and a proportion of mothers using the nurseries).

The distinctions offered by Armstrong (op. cit.) are detectable in the accounts provided by the nursery workers in this study – both in relation to themselves (as working mothers) and the differences that they identify between working and middle-class mothers and between different factions of those classes through their daily professional encounters. Precious, a working mother employed at Mulberry Bush, illustrates this concept well in her account of occupying both subject positions – working mother and nursery worker:

Jayne: What's difficult about the parents? Do you feel they respect what you do?
Precious: No, I think some parents do but there's only a few. And they are the
                 ones who wonder how we manage with ten children when they find
                 it hard to look after one or two, do you know what I mean? Some of
                 them can understand and some have worked in a nursery before so
                 they know. But then we've got some who have no idea, no clue at all
                 and probably think we are the worst staff on earth...
Jayne: How are you as a parent with a child in nursery? When you drop her
                 off or collect her?
Precious: I am nothing like any of the parents here which is why I think they,
                 [...] I've never fussed, I've never moaned, I've always been friendly, I
                 know exactly how it is and I don't see any point in stressing the staff,
                 do you know what I mean? When I know exactly what they've been
                 through during their day. I always just go, pick her up, have little
                 conversations with them obviously, see how things are but I've never
                 moaned or made their lives any harder than it already is. That's the one
                 thing, the parents that come in here they give you a mouthful and you
                 think 'gosh I don't get paid enough to be treated like this!'

Whilst the narratives offer illustrations of the effects of classed and 'raced' differences between (principally white) middle-class mothers and working-class nursery workers (from a range of ethnic and cultural backgrounds), exceptions were presented, so that we come to understand that 'not all', or only 'a small minority' or 'one or two', mothers behaved in ways that the nursery workers considered exploitative and prejudicial. But where relationships were shaped by differences in class practices and subjectivities, they were pernicious in their effects upon nursery worker constructions of a professional self. In offering a means to understand the reasons why some mothers invest so heavily in constructing nursery workers in particularly pathological ways, my intention is not to justify but rather to highlight the ways in which middle-class discourses about 'quality of childcare' are shaped by subjective encounters and classed assumptions.

Others become unwittingly implicated in sustaining dominant (middle-class) constructions of the 'inferior nursery worker'. An example of this can be found in the seemingly benevolent approach taken by the (white, middle-class) manager at Mulberry Bush Nursery. She had also identified the heavy costs of the negative discursive positioning of the nursery workers as worthless, untrustworthy and so on:

Delia: They [parents] treat me [nursery manager] differently to the girls. The girls are perceived as beneath the parents. I've seen it myself and it's shocking how they can treat them, it's just horrible. Obviously it is part of my role to stamp that out, and I do intervene when I see it going on but it doesn't alter the parents' perceptions. They [parents] don't see them [nursery staff] as being in anyway equal, they see them as relatively uneducated, maybe it's the language that they [nursery staff] use – strong London accents, and maybe the spelling in their record-keeping is not good and also they don't hold themselves as well as they could…many lack professional confidence, when somebody is good at their job, know that they are good at their job and put that across to parents then they become adored and perceived as incredibly professional…but where that is lacking, parents don't trust the girls to pass on a message or to give medication or whatever, which is totally unnecessary, unfounded because they are completely competent, but it is how they are perceived that is the issue.

Although Delia is protective of the working-class women working at Mulberry Bush, she nevertheless draws upon and sustains middle-class normalising discourses through her identification of markers of difference, such as accent, and presentation of self. Class is inscribed on the self, and it is repeatedly signified through distinctions: in lifestyle, food, aesthetics and so on. The mothers were engaged in deploying practical signifiers to locate 'the girls' in the broadest sense but also to locate them in relation to themselves. As Bourdieu (1986: 6) contends: 'Taste classifies and it classifies the classifier. Social subjects classified by classification distinguish themselves by the distinctions they make, between the beautiful and the ugly, the distinguished and the vulgar.'

The way that 'the girls' dress, the food that they consume, the way in which they speak – all come to distinguish them as lacking in terms of cultural capital (Skeggs, 1997). The failure of the girls to embody middle-classness marked them as deficient and worthy of suspicion and hence regulation. Delia argues that the parents were distrustful and sceptical of the nursery workers' professional capabilities based upon their embodiment of a classed identity (rather than their professional conduct), and consequently liaised directly with her (as 'somebody like us', i.e. white middle-class professional; see Ball, 2003b) to safeguard the well-being of their children and/or mark their superiority.

The analysis offered here paints a bleak picture of the professional lives of the nursery workers in the private sector. Whilst structural factors including low pay, poor working conditions and so on were identified by nursery workers from across the sectors – and were sources of dissatisfaction and cause of demoralisation – the symbolic and psychic costs of the classed relationships between carer and parent were more significant with regard to self-worth and ontological security. It is perhaps for this reason that the women at Mulberry Bush invested considerable energy in casting judgements about middle-class working mothers, as a form of defensiveness and a means of marking themselves as morally superior. Skeggs (1997) identified strategies of self-preservation employed by working-class women engaged in professional caring:

> A caring identity is based not only on the fulfilment of the needs of others and selflessness but also on their own desire to feel valuable. Their altruism makes them feel good. They are aware of their position in the social hierarchy of knowledge and to dissipate its effects they position themselves as morally superior caring subjects. In the process they become ethical beings, who define and regulate themselves according to a moral code which establishes precepts for conducting and judging their own lives.
>
> (Skeggs, 1997: 62)

As outlined in earlier sections of this chapter, the concept of becoming a mother was repellent to many of the younger women in this study. Maternal responsibilities were seen as a barrier to social mobility or because doing mothering required total self-sacrifice and commitment. Such views were undoubtedly informed by personal experience of being mothered, and in other cases doing mothering, and also their professional subjectivities of being engaged in work that is publicly constructed as 'mother-like'. But further, I would suggest that the painful encounters and negative discursive subject positions conferred upon nursery workers acted to promote the creation of counter-narratives – around the uncaring/neglectful/selfish professional middle-class mother. 'Dumping ground' was a commonly deployed phrase when referring to middle-class mothers' constructions of the purpose/function of nursery provision. Possibilities to invert class divisions and claim moral superiority to middle-class women who 'farm out' their children are afforded through the counter-narratives devised by nursery workers (located in the private sector):

Batinah: I personally don't think that a nursery is the place for tiny babies. I wonder what their mums are thinking when they leave them here. If you have a child then you should be there for them not dump them here so that you can carry on with your life like nothing's changed. When they [babies] first arrive they are not at all happy; because of the new atmosphere, the new environment, new faces, missing their mum basically, they probably experience a strange feeling like 'Oh my god! What am I doing here? Why have I been left here with all these strangers, why doesn't my mummy want me? What did I do wrong?' That's something I could never see myself doing, it's just too cruel.

The morally superior, caring self is both performance and subjective technique, used to generate a sense of responsibility and respectability. Or as Skeggs (1997: 69) argues, 'doing caring is fundamental to a sense of self.' Through this relational construction, of nursery worker as morally superior to middle-class working mother, the women manage to claim some purchase on a valued/ valuable identity.

Further to casting judgement about what the professional working mothers failed to do with their children (due to their absence during the working day), critiques were offered about what these women actually did with their children when in their care. The normative, middle-class model of sensitive mothering designed to promote self-regulation was constructed in alternative ways by the nursery workers. Precious, a working mother herself (but of necessity rather than choice), cast doubt on the merits of normative styles of middle-class parenting which she considered overly liberal and therefore deficient:

Precious: I think a lot of parents need to go on parent training classes because a lot of the children here have got no discipline, they've got no boundaries, do you know what I mean? So they [children] come here doing whatever they want and then it's down to us to set the boundaries because there aren't any at home, so I think what parents don't do at home makes our job a lot harder than it needs to be.

Davies (1992), followed by Lawler (2000), argue that mothering is a metaphor whereby mothering is represented as a series of activities involving a combination of nurturance and regulation. Nursery workers (the 'other-mothers') become charged with regulation whilst nurturance is left to the (middle-class working) mother. But at Mulberry Bush, professional middle-class mothers are deemed to fail on both counts; to either embody a caring self or to offer proper guidance and regulation so that their children can function in socially acceptable ways.

Nursery work as 'other(ed)-mothering'

Referring back to the quote provided by Ailwood (2008) at the beginning of this chapter, it is widely accepted that nursery workers variously invest in and reject maternalistic discourses in ECEC. The narratives of the women in this study support this. However, what I attempt to illustrate, through analyses of the data, is the implications of this for 'projects of the self' and the formation of a 'professional' identity. Unlike Ailwood (op. cit.), I refute that the acceptance or promotion of maternalistic discourses in ECEC act to compromise professionalism – particularly when an alternative form of professionalism is conceived where it does not rest upon masculinist, neo-liberal discourses (Osgood, 2006a, 2006b, 2006c). (I turn to a more detailed presentation of alternative constructions of professionalism in Chapter 7 but offer it here in the context of motherhood subjectivities.)

The nursery workers in this study held contradictory and/or ambivalent stances on public constructions of nursery work as 'mother-like' or a form of 'other-mothering'. Elsewhere, I have outlined the conflation of mother-like attributes of ECEC practice with doing mothering (Osgood, 2004, 2005, 2008). The principal similarities that lie in the nature of the work, the very physical nature of nursery work and an overriding concern with the physical well-being of the child are not unlike that expected and performed by mothers. But further to meeting the basic physical needs of a child, like a mother, the nursery worker is expected to safeguard (and nurture) the social and emotional self of the child – and this is achieved through a range of methods that rely on affective skills. Like the 'good/sensitive' middle-class mother, the effective nursery worker is able to nurture the child to become an autonomous, self-regulatory agent (Elfer *et al.*, 2003), or in the *Birth to Three Matters* discourse: a strong child, a skilful communicator, a competent learner and a healthy child (Sure Start, 2004). The highly emotional labour of nursery work is associated with the feminine and so comes to be accepted in public discourse as highly gendered work; and work that is further constructed through naturalising discourses as the work of (potential/actual) mothers. The mothers in this study readily drew upon such public constructions. For example, some were initially drawn into the profession because it offered opportunities to 'do what comes naturally', 'what I'd been doing at home with the kids already' – Toni, Gazala, Francelle, Ruth and Bertrise all entered careers in nursery work because they had helped shape their own children's preschool experiences as volunteers. When these women entered careers in childcare in the 1980s and 1990s, an implicit assumption was cast that motherhood was sufficient grounding for work in a nursery with groups of children. This was widely refuted by these women and others in this study; for example, Ysabelle was eight months' pregnant when she spoke about the distinction between nursery work and mothering:

> It is just not true. We work in partnership with other adults and we have five or six children to look after. What you do at home with your own child and what you do in a nursery is completely different, it could maybe help a little bit but in here you interact with children in a particular way – not a motherly way...of course, you would be emotionally attached to each child but it is a different kind of relationship because at five o'clock you are leaving to go home, you shut your eyes to it then, you can't really get too touched or you would crumble...as a professional you step back and you can see there are many explanations for a child whereas a parent would not want to see many of those things...our observations mean that we can be outside of where a parent would be.

Ysabelle's reference to boundaries, objectivity and the ability to disengage at the end of the working day shape her particular construction of professionalism; however, like the other women in this study, she acknowledges the emotional nature of the work and the psychic investments (that are necessary aspects of the profession but which act to position it outside of hegemonic masculinist discourses around professionalism; see Osgood, 2008). Although several of the mothers who came into nursery work by virtue of their maternal status and experiences then challenged assumptions that nursery work was a form of 'other-mothering', this was a position that emerged over time. Toni and Gazala both entered nursery work because it offered a means to spend time with their children and access employment, but both are now graduates in Early Childhood Studies and have many years of practical experience:

Toni: I don't think it's like mothering, no. You have to work at a professional level and that involves setting boundaries, umm I think many people have the perception that it [nursery work] is all lovey-dovey, cuddles and love, and yes you do get that but then there is the professional aspect which involves setting boundaries and you have to have that because otherwise you would have staff wanting to take on motherly roles and that is not workable, appropriate, you know and what's more parents can get very upset by that.

It is interesting that Toni demarcates emotional displays of affection and being professional. This is indicative of the ambivalent attitudes the women present when discussing their professional conduct and hence professional selves. In drawing upon hegemonic discourses about professionalism, the presence of a maternalistic disposition or motherly behaviours – whilst seemingly instinctive and intrinsic – is constructed as inappropriate and out of place in a 'professional' childcare environment. Throughout the narratives, the women appear to wrestle with the presence of maternalistic discourses when reflecting upon the formation and promotion of professional identities in nursery work. Maternalism is omnipresent but dismissed as if it were a 'guilty secret' – a disposition that is widely taken on but routinely hidden from view or actively suppressed. Gazala offered some clarity on the presence of maternalistic discourses and the interplay with professional discourses:

It [nursery work] always seemed to me something natural that women do; it wasn't a profession in my eyes – not before I came into it. I couldn't understand why anybody who wasn't a mum would want to work with very young children, why would it be of interest to them? How could they know what to do? But now obviously, with thirteen or more years of experience and, you know, training, qualifications under my belt I see things differently and can fully appreciate how specialised good quality nursery care is and how totally unlike mothering it is, it is about boundaries and expert knowledge, working *with* parents not replicating what they do.

The prevalence of maternalistic discourses that informed the initial impressions and expectations of these women when entering careers in nursery work are both pervasive and persuasive. For some, the motivation to embark upon a career in nursery work stemmed from an apparent proximity to mothering and therefore a means to reconcile inadequacies of personal mothering experiences (of being mothered or of doing mothering – in either case, working as a nursery worker was constructed as a means to address the failures to achieve/experience middle-class normativity). The motivations and initial expectations held by these women act to reinforce gendered understandings of nursery work as mother-like. In recognising the limiting effects of maternalistic discourses upon the professional status/identity of nursery work, the women appear troubled by their apparent complicity in sustaining negative constructions and so offer an alternative reading of their work. However, as others have argued (Katz, 1995; Friere, 1999; Moyles, 2001; Vogt, 2002), maternalism (or at least the affective characteristics associated with doing mothering) is intrinsic to working with very young children, and so hegemonic discourses remain in place as an undercurrent in the narratives:

Delia: It can't be like mothering; we will always be doing it differently because we have a group of children and they have one. Children have to wait for things in a nursery, they can't scream for an instant reaction, we can't whip them up and smother them in kisses and cuddles. We have more than one thing to do at any one time, we have to change a nappy, feed another baby, administer another child's medication; it's just a totally different situation. But that said, there is that, not maternal instinct, but you look after them according to their parents wishes...so in a sense you can be extending what Mum does at home, but you are not a substitute mother, it is just not possible.

Like the women in Ailwood's (2008) study, the women here were vociferous in their protestations that nursery work was qualitatively distinct from mothering. Yet the impassioned denials from within the profession, that doing nursery work was anything like mothering, appear to do little to alter the persistence of maternalist discourses in public constructions. Bhadra, a mother of one, was working as a volunteer at Mango Grove Nursery whilst in the second year of a part-time degree in Early Childhood Studies. Although her entry into nursery work was relatively recent (2004), it is possible to identify the persistence of naturalising maternalistic discourses:

If you are an individual who doesn't have a child and you are starting in a career in childcare then it must be very difficult, more so than if you are a mother and you step into it with all that experiential knowledge.

The role that nursery workers take on in the care, nurturance, regulation and 'love' of other people's children places them in a highly precarious position. The reference by Vincent and Ball (2006) to childcare as a 'market in love' signals the highly emotive and emotional nature of the relationships between carer and child, and parent and child. The terrain that nursery workers must negotiate in providing 'quality' care and remaining within professional boundaries is treacherous. Not only must nursery workers negotiate 'risk' discourses and implicit assumptions of ill intent and an air of suspicion (which is further amplified for men working in childcare – see Cameron, 2006), but the relationship with the parents of the children in their care must be carefully managed so that territorial boundaries remain intact. A nursery worker must be caring but not loving, nurturant but not motherly, professional but not austere – a complicated juggling act to perform as a project of the self. Parental expectations of a given nursery and the expectations of the individual nursery worker caring for their child vary widely and are inflected by classed, 'raced' and gendered assumptions and are ultimately dependent upon the subject position of the parent (Vincent and Ball, 2006). However, the discourses that are drawn upon, promoted and sustained throughout the social relationships around nursery provision appear to secure the prominence of maternalism in ECEC. At the time of this study, Natalia had worked in nurseries for over 15 years. She held a range of higher-level qualifications in nursery practice (including a recently completed MA in Early Childhood Studies) and had worked in childcare in three continents up to and including managerial level. Yet she judged her professional self as deficient because she did not have maternal status:

> I think I am lacking in that I may have a higher degree and years of experience but I don't have children of my own, I can't bring those experiences to my professional life, to my work with the children... I've worked with so many people, mums who don't have training, who are fantastic and they draw from their experiences or their personalities, but on the other hand, I think there is nothing that can't be learnt...whether you are a mum or not what needs to be done in the nursery can be learnt, you know. And ultimately we work equally as a team it is just that some bring other skills, qualities, insights - whatever you want to call it from their experiences of being a mum.

When dominant constructions of nursery work as mother-like come into play, the women in this research come to occupy contradictory subject positions – wherein active attempts to distance themselves from maternalistic discourses are made, but nonetheless they become constructed as mother-like in a highly gendered (and classed) profession. As illustrated here, the women become implicated in and instrumental to promoting these constructions and are acutely aware of the consequent challenge posed to embodying hegemonic forms of professionalism. As outlined in this chapter, there is congruence between maternalistic and authoritative ECEC discourses – at first glance it appears that there is considerable overlap and interplay. However, normalising middle-class discourses (about good/sensitive mothering; and about good/quality nursery provision) inflect and shape both maternalistic and authoritative ECEC discourse to provide a particular form of ECEC professionalism – one that allows a permissible quantity and form of regulated and controlled other-motherliness.

Summary

I have sought to demonstrate that personal biographies shape professional subjectivities so that professionalism comes to be understood as performance (Butler, 1990). But it is a performance that is shaped and determined by powerful actors, so that nursery worker professionalism manifests in different ways, and to differing degrees is dependent upon context; therefore, contextual specificity is crucial to the discursive construction of particular identities. Through an analysis of the maternalistic discourses that shape and inflect ECEC practice, it has been possible to explore and expose class difference as central to understanding professional subjectivity. 'Being professional' or the discursive positioning within and through normalising middle-class discourse can undermine the efforts of nursery workers to do professionalism in ways that are instinctive, intrinsic to the nature of the work and foundational to providing appropriate emotional nurturance and regulation to young children in nurseries. The ways in which nursery workers are constructed in public discourse is in large part based upon the partial and subjective experiences that some middle-class actors have of using private day nurseries. These experiences are shaped on the basis of competing agendas (profit making, commercial enterprise at the expense of investments in staff), yet these constructions inflect wider public discourses about the quality of early years provision and the professionalism of nursery staff. Where conditions exist for nursery workers to perform expertise and form part of a legitimate authoritative framework for children's services, they come to believe in their professional capabilities and become active in promulgating and sustaining an alternative construction – the (mother-like) professional.

Chapter 7

Negotiating professionalism
Challenges and resistance

As highlighted in earlier chapters, the notion of professionalism in the early years has become a central concern to a range of key actors. I have demonstrated the importance attached to 'professionalism' for policy makers, nursery staff and managers, others working with children, and parents/mothers. This sustained interest has attracted considerable media attention, which in turn has acted to promote/fuel hegemonic public discourses that then contribute to a construction of nursery staff in particularly narrow ways. My aim is to bring together a number of the issues raised in preceding chapters to further explore the complexities of doing professionalism/being professional in a highly gendered and devalued employment sector.

From the time that I began this study (2003), the terminology used to describe members of the early years workforce, and the concomitant career development pathways and opportunities, has altered considerably (which is reflected in my varying reference to the participants in this study as nursery workers, practitioners, childcarers, early years educators and so on). In Chapter 4 I endeavoured to deconstruct and problematise the labels that are applied to those working in nurseries and the symbolic meanings attached which construct members of a workforce in certain ways at different times. This refashioning of the 'nursery worker' stemmed from widespread acknowledgement that there was confusion around precisely what ECEC encompassed, and who comprised the workforce (DfES, 2005; Moss, 2006). This ambiguity provided justification for reform (through processes of top-down professionalisation) of a hitherto fragmented/heterogeneous workforce.

Introduced in 2005, the Children's Workforce Development Council (CWDC) had, as part of its central mission, the explicit aim to create order and clarity where there had been confusion, duplication and ambiguity surrounding career structures and pathways available in ECEC (www.cwdcouncil.org.uk). A key aspect to this reform agenda was the application of appropriate labels/job titles and the establishment of a clear hierarchy in the quest to achieve a graduate-led profession of the future. In 2007, the 'Early Years Professional' became a credentialised status that could be conferred upon nursery workers (and others working with young children in ECEC) through formal accreditation. This marked a significant moment in the field of ECEC whereby being 'professional' or having 'professional status' was an accolade that could be attained through evidence of demonstrating a series of competencies. The ongoing policy reform in ECEC workforce remodelling demonstrates a commitment to a particular form of professionalism, which I argue foregrounds a neo-liberal, technicist approach in which individuals must perform 'professionalism' against an external set of criteria by which they will be judged (Mahony and Hextall, 2000; Osgood, 2006c).

A number of international scholars, such as Cannella (1997); Goodfellow (2004), Dahlberg and Moss (2005); Kilderry (2006); Fenech and Sumsion (2007), wrestle with precisely what professionalism in ECEC can/does and should look like. Leading to this piece of work, I too have invested considerable time in exploring what is meant by 'professionalism', and in contemplating the related contradictions and ambivalences when the application of hegemonic discourses come to play out in localised sites and on individual subjecthoods (Osgood, 2004, 2005, 2006a, 2006b, 2006c, 2008). I have previously argued that neo-liberal discourses promote a form of professionalism that foregrounds masculinist values and cultures, a position supported by other commentators (Acker, 1995; Hearn and Parkin, 2001; Reay and Ball, 2000). As a highly gendered employment sector strongly associated with the affective realms of caring and nurturance, ECEC becomes understood as lacking in professionalism precisely because it is deemed hyper-feminine. The participants in this study wrestled with the gendered discourses surrounding the nature of their work and the consequences of this for its discursive positioning as lacking in professionalism. Yet they were also staunchly defensive of the emotionality and necessarily affective nature of the work that they do which they regarded as being central to their identity as working professionally with children (and their families). It is evident that a desire to be constructed in public discourse as professional is fraught with tensions, contradictions and ambiguities. This is further complicated when nursery workers invest in a sense of moral righteousness and by embodying and performing emotionality in their work.

I revisit and develop earlier theorisations of professionalism offered from within the academic community. Further, my aim is to draw upon the analyses offered in Chapters 5 and 6 to map the salience of discourses around 'imagined childhood' and 'othered-mothering' onto hegemonic constructions of the professional nursery worker. By doing this I am endeavouring to unearth and explore the tensions between policy formation/application and the subjective experiences involved in 'being professional' and doing professionalism in the nursery.

Theorising professionalism

In public discourse, 'professionalism' is commonly understood as an apolitical construct broadly defined by the acquisition of specialist knowledge/qualifications and the ability to meet high standards, to self-regulate and to exercise high levels of autonomy (*The Penguin English Dictionary*, 2000). In a series of articles published (Osgood, 2004, 2005, 2006a, 2006c), I endeavoured to deconstruct common-sense definitions by focusing upon the cultural, historical and political specificity of the concept in relation to ECEC. I argued that the current popularity of promoting professionalism within ECEC stemmed from the changing socio-political and economic landscape in England where the Labour Government invested heavily in promoting citizenship through full employment, especially the employment of mothers (Levitas, 1998). In order to realise that goal, nursery provision attracted much attention because it represents the means by which mothers can return to the labour market. Furthermore, the professionalism agenda in ECEC is attractive/seductive because it is seen as the key to a strengthened labour market position and increased respect for nursery staff. Yet various commentators such as Cannella (1997), Novinger and O'Brien (2003) and Fenech and Sumsion (2007) highlight a risk embedded within professionalism discourses; they argue that masking the progressive rhetoric is an implicit aim to control rather than empower:

> The discourses and actions associated with professional institutions and practices have generated disciplinary and regulatory powers over teachers (who are mostly women) and children. Standards have been created through which individuals judge and limit themselves, through which they construct a desire to be 'good', 'normal' or both.
>
> (Cannella, 1997: 137)

In Chapter 4 I demonstrated that hegemonic government discourses around professionalism in ECEC can act to effectively silence alternative debates and constructions about what it means to be professional. Counter-narratives founded on the subjective experiences of nursery workers engaged in 'doing professionalism' can become marginalised and/or pathologised against the hegemony of authoritative government policy discourses. In this chapter, through analyses of the narratives offered by a sample of nursery workers located in this specific policy climate, I explore the seductive power of, and the dangers of unreflexively accepting and adhering to, externally imposed normalised and normalising constructions of professionalism.

I turn to the work of Foucault (1978, 1980), who, through his theorisations of subject, power and political rationality, offers a means to understand control as achieved through 'disciplinary technologies of the self'. Through objectifying practices of constant surveillance and the promotion of normalising discourses, subjects come to regulate themselves in ways that render the exercise of state power invisible and therefore impossible to challenge or negotiate. I find applying Foucauldian ideas here helpful to understand the processes of subjectification that occur through the localised negotiation/application/rejection of policies designed to promote a certain form of professionalism in ECEC. Foucault (1972, 1980) conceptualises discourses as systems of statements, which construct objects and subjects within which the self positions, and is positioned through, interaction based upon a struggle for power. Because discourses are perpetuated by social structure and practices, the importance of deconstructing them lies in the possibilities available to provide alternative readings and examine multiple and shifting subject positions. Foucault's (1980) conception of discursive positioning explains the ways in which subjects can be positioned as powerful or powerless via different discourses.

Drawing on these ideas around discursive positioning through discourse, I unsettle and dismantle hegemonic discourses of professionalism and the less powerful, and therefore arguably marginalised, discourses that exist within the localised sites of the nurseries. In earlier chapters I began to undertake this exercise, so that, as illustrated in Chapter 5, it becomes possible to understand the nursery workers' childhood subjectivities as obscured, and hence marginalised, in the face of dominant pedagogical discourses that construct children in particular ways which in turn limits what practitioners will/can do with children. I used examples of 'taboo adult issues' – sexuality and racism – and in doing this, I exposed the limiting effects of hegemonic normalising discourses upon ECEC practice and the related emergence of ontological professional insecurity. Through deconstructing the social construction of childhood and its implications for professional practice, it was possible to identify dissonance and ambiguity when nursery workers become discursively positioned in contradictory and competing ways.

Earlier chapters afforded the opportunity to explore the ways in which hegemonic discourses are drawn upon, invested in and strengthened in a quest to be constructed as professional. The prevalence of counter, and albeit marginal, discourses are exposed and debated to illustrate the ways in which the self is discursively constructed and subject to change and manipulation dependent upon historical, cultural and social specificity. I build upon these theorisations and conceptualisations to illustrate the interconnections between the private and the public, the emotional and the rational, the individual and the collective – to reach an understanding of professionalism from within the nursery, as a culturally, socially and politically specific discursive construct.

Negotiating neo-liberal constructions of 'professionalism'

All of the participants in this study were asked to self-define professionalism in their work. They were asked what they felt made them good at their work and what skills/qualities were necessary to work effectively with young children in a nursery setting. In order to illustrate subjective constructions of professionalism, several participants drew historical comparisons. Reflections were offered about the fluid nature of the importance attached to nursery education and care over time and in relation to various policy/media priorities:

Debbie: I suppose it's a profession you never really, umm you're continually
learning because changes in the media and things that are going on in
the world, things change quite a lot, because in the time I've been in
childcare things have gone full circle, repeated themselves, I've come
back round to doing things the way they were done 10 years ago.
Learning through play, child-centred pedagogies and also like the way
people plan, procedures and all these sorts of things, they go out of
fashion and then they come back again, and you think 'well hang on
a minute I was doing that 15 years ago' so it all comes back as a good
idea… I don't feel people look and see what is behind early years practice though; all that we have to do to achieve where we are. Umm I still
feel that early years, is umm, how can I put it? Although we come under
the education umbrella we still seem to be the ones who are continually,
how can I put it, fighting for recognition, to be taken seriously in the
eyes of others I suppose.

The dual concern raised by Debbie, that ECEC is frequently driven by authoritarian discourses (promoted by and through government and the mass media),
and that ECEC continues to lack recognition for the contribution it makes to
society broadly and children's lives specifically, was echoed in other narratives. By
offering accounts that draw on previous eras of ECEC, the participants mapped
professional journeys through training/qualifications against the application of
a sustained period of reform through top-down policies. Through retrospec-
tive frameworks it becomes possible to identify the shifting and fluid nature of
professionalism discourses and further to track the junctures and ways in which
particular constructions of the 'effective/good' nursery worker foreshadow others and assume dominance in ECEC practice and rhetoric at particular moments.
Through highlighting perceived inadequacies of ECEC practice in the past,
practitioners felt able to construct professionalism as evolving from necessary,
progressive and external demands:

Ruth: I've been working in nurseries for about 23 years, it has changed a lot
because when I first started I was working with this lady…in an old church
building and umm there was like 23 children and only three staff. Well
I was never a smoker, but this old woman used to sit there and smoke a
cigarette and drink coffee and the children were racing around her, but
now you couldn't dare do that, you know. One member of staff would be
left with all these children while you were waiting for another member of
staff to come in and they weren't due to come in until about ten o'clock.
It was much more casual; very laid back.
Jayne: Was there any structured learning at that time, like early learning goals
and the curriculum, birth to three and so on?
Ruth: I mean there was some structure but not in the way that it is now… It
wasn't so deep, we now have to measure and demonstrate and record and

in some ways I suppose it is an improvement and in another way it is not, because at the end of the day they are still learning whether the measurable outcomes are measured or not... In those days you didn't have to do them, you didn't do them full stop, but there was nothing wrong, the children still progressed just as well.

The 'audit culture' (Rizvi and Lingard, 1996; Ozga, 2000; Strathern, 2000) is detectable in Ruth's appraisal of the ways in which ECEC practice has altered over time. Like others, Ruth recounted the effects of the application of national policy developments in localised sites. Her reference to greater depth indicates that an application of more structured approaches to learning encounters results in greater reflexivity and ongoing analyses of pedagogical practices and outcomes. However, there was widespread scepticism about developments to ECEC practice; performativity discourses (Butler, 1990; Ball, 2003a) were variously drawn upon to make sense of the ways in which nursery work was refashioned through a range of policy developments designed to improve accountability, transparency and measurability. Ofsted inspections were most frequently cited as the embodiment of neo-liberal demands for accountability and constructed as the primary means of assessing quality. Inherent within appraisals of Ofsted (as a mechanism to ensure quality through professional standards) were scepticism and doubt over the appropriateness of demands for standardisation, measurable outcomes and the related goals of efficiency, effectiveness and accountability (Sachs, 2000, 2001; Alexander, 2002).

In this study neo-liberal mechanisms designed to regulate, standardise and judge were variously constructed. For example, Ofsted was considered something of a 'poison chalice' (Orla, Mulberry Bush), offering the promise of heightened attention but at a considerable cost to the professional conduct and subjectivities of those working in the early years. In some respects Ofsted inspections were seen to signal that nurseries, and the professionalism of staff working within them, were regarded as equivalent to schools. Inspection and regulation were considered vital and effective at 'weeding out the worst' (Terry, Apple Tree) and assuring 'minimum standards are met' (Bhadra, Mango Grove). However, scepticism and suspicion were also evident in the narratives. The partial nature of Ofsted inspections (as in some cases amounting to little more than a two-hour visit) was considered a weakness, and so too was the fact that Ofsted inspectors appeared to lack expertise in the field of ECEC:

Toni: My experience of Ofsted, the recent ones have been absolutely dreadful, not because they have found any fault with us, but because they arrive at 11 o'clock in the morning, they spend an hour or two in one room, about ten minutes in another, I just don't see how they can go away from that and have a proper picture of the nursery... I would much prefer, and the staff team have said this too, that we would much prefer one or two people to come in and spend a week with us, because then they will go away with a better picture than someone who spends a very brief time. You know it is like if you or me go into a room and see something happening we only get a glimpse, whereas if you are there and you have seen the situation unravel then you'd have a better understanding. I think when it changed a few years ago, Ofsted was centralised, because once upon a time we used to have inspectors here and we used to be inspected as an early years centre and then the government got it all together and so all the Ofsted inspectors are together now, so a single inspector can go out and inspect nurseries, secondary schools whereas before you had people who were experienced in the early years and knew about it, so now you may get an inspector in who has perhaps been a teacher of teenagers who doesn't have an understanding of the early years... In the past it was so much better with an early years specialist spending two days sometimes with us, going through everything with a fine toothcomb – through the planning, record keeping as well as observation, more rigorous. That used to make me feel comfortable that they were in tune with what we are doing and why we are doing it the way we do.

Toni's views were reinforced by others and act to indicate an acute distrust of Ofsted's capability to assess quality and professionalism in a rigorous and special-ised way. Throughout the second interviews with participants, a disproportionate time was devoted to reflecting on inspection and regulation. The semi-structured nature of the interview allowed for participants to focus more or less intently on a range of issues relating to professionalism in their work. Therefore it is interest-ing to note the significance placed upon authoritative forms of surveillance and assessment. Self-reflexivity and team reflection with a view to improving prac-tice and professionalism were also discussed at length (and are presented later in this chapter). However, the descriptions and reflections upon Ofsted inspec-tions dominated subjective constructions of professionalism and were highly emotive. Performing professionalism was felt to rest upon a combination of per-sonal/moral commitment *and* the embodiment of externally defined notions. Authoritative constructions of professionalism and quality encapsulated in Ofsted assessment criteria were considered overly prescriptive and narrow in focus, deny-ing space for subjective representations of professionalism:

Natalia: I know that I am conscientious, well qualified, experienced and reflect on what I am doing, I also recognise that there is always room for improvement. If that was what Ofsted was about then great. But I just felt that there was an air of distrust; that my professionalism was being doubted and unfairly judged... I would say that to get a sense of my professionalism and an understanding of what I am doing, then come and take a *good* look before making any sorts of assumptions...it goes back to what I was saying before about your personal philosophy and working ethos and finding a balance between what you hold dear and

> what is expected of you from external agendas…you always feel under
> scrutiny in this line of work but if judgements are being made then they
> should be informed and considered.

The tension identified by Natalia between external agendas/public scrutiny and
personal philosophy/working ethos offers a vital insight into the ways in which the
participants wrestle with hegemonic discourses and practices designed to assess
professional competence (Rees and Garnsey, 2003). Authoritarian discourses are
constructed in multiple and contradictory ways as necessary, affirming and legiti-
mating whilst simultaneously as unjust, partial and containing. The discursive
landscape in which the participants are located, and to which they contribute, is
inflected with neo-liberal technicist assumptions and expectations. Nevertheless,
as Natalia's account testifies, investments were made to find space, to both challenge and refashion mechanisms designed to contain and control; this is an issue
I explore throughout this chapter.

Another key factor to saturate the data was a sense that workload had inten-
sified; this was chiefly attributed to a cultural shift in nursery provision that
demanded greater evidence of effectiveness (e.g. increased record keeping and
monitoring, performance appraisals, strategic planning and preparation for
inspections). This process of intensification has been hotly debated within the
field of the sociology of education (Ball, 1990; Reay and Ball, 2000; Avis, 2003)
with commentators concluding that such reforms lead to reduced autonomy as
a result of a regulatory gaze and accompanying directives which leave educators
too preoccupied with work to negotiate and construct a subjective/collective
sense of professionalism (Novinger and O'Brien, 2003; Osgood, 2006a, 2006b).
The policy attention that ECEC has received since 1997 met with mixed reactions within this study. The seductive promise of being projected centre-stage in
neo-liberal policy formation was palpable:

Terry: It's great that we are finally getting the recognition that we deserve. What
         we do is so important on so many levels and we finally have the chance to
         show what we do.

Although participants remained suspicious of the implications that such attention
might have for professional identity and pedagogical practice:

Delia: I think over the years that I've been doing the job, I mean I have been in
         childcare for many years and for me I have seen how umm it can be more,
         it is quite stressful at times in respect that the ratios have gone up. And
         you've then got report writing to do if you're an educator, you have obser-
         vations to write up, so that's quite a burden to keep your records updated
         umm so I think as time has gone on the job has become increasingly
         hard in that way… So I think for some staff it may get to them at times,
         it's extremely hard when you are working with very young children…it's

very demanding physically as well as emotionally. It's totally draining at times...umm so I think from the time that I first came into childcare it has changed quite a lot, for the staff on the ground and for the management team. The management team have vastly more work to do than was the case in the past and I think also what has changed is that staff are expected to have more skills, there are endless learning curves to climb, there are obstacles and stresses along the way I think. Umm what I have seen is that quite a lot of staff have opted out of becoming educators and taken on the role of practitioner because they feel they don't want the added stress of report writing, record keeping and all those other chores as well.

Delia's reference to 'other chores' is indicative of the perceived laboriousness of current expectations in nursery practice. Throughout the narratives there was acute awareness of hegemonic discourses through and within which particular forms of professionalism are extolled at the expense of others. The hegemony of the 'enterprising neo-liberal subject' (Walkerdine, 2003) within government discourses was identifiable, and the ways in which this played out in localised discursive practices were variously reflected upon. The need to perform professionalism in particular ways at particular times was a theme to emerge from the narratives. In attempts to satisfy the demands of the regulatory gaze and hegemonic constructions of the 'professional nursery worker', the theorisations offered by Morley of 'a form of ventriloquism' (cited in Ball, 2003a) and Butlerian ideas around 'enacted fantasy' (Butler, 2004) were in evidence. Practitioners were busy demonstrating an approximation to hegemonic forms of professionalism whilst remaining unconvinced of its appropriateness or authenticity in their work:

Gazala: That is the way that we need to be now, you have to sell yourself, you have to promote yourself as being a certain type of professional, hand over examples that demonstrate that, convince the powers that be that we are doing what is required...but then again, whether the powers that be really know what is best, you know, for us, umm performing well during an inspection is a very different thing from being, well...knowing... umm that you are good at this sort of work, do you know what I mean? Well that's a totally different ball game.

The pressures to embody a particular form of professionalism were widely identified and questioned. As demonstrated above, these pressures were felt to stem from the introduction of regulatory and inspection frameworks, accountability structures and a heightened audit culture (Gee et al., 1996; Luke and Luke, 2001). Despite scepticism, these various neo-liberal mechanisms were frequently constructed as a necessary means of assuring quality.

Ysabelle: You feel the pressure because you try to do your best but you know somebody is watching you, judging your every move and I think this

> can make you make mistakes…but I do think that it does assess quality quite well, it has had the effect of raising standards and to be honest I don't know how they could do it differently.

Despite counter-narratives that constructed the need to meet increasing demands for accountability and performativity as unreasonably burdensome and seemingly inappropriate or ineffective, the conceptual rationale for their existence was left largely unchallenged – the rationale being that inspecting and measuring quality inevitably leads to better outcomes (improved professional standards/quality provision and hence 'school readiness' for children). The seductive power of this discourse was detectable in the narratives; participants were aware of the paradoxical positioning of the nursery worker as central to delivering 'quality' and hence learning 'outcomes', whereby professionalism is increasingly constructed as assured through measurement and documentation of practice with respect to frameworks of standards (Stronach *et al.*, 2003). Such cultures of accountability are expressions of governmentality (Foucault, 1983), which induce cultures of performativity through the use of simplified assessment data, with adjudication performed through discourses of 'quality assurance' (Luke and Luke, 2001: 7). Quantifiable surveillance within a culture of coercive accountability allows for centralised control over the local through largely self-monitoring responses or 'disciplinary technologies of the self' (Foucault, 1983). This process is argued (Ball, 2003b) to construct education/teaching as being fashioned in such a way that governments and their instrumentalities can lay claim to measures of 'quality' to present to the 'market' to guide 'choice'. The interrelationship between these concepts, if left unproblematised, can appear completely reasonable and hence impossible to challenge. The consequence is that self-regulating 'professionals' under the panoptic gaze are deemed consummately capable of achieving a narrowly defined version of 'quality' by virtue of dual accountability – to the self in the first instance, but ultimately to 'society' (children, families, government, the nation state). The processes of individualisation (Beck, 1992; Adam *et al.*, 2002) and the symbolic importance attached to professionals working in ECEC were evidenced in the narratives. The power of government discourses to construct 'professionalism' and 'quality' as entities that can only be assured if measurable, auditable and documented shaped resigned acceptance amongst nursery workers:

Elspeth: So it is about being seen to be doing something but you're really just doing it for the sake of it *not* because it improves the child's learning or your practice you know. Time could be better spent, you'd still do your planning but keep it a lot simpler because then you'd actually have time to carry out things that you actually planned to do instead of just writing things on a piece of paper and because you are so busy writing down what you were going to do you didn't have time to do it. Yeah so it is just an exercise in paper at the end of the day. That said though, some of it, it's quite important to keep records of what the children are doing and where the children are at, and plan activities around that. But I think things like your yearly planning, when you look at that it's just completely stupid, it's a complete waste of time because yeah they say you can be flexible but then what's the point of doing it for a whole year? Yeah, you can map out what you might do for your themes or whatever but I don't think you have to be so hell bent on writing and planning everything. And the learning intentions, writing down every little detail, it's just duplicating work... But then you get told different things, like support teachers come in and tell you to do one thing, Ofsted come in and look at things and say 'oh no, I don't like the look of that', so we are at the behest of all these different people, telling us to do different things and so we're just stuck in the middle doing it because we have to be seen to be doing, it's total madness!

The language used within the narratives, for example 'powers that be', 'the behest of all these different people', and frequent reference to 'they' when referring to regulatory bodies, indicates the ways in which the nursery workers feel positioned in marginal and compromised and/or powerless ways. The ambivalence stemming from a new/unfamiliar and elevated positioning with policy discourse was variously articulated throughout the narratives. In many ways the application of top-down measures designed to enhance the quality of nursery provision was viewed as inherently benign and overwhelmingly positive. Further, the sustained central government investment in ECEC, in terms of time, policy development, assessment, regulation, and so on, was broadly interpreted as overdue but welcome. Yet these sentiments were mitigated by criticisms that reform had resulted in unreasonable demands to alter practice in unacceptable ways: demands that have been made in a narrow quest to enhance accountability/transparency (often at the expense of the form of professionalism valued by nursery workers – something I attend to in subsequent sections of this chapter). Despite the concerns, criticisms and doubts raised throughout this study in relation to regulation/surveillance, the taken-for-granted assumption of an unproblematic and linear causal relationship between 'quality' and 'professionalism' within an audit culture remained largely unchallenged. Within government discourse, professionalism can be viewed as synonymous with quality. Throughout this study I have troubled the notion of professionalism and sought to offer alternative readings and constructions. In similar ways, others working in the field of ECEC (Dahlberg *et al.*, 1999; Dahlberg and Moss, 2005; Alexander, 2008) have sought to deconstruct and trouble 'quality' to expose it as politically motivated and permeated with modernist values and assumptions:

> The concept of quality is about a search for a definitive and universal criteria that will offer certainty and order, and a belief that such transcendental criteria can be found. It asks the question – how far does this product, this service or this activity conform to a universal, objective and predetermined standard?

It has no place for complexity, values, diversity, subjectivity, indeterminacy and multiple perspectives.

(Dahlberg *et al.*, 1999: 108)

The constructions of ECEC staff as deficient and hence in need of reform, through processes of professionalisation, contain nursery staff in certain ways. Public constructions of nursery staff as lacking (qualifications, status, etc.) played out in the narratives and provide some explanation for the acceptance (and in some cases embracement) of neo-liberal policies offering the promise of 'professional' standing.

Juanita: The public don't see people working in nurseries as very intelligent, and often we are, I have a Degree in Social Science and Masters in Pedagogy, but nobody would expect that of me, you know?... People don't respect people who work in nurseries mostly because of the money, you can see it in their eyes, that to work for little money then the nursery worker she can't be intelligent...in a society obsessed with money that is what counts right?... But I guess that things could change now that the government have become so obsessed with us, maybe the spotlight will mean that we start to be seen differently, maybe some respect will come our way [laughs] and all this extra work [additional record-keeping, etc] will be worth it...hey, perhaps some more money too! [laughs]

As others have observed, the rate and pace of policy change and a sustained intensity of attention upon the workforce can leave a sense of ontological insecurity (Ball, 2003a). In effect, the participants in this study were rendered incapable of resisting (sometimes) seemingly nonsensical reform, and left feeling doubtful of their experiential wisdom and hands-on capabilities. As I demonstrated in Chapter 4, hegemonic discourses that promote certain forms of professionalism over others are embedded within and promoted by current ECEC policies designed to modernise, restructure and improve. Located within this discursive landscape, participants are left to variously negotiate, resist and embrace hegemonic discourses whilst simultaneously creating, modifying and sustaining counter-discourses from within their localised networks or communities of practice (Fleer, 2003). My intention is to attend to the counter-narratives and discourses that were generated by those working in nurseries.

'Professionalism from within'

As the analysis presented above demonstrates, the hegemony of government discourses around professionalism in ECEC stemmed from a range of objectifying practices and was (reluctantly) accepted by the participants in this study. However, when questioned about the qualities and skills that equated to 'being professional' or doing professionalism, considerable dissonance could be identified.

Rationalism, accountability, measurability and other traits encompassed within hegemonic government professionalism discourses were notably absent (or qualified) from practitioners' self-definitions of professionalism in the nursery. Whilst performing hegemonic forms of professionalism involved adhering to demands to demonstrate measurable outcomes and 'enact a fantasy' (Butler, 2004), claims to more authentic professional subjectivities rested upon a set of different (and often competing) performances.

I refer back to the previous chapter where reflections were offered on the presence/rejection/negotiation of maternalistic discourses in relation to 'professional' subjectivities. The struggle to reconcile the necessarily emotional and affective aspects of ECEC practice with demands for more widely accepted constructions of professionalism occupied a significant space in many of the narratives. Stronach *et al.* (2003: 125) 'criticise reductive typologies and characterisations of current professionalism'; instead they argue that the 'professional self' is constituted by a series of contradictions and dilemmas. The authors offer an 'uncertain theory of professionalism' shaped by lived experience and characterised by plurality, tension, juggling, ambiguity and inconsistency. Analyses of the data from this study are usefully shaped by this 'uncertain theory of professionalism'. Above I have demonstrated the persuasive and pervasive effects of government discourses upon subjective understandings of ECEC staff as professional – the ways in which these discourses were encountered were typically inconsistent and ambiguous. In Chapter 6 my analysis revealed that participant engagement with maternalistic discourses was similarly contradictory and uncertain. Here I want to explore further the ways in which competing discourses play out in the narratives and to highlight the existence/emergence of counter-discourses which act to offer alternative versions of professionalism (shaped by personal histories and subjective experiences) that reside outside the professional context but come to inflect and shape practitioners' self-understandings as more/less professional in their work.

Professional subjectivities or 'ways of being' come about from an active engagement and negotiation of the discourses through which individuals are shaped and in which they are positioned. Whilst neo-liberal discourses place an emphasis on modernist rationalism, counter-discourses that emerge from the narratives tended towards prioritising an ethic of care in the quest for a version of 'professionalism from within'. A substantial body of literature has established that emotionality is necessary and integral to ECEC practice since the work involves strong feelings towards children, a child's family and the wider community, and supporting and caring for colleagues (see Claxton, 1999; Friere, 1999; Nias, 1999; Vogt, 2002; Dahlberg and Moss, 2005). This study provides further evidence of the considerable personal and collective investments that are made towards achieving a culture of care characterised by affectivity, altruism, self-sacrifice and conscientiousness.

Each participant was asked to find specific words that they felt best described their subjective construction of working professionally. In Table 7.1 I outline the frequency with which the 24 participants cited each characteristic.

Table 7.1 Practitioners' constructions of professionalism

Professionalism trait	Frequency
Caring/loving/compassionate	15
Non-judgemental/fair	14
Collegial	11
Self-reflexive/critical	10
Confident	9
Effective communicator	9
Fun-loving/GSOH/playful	9
Detached (avoiding emotionality)	8
Professional as part learnt, part innate	7
Pragmatic/flexible/reactive	6
Demarcates private self from professional	5
Expertise	5
Energetic/healthy/brawny	5
Intuitive/instinctive	4
Reliable/dependable	4
Committed/dedicated	3
Empathic/altruistic	3
Conformist/adherent to externally set standards	3
Patient	3
Organised	3
Creative	2

The table illustrates that counter-discourses exist amongst this group of professionals. Amongst the most frequently cited and hence highly regarded attributes
that were felt to constitute a professional self were those associated with the
affective domain. In itself this is perhaps unsurprising, but this insider construction of professionalism from localised sites sits in tension to dominant discourses
that promote rationalism, which allows little or no space for displays of emotion.
The values included in Sevenhuijsen's (1998) 'feminist ethics of care' include
empathy, intuition, compassion, love, relationality and commitment, with the
central values being responsibility and communication. Clearly this model
resonates loudly with Table 7.1. But there is a degree of ambiguity and contradiction in the list of traits offered; I would suggest that the relative importance
placed on 'detachment' (8), 'demarcation of private from professional self' (5)
and 'conformity to externally prescribed standards' (3) provides evidence of the
struggle that this group of nursery workers is engaged in when trying to negotiate

hegemonic policy discourses and collective professional subjectivities in localised communities of practice (Wenger, 1998).

By offering a conceptualisation of professionalism in the nursery as performance (Butler, 1990), it becomes possible to identify the inconsistencies, ambiguities and tensions that come to shape 'doing professionalism' in daily practice (Stronach *et al.*, 2003). Whereas the demands to demonstrate neo-liberal technicist competence occupy space in nursery practice, this is frequently superseded by subjective and collective commitments to an 'ethic of care' performed through emotional labour. As I have endeavoured to demonstrate, participants exerted a degree of scepticism around reforms encapsulated within the neo-liberal 'audit culture' and, whilst seemingly complying with its demands, small acts of subversion were in evidence. This was clear in Elspeth's claim to 'being seen to be doing', and Gazala's reference to 'marketing a certain form of professionalism' during inspections. But these performances were designed to satisfy externally set demands for competence at a particular moment. The hegemonic construction of professionalism that typically played out through the narratives and was reflected in practice in the nurseries was more closely aligned to Sevenhuijsen's feminist ethics of care model (characterised by the foregrounding of emotional labour):

Natalia: It is simply not a profession that you can't care about. It requires a high level of emotional investment; you need to have a love for the job and a love for what you do and realise that everything that you do in this job has far-reaching consequences; it can be totally exhausting to invest so much of yourself into this work but if you don't then you are doing everyone a disservice: yourself, your colleagues, the children and ultimately their families. This is the bedrock to what we do but I suppose it's kinda hidden from view, it's…implicit I guess would be the word.

Professionalism as emotional labour/emotional capital

The sentiments raised by Natalia were echoed in other narratives. The central role of emotional labour in participant constructions of 'professionalism from within' is worth unpacking and reflecting upon, since emotionality has been the subject of debate in a range of academic fields (including sociology, education, employment and feminist writings). The current debate follows the influential theorisations offered by Arlie Hochschild in *The Managed Heart* (1983). Hochschild offered an interpretation of emotional labour as an oppressive and totalising form of control, which she linked to high levels of anxiety and unreasonable demands for performativity. She argued that women perform disproportionate emotional labour and are routinely required to take responsibility for the feelings of others. Emotional labour through work processes can be understood as scripted by employers and directed/supervised by others for payment, and therefore represents a colonisation of worker subjectivity and form of control. Further,

Hochschild highlighted the potential for 'the managed heart' to become an act of subjective alienation through which the worker engages in 'surface acting' in a way that lacks authenticity and can be psychically harmful when the chasm between the 'natural self' and 'performing self' becomes too wide.

Hochschild's theorisations have been variously challenged for the depiction of workers as lacking agency (Hughes, 2005; Payne, 2006) against managerial demands. Studies of caregivers (Ashforth and Tomiuk, 2000) indicate that despite exceeding contracted obligations workers still maintain control over 'bounded emotionality' performed through working practices. As Table 7.1 indicates, attributes belonging to the affective domain were considered vitally important in nursery settings. Furthermore, analyses of the narratives from this study would indicate that not only are emotions central to ECEC practices (with children, colleagues and families) but that the management of emotions is central to effective conduct and a sense of professionalism. The importance of detachment and the ability to demarcate home life from work (see Table 7.1) are part of this process of emotion management.

Francelle: I think that professionalism is about separating your social issues from your work, because in this job you can easily get too emotional and too much emotion can interfere with your work and that is where you have to know where, when and how to draw the line. But you can still be emotional, you have to be, you know?... You need to show emotion to the children and to love them to be able to teach them and nurture them but you can do that so that they understand discipline, boundaries and so on, and it is possible to do that without losing balance and respect.

The careful balancing act required to work empathically, to allow subjective experience to inflect practice whilst maintaining a 'safe distance' between the private and public, is conveyed in this quote. The embeddedness of emotional labour to the work of nurseries was recognised, and (in many ways) understood as challenging. Whilst emotional labour is central to practitioner constructions of professionalism, for that labour to be credible, and have a degree of status conferred upon it, emotions were constructed as requiring skilful management and containment. As skilled emotion workers and managers of subjective affectivity, the participants in this study can be understood to have an insightful and astute grasp on the role that emotions play in effective ECEC practice and workplace relations:

Orla: The type of caring that you do depends on how professional you are; what 'professional' means to you, if you get me? I mean people quickly realise that you wouldn't come into this [nursery work] unless you were committed, like emotionally committed...that you care and can be caring... But it boils down to doing it in the right way...umm, with children you have to treat them with compassion and really mean it...children can tell if you're faking it in ten seconds flat, it has to be natural and if it doesn't come naturally then it becomes calculated and nobody can keep that up for long, that's why you've got so many people leaving. It's like if you come into nursery work and you 'get it' and you know if you can genuinely do the sort of caring I'm talking about then you stay for life, or for a long time at any rate, but if you can't – you don't last five minutes. Like the owner of this nursery, she hasn't got a clue, she has absolutely no idea, totally disconnected, no feeling for it. She can't ever have worked with children, her interest is making money and you can see that – she doesn't know how to be with the children, or the staff, or the parents for that matter which is why she leaves it all to us.

An analysis of the narratives indicates that the tensions between subjective authenticity and surface acting (identified by Hochschild) were incongruous in the nursery context; in effect, space and opportunities to 'fake' emotional labour in the nursery were denied. Ashforth and Tomiuk (2000: 195) argue that emotion management is constructed as integral to subjectivity – as a means of supporting authenticity and expressing identity, which is borne out in the narratives offered in this study. Orla's reference to 'doing it the right way' is suggestive of emotional labour as scripted performance. However, her claims to commitment, genuineness, authenticity and 'ways of being' and so on indicate that doing emotional labour as a professional performance is embedded in personal subjectivity. Her interpretation of emotionality indicates that the occupational demands of nursery work amount to more than the mere execution of a set of preordained competencies. Shavarni reflected upon the ways in which subjective experiences in childhood played out in her professional interactions with children and the central role of emotionality to doing her job effectively to meet the needs of children in the nursery:

Jayne: When I came in yesterday I saw you with the Russian boy and that got me thinking about what you had said – about your earliest experiences of school and the language barrier...

Shavarni: Yeah I recognise the look, although he can't understand and speak English if you do hand movements and gestures for now – then you know he should be fine in the long-run. But for now it's important that he feels secure that's the main thing for him right now; that he should feel secure and be given cuddles and reassurance when he needs it...he was distressed the other day and so we took him away from the other children, they probably overwhelmed him because I think he is used to being surrounded by adults and so he just needed to feel loved and be shown some TLC... I totally understand what he's going through from what I was telling you before about my own experiences of school and not understanding the language, it can be quite difficult and recognising what he needs during those moments, that is where we can make a huge difference, it's not just about the curriculum, learning outcomes, they need to feel safe, loved, you know?

The quote from Shavarni's narrative indicates that 'intuitive practice' (Claxton, 1999) is central to effective ECEC practice, yet there is little space for 'cuddles', 'TLC' and 'love' in neo-liberal discourses. Demands for strong feelings towards protecting, supporting and engaging empathetically with children are acknowledged in the academic community (e.g. Elfer, 1994; Moyles, 2001; Elfer *et al.*, 2003). A body of research argues that emotionality is central to ECEC practice (Claxton, 1999; Friere, 1999; Nias, 1999; Vogt, 2002). However, Katz (1995) recognises that emotional labour in ECEC extends beyond meeting the exclusive needs of children to interactions nursery staff have with colleagues and parents in the local community which they serve. This is something that Debbie reflects upon in her narrative:

Jayne: How does the public perception of what you do for a living fit with the type of person you've had to be in your life?

Debbie: Well I suppose it does fit, I've had people lean on me all my life. I guess you could say that I am a giver, I care *about* people and so I care *for* people, and in the early years...well it's a caring profession so it figures that I would come into this or something like it because that's what I am about, that's what I do, that's what I know how to do...what I've always done so you know, yeah there's a fit between who I am and what I do if you like... I suppose something that strikes me is it's not only caring for the children and the parents, but it is for the staff. If you've got over 30 staff I find myself doing counselling, you're supporting people, you're motivating people, you're developing people, that's what I've always done, of course it's different in a formal setting, like you do it for your family, your friends or whoever but when it is a staff team then it's slightly different but of course you still bring yourself to it if you like.

The 'fit between who I am and what I do' runs through the narratives of others in this study and offers a challenge to Hochschild's (1983) conceptualisation of emotional labour as a surface-level performance.

Bertrise: It has to be within you; you can learn to a certain degree but if it's not in you then it's always going to be a struggle...the bottom line is that you can't learn love, you can't learn patience; if you haven't got it to give then you can't learn it. But if it *is* there then it can be brought to the surface and nurtured – so in that sense it can be learnt – although no, not learnt so much as developed if you know what I mean?

The emotional labour referred to in this study, and the skilful and meticulous management of emotionality amongst this professional group, offers a counter-discourse to that offered by Hochschild. One interpretation of the narratives given in this study is that certain forms of emotionality have come about through 'gendered processes of socialisation' (Hochschild, 1983: 167), so that the women in this study are understood to have been channelled into caring professions through their childhood socialisation and through societal expectations of what is expected of (working-class) women (which is identifiable in Debbie's reference above to 'that's what I know how to do...it's what I've always done' and is further substantiated by the findings and analysis presented in Chapter 6). Yet a counter-discourse is identifiable and relates to the ways in which these women manage and deploy that emotional capital in their professional lives (Nowotny, 1981; Reay, 2000; Manion, 2006). I would argue that it is possible to construct the participants in this research as professionals exercising agency and a large degree of autonomy through emotional subjectivities that are brought into play through routine daily social interactions in the nursery. An example of this can be found in 'boundary setting'; setting emotional boundaries was a recurring issue throughout the narratives and was variously referred to through pedagogical practices with children, to interactions with colleagues and to the self-regulation of emotions to safeguard their own psychic well-being:

Ruth: You have to look out for yourself in and amongst it all. When I come through the door in the morning I am Ruth the Educator and my priorities are the children, their learning, their happiness and what I can do to promote that but when I leave I am mum and wife – I have learnt to switch off. But when I am here you have to consider the feelings of your team-mates – you can't work well in a nursery unless you work as a team – so there is a whole lot of stuff going on there that you have to manage, you know different views, approaches, sensitivities – and your own, umm, you have to manage yourself, bite your lip sometimes, which ain't always easy. So it's all a careful balancing act, you've got to, you know...well... when I am here I am in a professional zone if you like and I get into it, that's about knowing when to step back, put a bit of distance in place and know where the boundaries are at each level...

I have endeavoured to highlight the agentic potential of emotional labour by identifying positive uses of emotion in constructing and sustaining particular identities. Through this analysis I illustrate that it becomes possible to understand emotionality in the workplace as potentially empowering. For the participants in this study, the capacity to effectively manage emotions and deploy them in a range of ways – throughout pedagogical practices with children, in work with colleagues, and interaction with families – means that potential opportunities to construct themselves as worthy professionals are opened up.

Referring back to the theorisations offered by Sevenhuijsen (1998) is useful at this juncture. She argues that a feminist ethics of care provides opportunities to reflect on the importance of interpreting and fulfilling responsibility to others;

for her an ethics of care both requires and enables a relation to the Other that assumes difference:

> The central values in the ethics of care...lead to a commitment to deal with difference, not only between individuals and social groups, but also within the self. This is made possible because a definition of the self as multiple and unstable is no longer seen as a threat but rather as a part of life... A feminist ethics of care grafted onto postmodernism thus has the capacity to deal with diversity and alterity, with the fact that subjects are different and in this sense both 'strange' and 'knowable' to each other.
>
> (1998: 60)

The various articulations of participants recounted above indicate that, through emotional labour and the opportunities that are afforded to manage the self in ways that take into account the effects of professional practices on others, a discourse of professionalism emerges that represents a direct challenge to the limiting and containing version offered in neo-liberal government discourse. For example, participants placed a high degree of importance upon acting in non-judgemental and socially just ways (14), to working collegially (11) and to being self-reflexive/critical (10). The professional subjectivities constructed through the narratives tended to run counter to neo-liberal discourses that promote standardisation and individualist, publicly accountable approaches to assuring effectiveness, quality and hence professionalism. In attempts to 'stay true to your own belief system' (Natalia) and 'hold dear what you believe to be the right way' (Bertrise), contestation and tension played out in the narratives when seeking to negotiate hegemonic constructions promoted through discourses of governmentality and standardisation.

In England, the ECEC workforce is readily constructed through neo-liberal discourses as comprising 'docile bodies that yield to the discourse' (Foucault, 1980) – as 'technicians', willing to comply and unquestioningly deliver pre-scribed practice and meet externally set occupational standards (Moss, 2006). This study has demonstrated that counter-discourses can and do exist within localised sites and these resonate with feminist theorisations of 'doing quality' and 'doing professionalism', which are in stark polarity to that intended through policy prescription. The 'worker as technician' discourse renders the early years workforce in many ways powerless to hegemonic discourses that play out through unprecedented policy reform. Applying a Foucauldian (1980, 1983) lens to the related issues of power relations and the effects of discourse makes space to view resistance as both possible and necessary. Foucault argues that local politics and local actions are the most effective means of introducing change to larger power structures. So I would suggest that, whilst the participants in this study are technicians at certain moments in their professional lives, alternative subjective constructions of professionalism are offered, and these professional subjectivities can/do have important effects at the local level.

Within local sites (the nurseries), counter narratives emerge that can represent a challenge to neo-liberal technicism.

The analysis of 'professionalism from within' presented in this chapter reveals an adherence to collective, democratic practices that promote interdependence, collaboration and an ethic of care through carefully executed forms of emotional labour. Like other feminists (e.g. Hochschild, 1983), I have endeavoured to expose the commitment to emotional labour as problematic, although I offer a challenge to theorisations that argue emotional labour represents a means to control and oppress (working-class) women in the care of others. For example, Skeggs (1997) and later Colley (2006) argue that learning to do emotional labour (through further education training courses) acts to mask structural inequalities such as low pay, poor working conditions and so on. Whilst I do not refute these claims, I offer an analysis that recognises that emotional labour is a contradictory concept that in some ways can be empowering to a professional group caught in a moment of intense policy reform framed by neo-liberal technicist discourse. For the women in this study 'a caring self' was intrinsic to subjective identity formation and in many ways afforded an opportunity to invest in the construction of alternative forms of professionalism.

Within this analysis, emotional capital is conceptualised as a counter-narrative deployed in local sites as a form of resistance to unprecedented policy reforms that pose a serious threat to the authenticity and effectiveness of 'professionalism from within'. The sorts of emotional capital and the forms of emotional labour played out in the narratives were markedly distinct from those offered by Hochschild (1983) and later Skeggs (1997) and Colley (2006) – perhaps because the participants in this study were relatively experienced and mature practitioners, frequently engaged in self-reflection (indeed commitment to this study stemmed from a desire to establish a deeper understanding of professional identities and consider possibilities for change). Unlike Hochschild's focus on flight attendants, and Skeggs' and Colley's focus on teenage trainees enrolled on vocational care courses, many participants in this study offered critical reflections on emotionality and exercised informed judgement about how, when and in what ways emotions played out in their professional performances and the personal costs of emotional mis/management. Within the narratives, an understanding of emotional labour as concerned with reciprocity emerges; my analyses indicate that ECEC practice necessarily involves emotion, but the nature of the emotional labour exchange is carefully managed, which nonetheless has both costs and benefits to all parties involved. In a similar way, Elfer et al. (2003: 27) acknowledge the need for boundaries and detachment and the careful management of emotion in early years practice:

> The emotional demands are great...in a professional role she must develop a very personal and intimate relationship with each of the babies and children with whom she is working. There are bound to be some painful feelings involved, as the work cannot be done in an emotionally anaesthetised way...

Maintaining an appropriate professional intimacy, which every child needs in order to feel special, while keeping an appropriate professional distance requires emotional work of the highest calibre.

The analyses offered in this chapter indicate that this emotional work reaches beyond interactions with children to that undertaken with colleagues and families. Rather than conceptualising the women in this study as oppressed, docile bodies routinely performing emotion through their work by virtue of a gendered professional script provided for them, a competing construction emerges whereby participants constantly negotiate and assess the role and interplay of emotions in their work. Furthermore, the notion that emotionality can be taught, measured and demonstrated in the form of 'vocational competencies' (see Skeggs, 1997; Colley, 2006) is further complicated in this study; this is something that I offer further reflection on in the next section.

Professionalism as learnt

Reflecting further upon Table 7.1, participants considered self-reflection (10); professional confidence (9); professionalism as learnt (7); and expertise (5) as fundamental to a sense of professionalism in ECEC. The data indicate that these factors were inextricably related to training, qualification pathways and professional development activities. In this section my aim is to explore the narratives so that understandings about the forms of training that best cultivate and support the version of professionalism favoured by this group of nursery staff can be had. Many commentators (e.g. Wolf, 1995; Hodkinson *et al.*, 1996; Taylor *et al.*, 1997; Tomlinson, 1997; Bates 1998a, 1998b; Bates *et al.*, 1998) have troubled the narrowly prescriptive nature of much vocational training provision available in the form of G/NVQs and BTEC National Diplomas. Since this was the dominant route that many of the participants had travelled, my intention is to expose both strengths and weaknesses and reflect upon alternative routes that are available and that some of the participants experienced (e.g. Juanita studied pedagogy at masters level in Spain, Natalia pursued an ECS degree in Australia, and several participants were actively engaged on degree courses as part-time and/or distant learners).

The attention that government has placed upon establishing greater clarity around training routes and parity between different qualifications in the children's workforce indicates the significance of training to the professionalisation of those working in ECEC. However, it can be argued that particular types of training/qualifications are valued above others. It would appear that qualification routes founded upon neo-liberal principles (designed to assess measurable technicist practice through prescribed competencies) continue to prevail.

Others, for example Dahlberg and Moss (2005) and Moss (2006), offer theorisations and ways to navigate through limiting neo-liberal discourses to envision the future of professionalism in ECEC. These authors (op. cit.) argue that change to the ECEC workforce is both necessary and inevitable. Furthermore, Moss (op. cit.) offers a conceptualisation of occupational professionalism, which principally rests upon appropriate qualifications and training. The extensive comparative European research undertaken by Moss and colleagues (Brannen and Moss, 1998, 2002; Dahlberg *et al.*, 1999; Moss and Petrie, 2002; Cohen *et al.*, 2004; Dahlberg and Moss, 2005) has been key in shaping policy developments in England; whilst many recommendations have been embraced and taken forward, others (such as the Danish pedagogue model) have fallen from view. Although Moss and colleagues bemoan the two-tiered ECEC workforce in England (with teachers assuming an elevated position in all respects – pay, working conditions, qualifications – to a secondary layer of 'workers'), the policy developments in ECEC indicate a commitment to a graduate-*led* workforce, so the maintenance of a tiered system looks set to remain.

For those working in ECEC, the changes described above are subtle and so remain largely undetected. This study exposed the pursuit of training and the acquisition of qualifications for nursery staff as typically characterised by a series of obstacles and constantly shifting goalposts. The most frequently cited challenge to pursuing structured training programmes was the incompatibility of part-time study and full-time work. This was more acutely felt in the private sector, when at the time of the fieldwork the participants were required to personally fund and allot time outside of working hours, which for those on relatively low incomes, typically working long hours, was simply not feasible. Orla described her repeated attempts to complete NVQ Level Four in Early Childhood. She was forced to abandon the course due to ill health. Despite nearly completing the course, when she came back to it (18 months later) she was advised that she would need to repeat the entire course. Orla found the assessments and content of the course unchallenging and constructed it as 'a means to an end'. She held derisory views of the 'tick box' culture of vocational training routes. Applicability and usefulness of what was covered on the course was limited for her:

> It's not necessarily hard, in fact I don't think I have struggled at any point – it is more going through the motions…but what it is – is very time consuming and when you come home from here at the end of the day you are totally exhausted and the last thing that you want to do is a paper exercise.

The combined challenges of balancing the demands of nursery work with study are further compounded when the course content is deemed to lack resonance with professional life in a nursery. Nearly all the participants in this study were engaged in some form of training or working towards one of a range of relevant qualifications (see the tables in Chapter 3). The costs (financial, emotional and practical) of undertaking study in addition to work were considerable. The working mothers in this study felt it more intensely, since the challenge of balancing competing demands of domestic, professional and student life meant that pursuing higher education was often a protracted and frustrating endeavour (Maguire, 1997; Reay, 1998, 2001, 2004):

Debbie: I need to complete my degree, I'm part way through. I am doing the Early Childhood Studies degree, which as I say I'm part way through, five modules on the second level. I started it...god, I don't know... I mean it's years ago, it's got to be five years that I've been doing it. But the reality is that there's only so much you can do, but when I find the time or make the time then I really enjoy it, can see the value in it...but yeah I *have* to finish it, I *want* to, I *need* to – for me as much as anything, but I suppose that's the issue – stuff for me can easily get pushed to the bottom of the pile. [emphasis in original]

The heavy investments that many of the participants made to professional development and the acquisition of qualifications were variously recounted. Single-minded determination and what many of the women constructed as uncharacteristically 'selfish' approaches were adopted to complete part-time courses:

Gazala: I remember breastfeeding my youngest one... I'd sit at my computer determined to get the work done...then at points throughout the night he'd wake up and need feeding, so I'd stick him on and carry on with the assignment. Looking back I see that was ridiculous, I was working full time, with two older children, a babe in arms and a mountain of work to do for my degree. But some how I have got through it, I've had to, but I can see now that was madness, not how it should have been done.

Other examples included working on assignments on Christmas Day (Toni) and sacrificing family holidays to study (Debbie). Debbie's reference to her 'need' to complete the degree for self-gratification is significant and marks the complex relationship that (mature, female) students from working-class backgrounds have towards higher education (Archer *et al.*, 2002).

Yet the exchange value (Skeggs, 2003) of ECEC qualifications, in terms of economic capital and status is widely recognised as limited and acted to deter many from either engaging in higher levels of study, or where commitments were made then those commitments were protracted or ultimately abandoned. Other than compulsory INSET and non-accredited training days, Iesha, like others in this study, remained unconvinced of the importance of making heavy commitments to additional study. The pursuit of further and higher education was constructed as unnecessary and incompatible to home life; and the relationship of a relatively low income to higher level qualifications, incongruous:

Jayne: Will you go on to study any further?
Iesha: No, I'm not prepared to do any more study... I think if I was going to

do it I should have done it years ago, but now when I finish work, I finish work I don't want to be thinking about dissertations and things like
that, once I'm home – exhausted – then that time is mine... And besides
where's the incentive, you could invest years, and I've seen people here do
it, practically kill themselves getting a degree for what? Salary's the same;
job's the same, and before you know it you've spent the last five, ten years
or whatever slogging your guts out for a piece of paper that means diddly.

Despite this recognition (of limited exchange value); those participants engaged
in part-time degree courses invested heavily in identifying the 'subjective value'
involved. For Gazala, Toni and Debbie, a degree acted as symbolic representation of their academic potential, their determination, and their commitment
to ECEC. However, the extraordinary effort required to engage in further and
higher education whilst working full time was compounded by issues of class, age
and gender (Maguire, 1997; Reay, 1998, 2001; Archer *et al.*, 2002; Osgood,
2005). A number of the more mature women from working-class backgrounds
had embarked upon degree courses either as distance learners and/or on a part-
time basis:

Toni: I wanted to get a recognised qualification. I'd been doing this for a number of years and felt totally committed to it on so many levels and I was
eager to gain a deeper understanding...but the mere mention of university and I was like 'Oh my goodness! I can't manage that!' You have to
remember I left school at fifteen with a few average grades, got married
not long after then I was mum to my boys. University had not been on
my radar so coming to it later on I had all these terrible thoughts, doubt-
ing myself you know...umm, but I put them to one side and just took it
a step at a time. I had to give it a try and now that I've done it I can't tell
you how proud I am and what a difference it has made to how I feel about
myself professionally.

In previous work (Osgood, 2004, 2005, 2006a) I argued for the importance of
appropriate training and continuing professional development for the ECEC workforce. I proposed (Osgood, 2006a) that training of greatest appeal, relevance and
effectiveness to early years practitioners was that which provided scope for reflexivity leading to heightened professional confidence. I articulated (Osgood 2004,
2006a, 2006c) concerns that narrowly prescriptive vocational training which results
in poorly recognised qualifications can have detrimental effects upon those engaged
on such courses because of perceived deficiencies in terms of status, practical application and high order thinking. My concerns are shared by others (Tomlinson,
1997) and supported by the findings from this study:

Elspeth: I do think it's important as well for people who work in this field to have
a grounding in child development and insights into theory, sometimes

> I am a bit disappointed about the NVQ courses that seem to run now because they seem to be dwelling on the practice side of things...in my opinion anyway I think it is really important for people to have a knowledge or engage with theories in childcare in addition to child development theories, there's all the stuff about your role as an educator and the societal, philosophical aspects – none of that is covered on vocational courses but it's what should be known. In my opinion anyway everything hangs together more if you have the theoretical stuff that forces you to question, you know? I mean, I suppose the NVQs and what have you have their place but most of it is just 'checks and balances' for what you have to do anyway – the practical stuff.

It has been argued that specialist authoritarian discourses perpetuated within vocational competence-focused training courses can act to promote certain (narrow) forms of professionalism (Tomlinson, 1997; Bates, 1998a). It is interesting to note that the participants in this study that either held or were working towards a degree in Early Childhood Studies (or a similar relevant subject) offered more enthused views about the value and relevance of the courses:

Jayne: So what has doing the degree meant for you in a professional sense?
Toni: In a professional sense it's made me one, er within my work it's given me the recognition; and the process of obviously doing the degree was in itself a huge eye opener. I have a deeper understanding and I'm not so ready to... I'm not so accepting, I question the rights and wrongs. More reflection on all aspects I suppose, from the pedagogical with children to aspects of managing and where it all sits in a broader philosophical, urmm like political sense I suppose.

Hughes and Menmuir (2002) highlight the importance of depth of knowledge and reflection on practice as the keys to professionalism in the early years. The narratives of those engaged in higher level education and those who had graduated from degree courses prior to embarking upon careers in ECEC in England tended to convey greater self-confidence. Graduate status in the early years was a complex identity to negotiate. As illustrated, attaining a degree was quite often a lengthy struggle, and once achieved convincing others of the intrinsic and professional value was challenging. The collegial and collaborative ethos promoted and valued in nurseries was cultivated and maintained by flattened hierarchies, so that graduates came to conceal their ownership of higher level qualifications. A complex situation emerged where the legitimation as 'expert' to come from holding a degree required careful management:

Natalia: What all the years of study has given me is confidence I guess. I have got to the point now where I feel confident with the way I do things – that's not to say I am not open to change – but I am comfortable with the way I work and the appraisals my colleagues give of me, that's where your professional confidence comes from; when you realise that is the way that you want to be. So I think it is something that comes with age, experience and from respect from other people and having knowledge and expertise behind you. And professional confidence means that you can be true to your own philosophy and stand up for what you believe in. But being one of only a handful of people in a workplace that has a degree can be tricky... I never thrust it in people's face if you know what I mean, they know that I have it, I am proud to have it and know that it makes a different to my professionalism but until and unless there are more degrees...the graduates out number the non-graduates – then it is always going to be a, er well have to be handled sensitively. I don't want to set myself up as the all-knowing, and I am certain that all the staff here could get a degree but for whatever reason they don't...all the time I've got one and they don't, I have to be careful with it'

The pursuit of training and qualifications in ECEC is complex, as this quote indicates. Whilst there is tension and ambiguity around precisely what particular qualifications come to symbolise, the intrinsic value of different forms of training indicate that those which cultivate self-awareness and reflection are more highly prized than prescribed courses aimed to assess sets of practical/technical competence (Sachs, 2001). Degree courses were praised for the space afforded to reflect on the ways in which theory could be applied to practical situations and the scope for experiential professional wisdom to be brought into play (Goodfellow, 2004). As I have argued elsewhere (Osgood, 2008), through professional confidence (as described by Natalia in the quote above) those working in nurseries engage in critical reflections about all aspects of their work, and crucially to establishing understandings of the ways in which they are positioned through discourse and the alternative positionings available to them through the articulation and performance of alternative discourses of professionalism.

Other investments in professional development

Summative support via formal mechanisms (e.g. staff appraisals) where managers facilitate shared reflection on professional development was often cited as a means to effectively reinforce training. However, with the exception of Apple Tree, such activities were noticeably infrequent/absent. Methodological reflections indicate that throughout field visits I was frequently questioned about the suitability of various qualifications and asked for advice on how to access courses. I also encountered difficulties carrying out a CV deconstruction exercise (in all three nurseries). Whilst the dearth of CVs represented a challenge in a methodological sense, it is also significant in terms of the ways in which the participants approached professional self-reflection. The most common reason offered for not providing a CV was that a documented account of professional life/career trajectories was unnecessary in ECEC; the only time participants would collate information about training, qualification, skills, etc. would be upon applying for a new post. The request made for copies of CVs and the questions in the second interview about career trajectories, training/qualification, skills/attributes and so on alerted most participants to the fact that very rarely were opportunities available for them to 'take stock of where I am at' (Terry) or 'identify the gaps' (Ordina). A picture emerges whereby those working in nurseries are principally charged with a responsibility to meet the needs of children, each other, parents and the external demands to deliver standardised and accountable provision. The glaring absence in this illustration, though, is the individual professional development needs of the participants themselves.

Despite commentators (Dahlberg and Moss, 2005) and policy makers (CWDC) declaring that the workforce is central to the success of early years provision (and in government discourses, the 'salvation of society' – Rose, 1999), the priority afforded to investing in each professional appears to sit low. This chapter has demonstrated that hegemonic discourse and policy reform that foregrounds measurability, accountability and technical competence diverts attention from the subjectivities of those that constitute the workforce. Whilst the participants in this study were in part seduced by the elevation of ECEC in public discourse, there remained a level of scepticism that authentic investment was being made to the form of professionalism that is needed and valued within nursery settings. This study has revealed that training committed to/founded upon neo-liberal principles of measurable technical competence denies space for subjective experience to inflect professional practice. The preoccupation with satisfying the regulatory gaze means that nursery workers struggle to find space to engage with children, colleagues and parents in ways that demonstrate professional confidence, expertise and authenticity. That form of professionalism – what I have termed 'professionalism from within' – is shaped by life history and gendered, 'raced', classed subjectivities. The findings from this study indicate that where space is made for life experience and wisdom to play out in professional subjectivities then opportunities for deeper-level appreciation for the work (i.e. professionalism) become available.

Summary

In this chapter, through an analysis of the data, I have illustrated that emotionality is central to professionalism in ECEC. Further, I argue that rather than viewing emotional labour/emotional capital as a means of exploitation opportunities should be taken to reclaim emotions as vital and credible in ECEC practice. However, I recognise that emotional labour can and often is costly to practitioners – whilst there is clear demonstration of effective emotion management, this activity can/does deplete the psychic reserves of participants who invest heavily in the construction of a 'caring self'. Effective examples of this include Debbie, who experienced recurring depression, which she attributed to the emotional toil undertaken in all aspects of her life. Natalia similarly reflected on bouts of (emotional and physical) exhaustion leading her to take time off work.

Bringing subjective experiences from personal history is clearly hugely beneficial in terms of authenticity in ECEC work but it evidently carries heavy costs since participants can feel exposed and vulnerable. Where mechanisms were in place to supervise/support ECEC workers to do emotional labour and have an outlet for the (damaging) effects it might have, emotional labour was understood as vital and beneficial. A chance to debrief and reflect upon the impact/implications of 'giving of oneself' through the emotional toil that has been expended ensures that this form of professionalism is sustainable and not a form of 'violence against the self' (Sawicki, 1991; Segal, 1994). The current reform agenda, and relatedly narrow focus in training programmes, effectively banish emotions or at least hide them from view because 'emotional professionalism' runs counter to hegemonic masculinist constructions.

The analysis offered here indicates that it is imperative that recognition is made that pedagogical practices in nurseries; working collegially in emotionally demanding work environments; and managing the emotions and expectations of angst-ridden parents requires emotional labour 'of the highest calibre' (Elfer *et al.*, 2003). Following this recognition, emotional professionalism could become celebrated and acknowledged rather than denigrated and obscured from public discourse. What children need, what parents want and what practitioners intuitively extend is well-managed and appropriate emotional practice through daily professional interactions.

Chapter 8

Conclusion

Towards critically reflective emotional professionalism

This final chapter summarises the findings concerning nursery worker constructions of professionalism and the interplay with gendered, classed and 'raced' identities. I synthesise the findings and analyses offered in preceding chapters to highlight the implications for ECEC. I begin by reflecting upon the methodological approach taken in this study, and then move on to review the findings from the data chapters and, finally, to outline the implications for professionalism in ECEC.

The broadly ethnographic methodology, involving life history interviews, observation, semi-structured interviews and focus group discussions, enabled an analysis of the identity construction of nursery workers. The approach was justified by the opportunities it afforded to consider the importance of class, gender, 'race' and other markers of identity upon constructions of, and the performance of, professionalism. The life history interviews were especially valuable in meeting the feminist aims of the research. Narrative and autobiographical research methods hold the potential to pose questions about the essence of identity (Goodson and Sikes, 2001). By inviting the participants to construct subjective experience through personal narrative, identity becomes socially constructed. As argued by Middleton (1992), life history research enables the deconstruction of discursive practices through which subjectivity has been constituted.

The methods used to gather primary data from the nursery workers acted in a cumulative and complementary way. Following on with a more focused, semi-structured interview about professionalism meant that participants were able to determine whether or not to revisit issues raised in the previous life history interview. The final focus group discussion provided an interactive space where individualised perspectives and values could be collectively debated.

As discussed in Chapter 3, research is inevitably shaped by power and inequity. The use of qualitative ethnographic methods are often claimed to hold the potential for greater reciprocity in the research process (Moll and Greenberg, 1990). My feminist poststructuralist ethnographic position resulted in a heightened attention to issues of power and a commitment to reflective and reflexive research practice (Harding, 1987; Lather, 1988; Stanley and Wise, 1990). The feminist methodological reflections offered in Chapter 3 indicate the significance of my subject position throughout the entire research process, but notably during interviews with participants (Dyck *et al.*, 1995). I endeavoured to manage research situations so as to recognise power relations and limit the potentially damaging effects upon the participants involved (Phoenix, 1995; Reay, 1996). Rather than claiming to seek some authentic truth through scientific method, I endeavoured to make known my subjectivity and the political aims of my research. Furthermore, I stressed the likely costs (and benefits) of being involved and sought to engage the nursery workers in the research process through inviting their reflections about the study at various points. However, I was troubled by certain claims that research founded upon commitments to reciprocity could achieve emancipatory objectives (Skeggs, 1997). Like Denscombe (1998), I identify a narcissistic danger in attempts to (over)claim that research is conducted 'from within' for 'emancipatory goals'. Therefore this study employed a hybridised methodology that encompassed ethnographic, social constructionist and feminist epistemologies. This approach enabled an in-depth and sensitive approach in the field. Furthermore, the data was treated in a reflexive way so as to unearth and problematise taken-for-granted assumptions but avoided reaching claims to absolute truths grounded in realism.

The method of critically analysing discourse that I undertook was shaped by Foucauldian ideas. I drew heavily upon his theorisations of power and discourse, and in particular his ideas around discursive (re)positioning through discourse. By applying this approach I was able to identify how identities are constructed, resisted and (re)negotiated when prevailing hegemonic discourses and less powerful (marginalised) counter-discourses intersect and are exposed. My aim was to problematise, disentangle and expose the ways in which power plays out within/through discourse to highlight the implications this has for the professional identities of the nursery worker. However, as outlined above, as a poststructuralist feminist researcher, I acknowledge my subjectivity when coming to the issue of professional identity construction.

The broadly ethnographic approach taken in this research represents my feminist ontology (Skeggs, 1995). The aims of the study, choice of methods and each stage of the research process were shaped by subjective motivations. This has meant that the lens applied when gathering and analysing the data was politically motivated and therefore inevitably partial (Parker, 1998). The naming of particular discourses is based upon subjective assumptions about the nature of the discursive practices that position nursery workers in particular ways. I do not claim to have identified the full range of discourses that come to inflect and shape nursery workers' understandings of themselves as professional.

Allied to my subjectivity and feminist ontology is the specificity of this study. I undertook this research within a particular socio-economic and policy moment, and consequently the examination of nursery worker subjective identities against the backdrop of intense policy reform is embedded within a specific context (Cannella, 1997; Jones *et al.*, 2005). However, the discourses identified from analyses of the data resonate with studies conducted in broadly similar contexts, for example, Robinson and Jones-Diaz (2006) and Ailwood (2008) in Australia, and Otterstad (2008) and Ulla (2008) in Norway. Furthermore, a focus upon the subjectivities of nursery workers in the context of debating professionalism has provided a starting point for further, comparable investigations in England (Luck, 2008; McGillivray, 2008; Miller, 2008; Miller and Cable, 2008).

Arguments that highlight the hegemony of authoritative discourses to promote a particular form of professionalism (Mahony and Hextall, 2000; Avis, 2003; Ball, 2003a; Dahlberg and Moss, 2005) are supported by the findings of this study. As these authors (op. cit.) contend, narrowly defined constructions of professionalism serve to meet broader political/societal goals grounded in human capital theory (Levitas, 1998). This study has illustrated the means by which nursery workers become discursively constructed (as a means to an end) in policy terms. Through identifying and deconstructing policy discourses that construct nursery workers in particular ways, it has been possible to identify a process of objectification (Foucault, 1990). Within policy discourses, space to critique discursive positioning becomes compromised because the rationale for workforce reform is presented as entirely justified and necessary. Other research (e.g. Cannella, 1997; Ball, 2003a) has demonstrated that hegemonic policy discourses construct the embodiment of particular forms of professionalism (the competent technician) as reasonable, rational and taken for granted. I found that nursery workers variously drew upon, negotiated and rejected these discourses when doing professionalism. As noted in Chapter 7, the dominant construction of professionalism, cultivated in policy discourses is not straightforwardly taken up. Whilst elevation in policy terms was seductive, and investment into the workforce regarded positively, the narrowly prescriptive discursive construction of professionalism was questioned. Moreover, the construction of professionalism as rational/objective was challenged and resisted.

The aims of this study were concerned to investigate multiple subjectivities and the implications of doing class, gender and 'race' (Butler, 1990) for professionalism in ECEC. The narrative methods used in this study allowed space to reflect upon aspects of life that are not readily assumed to shape professional subjectivities – delving into the personal to seek to understand the public/professional identities of nursery workers generated a rich body of data. By giving the nursery workers space to construct autobiographical accounts, it became evident that subjective childhood experiences are often marginalised and silenced in, and by debates about, professionalism. The findings from this study indicate that the nursery workers invest heavily in childhood – both as a discursive construct and in their daily pedagogical practices in nurseries. By reflecting upon childhood subjectivities, the nursery workers were able to identify the investments that they make in promoting/sustaining an 'imagined childhood'. Through the research process the nursery workers came to draw connections between subjective experiences of childhood (that sat outside normalised constructions) and their pedagogical practices. This study indicates that opportunities to reach critical understandings of the child and childhood as socially constructed are vital to reflecting upon professionalism.

The findings from this research contribute to an ongoing debate around the proximity of maternalistic discourses to ECEC practice and professionalism (Riley, 1983; Cannella, 1997; Skeggs, 1997; Uttal, 2002; Vogt, 2002; Vincent and Ball, 2006; Ailwood, 2008). This study has contributed to understandings that ECEC practice is inflected by maternalistic discourses. Further, I found that hegemonic discourses around normative middle-class mothering (Walkerdine and Lucey, 1989) are taken up by the nursery workers and contribute to a series of tensions when engaged in work with young children. The findings indicate that maternalistic assumptions can be limiting for nursery workers when subjective experiences are positioned outside of normalised middle-class models of mothering. Through a critical analysis of maternalistic discourses that shape and inflect ECEC practice, it has been possible to explore and expose class difference as central to understandings of professional subjectivity.

Moreover, the ways in which nursery workers are constructed in public discourse rests upon partial and subjective experiences of middle-class actors (policy makers, parents and related members of the children's workforce). This study demonstrates that the discursive positioning of nursery workers within (and through) middle-class discourses acts to undermine efforts to 'do professionalism' in ways that are intrinsic to the nature of the work (Claxton, 1999; Elfer et al., 2003; Dahlberg and Moss, 2005). Following Vincent and Ball (2006), I analysed the class-inflected relationship between nursery worker and mother to reveal that the professional identities of nursery workers can be seen as fluid and shifting depending upon the social context. Where nursery workers have professional status conferred upon them by parents (and related professionals), there is evidence of heightened ontological security.

By reflecting upon the discursive landscape in which the nursery workers are located, and considering childhood and maternal subjectivities, it is possible to dismantle the notion of professionalism and offer a reconceptualisation. The findings from this research support literature that troubles dominant discourses that promote professionalism as an apolitical construct (Dahlberg et al., 1999; Ozga, 2000; Stronach et al., 2003). Like others (op. cit.), I have found professionalism to be socially constructed and furthermore to rest upon hegemonic normalisations stemming from a precise socio-political and economic moment. As illustrated in Chapter 4 through a critical analysis of policy, policy makers have invested heavily in cultivating normalising constructions of 'the early years professional'. As noted in Chapter 7, the hegemonic constructions cultivated within policy discourse effectively deny space for alternative internal constructions to flourish. The findings indicate that the ways in which nursery workers come to conceive of themselves, as more or less professional, rests upon their (life-long) subjective experiences and the wider discourses in which they are located and upon which they draw, reject and negotiate.

I turn now to an outline of the implications of the findings from this study for the professional identities of nursery workers. Through an engagement with recent policy around workforce reform and a heightened professionalism in ECEC, this study indicates the importance of top-down policy to the professional identities of nursery workers. The ways in which nursery workers are variously constructed through policy and in related authoritative discourses indicates a need for nursery workers to critically engage with policy discourses. Chapter 3 notes that this study is committed to 'hearing stories' rather than 'giving voice'. It is my contention that the discursive practices, which can construct nursery workers in marginalised ways, must be challenged from within the workforce. This research has demonstrated that nursery workers variously occupy positions of significant power. As I argue elsewhere (Osgood, 2006a, 2006c), discursive space is available for nursery workers to manage (and challenge) public constructions of professionalism in ECEC. Furthermore, through critical engagement with policy, resistance to narrowly prescriptive forms of professionalism becomes possible.

This study has demonstrated the existence of an alternative construction of professionalism 'from within' (Stronach et al., 2003). By bringing subjective experiences from their autobiographies, nursery workers experience greater authenticity in their pedagogical practices and sense of professionalism. The analyses I offer in this study indicate that the emotional nature of nursery work is acknowledged and valued by practitioners. Pedagogical engagement with children, collegial working practices, and the careful management of emotionally charged relationships with parents all require the deployment of emotional capital (Reay, 1998; Colley, 2006). My central proposition is that 'the emotional professional' should become celebrated and acknowledged rather than denigrated and obscured in public discourse.

However, doing 'emotional professionalism' is costly to practitioners and therefore a series of implications can be identified. In order to encourage greater reflexivity, so that nursery workers are willing and able to relate their subjective experiences to their pedagogical practices, requires adjustments at different levels of ECEC. Training providers and universities that extend professional development courses to nursery workers could go beyond narrowly prescriptive programmes that cultivate 'competent technicians'. This study has illustrated the importance of critical reflection on subjective experiences and the implications this has for practice. As extensively debated in Chapter 7, the potential for practitioners to build upon empathic motivations and commitment to their work is significant. The findings lead me to argue that the moral, political and emotional commitment to nursery work demonstrated in this study is at risk of being eroded where time and energy becomes diverted to technicist concerns (Novinger and O'Brien, 2003). Moreover, by enhancing the authenticity of the professional work that nursery workers undertake with children and their families, doing professionalism can go beyond the demonstration of technical competence.

Within the wider literature there are examples where nurseries demonstrate a commitment to greater reflexivity through localised practices. Perhaps most frequently cited are the municipal preschools in Reggio Emilia, northern Italy

(Dahlberg *et al.*, 1999; Giudici *et al.*, 2001; Dahlberg and Moss, 2005). These preschools have attracted much attention because they represent examples where ethics and politics are foregrounded without discarding technical practice. As Dahlberg and Moss (2005: 135) outline these preschools 'develop distinctive pedagogical practices, which can be seen as a highly political process of making choices – about understandings of the child, of knowledge and of learning'. This study has found that as local sites (comprised of 'emotional professionals' capable of critically reflecting upon their discursive positioning and committed to early childhood) nurseries hold the potential to promote the exercise of 'minor politics' (Rose, 1999). Minor politics involves a collective process of critical thinking (Rose, 1999: 20) it is

> a matter of introducing critical attitude towards those things that are given to our present experience as if it were timeless, natural, unquestionable: to stand against the maxims of one's time, against the spirit of one's age, against the current of received wisdom. It is a matter of introducing a kind of awkwardness into the fabric of one's experience, of interrupting the fluency of the narratives that encode that experience and making them stutter.

This study can be constructed as contributing to a collective process of critical thinking. Through their participation, the nursery workers were able to critically reflect upon the hegemony of particular forms of professionalism and the relationship of their subjective experience to their pedagogical practices. They took up an invitation to question and challenge regimes of truth (Foucault, 1980) that construct commonsense understandings of what constitutes professionalism in ECEC. The findings from this research lead me to advocate space for 'minor politics' to play out in nurseries. Participation in external research such as this study, the conduct of action research (Rhedding-Jones, 2005b) and other opportunities to become more critically aware, such as the use of professional development portfolios (Goodfellow, 2004), represent vehicles for minor politics to play out in the nursery. However, like Dahlberg and Moss (2005: 151), I suggest that such activity should become routine:

> Minor politics involves a *constant critique* and takes a reflective attitude. It is questioning and induces stuttering, disrupting discourses and destabilising accepted meanings, denaturalising the taken for granted, opening up issues to confrontation and contestation. It makes us aware that our constructions are constructions, which are produced in particular contexts and shaped by particular discourses. [emphasis in original]

For minor politics to become foundational to nursery worker professionalism, space and opportunities for critical reflection must be made available. This rests on the commitment of nursery leaders and managers to facilitate such processes. By making the discourse of professionalism 'stutter', public constructions of nursery workers can become disrupted and open to change. The nursery workers in this study frequently cited inadequate or insufficient continuing professional development opportunities, and related lack of professional support and guidance. The training and professional development activities most frequently attended were compulsory (i.e. in relation to national curriculum and frameworks, health and safety and so on). There was a demonstrable lack of importance attached to activities designed to promote critical reflexivity; other commentators have identified this trend. For example, Novinger and O'Brien (2003: 4) in the USA make reference to moving beyond 'boring meaningless shit' when discussing the enforced preoccupation with a standards agenda:

> The focus on standards and regulation has moved beyond 'just' being boring and meaningless to being deliberately destructive. Boring, meaningless shit keeps all of us in education – children, classroom teachers and college professors – too busy to engage in meaningful critiques of the status quo and that is bad enough. But the recent heightened and overt emphasis on control and compliance is harmful in that it is about dismantling the very idea, never mind the practice, of education for democracy.

To conclude, this study intended to seek an understanding of the way in which the professional identities of nursery workers are discursively constructed. Through a problematisation of hegemonic discourses, it has been possible to expose alternative discursive positionings. In order that alternative constructions of the nursery worker as a classed, gendered, 'raced' subject might be taken up will require critical engagement from a range of influential actors. For the 'critically reflexive emotional professional' to take the place of the 'competent technician' will necessitate making space to 'hear the stories' of those that make up the nursery workforce and to act upon constructions of 'professionalism from within'.

References

Acker, S. (1995) 'Carry on caring: the work of women teachers', *British Journal of Sociology of Education*, 16 (1), 21–36.

Adam, B., Beck, U. and Van Loon, J. (2002) *The Risk Society and Beyond: Critical Issues for Social Theory*. London: Sage.

Ailwood, J. (2008) 'Mothers, teachers, maternalism and early childhood education and care: some historical connections', *Contemporary Issues in Early Childhood*, 8 (2), 157–164.

Ainsworth, M.D.S. (1969) 'Object relations, dependency and attachment: a theoretical review of the infant–mother relationship', *Child Development*, 40, 969–1025.

Ainsworth, M. and Bell, S. (1974) 'Mother–infant interactions and the development of competence', in K. Connolly and J. Bruner (eds) *The Growth of Competence*. London: Academic Press.

Alexander, E. (2002) 'Childcare workers: learning or imitating?' *Forum*, 44 (1), 24–26.

Alloway, N. (1997) 'Early childhood education encounters the postmodern: what do we know? What can we count as "true"?' *Journal of Early Childhood Education*, 22 (2), 1–5.

Althusser, L. (1971) *Lenin and Philosophy and Other Essays*. London: New Left Books.

Anthias, F. and Yuval-Davies, N. (1992) *Racialised Boundaries: Race, Nation, Gender, Colour and Class and the Anti-Racist Struggle*. London: Routledge.

Archer, L. (2002) 'It's easier that you're a girl and that you're Asian: interactions of "race" and gender between researchers and participants', *Feminist Review*, 72 (2), 108–132.

Archer, L., Hutchings, M. and Ross, A. (2002) *Higher Education and Social Class: Issues of Exclusion and Inclusion*. London: Routledge.

Aries, P. (1962) *Centuries of Childhood*. London: Cape Publishing.

Armstrong, J. (2006) 'Beyond "juggling" and "flexibility": classed and gendered experiences of combining employment and motherhood', *Sociological Research On-line*, 11 (2), www.socresonline.org.uk/11/2/armstrong.html.

Ashforth, B.E. and Tomiuk, M.A. (2000) 'Emotional labour and authenticity: views from service agents', in Stephen Fineman (ed.) *Emotion in Organizations*. 184–203. London: Sage.

Aveling, N. (2002) '"Having it all" and the discourse of equal opportunity: reflection of choices and changing perceptions', *Gender and Education*, 14 (3), 265–280.

Avis, J. (2003) 'Re-thinking trust in a performative culture: the case of education', *Journal of Education Policy*, 18 (3), 315–332.

Ball, S.J. (1990) *Politics and Policy Making in Education: Explorations in Policy Sociology*. London: Routledge.

Ball, S.J. (2003a) 'The teacher's soul and the terrors of performativity', *Journal of Education Policy*, 18 (2), 215–228.

Ball, S.J. (2003b) *Class Strategies and the Education Market: The Middle Class and Social Advantage*. London: RoutldgeFalmer.

Ball, S.J. and Vincent, C. (1998) 'I heard it on the grapevine: "hot" knowledge and school choice', *British Journal of Sociology of Education*, 19 (3), 377–400.

Barrow, C. (1996) *Family in the Caribbean: Themes and Perspectives*. Oxford: James Curney Publishers.

Barthes, R. (1990) *The Pleasure of Text* (translated by R. Miller). Oxford: Blackwell.

Bassey, M. (1999) *Case Study Research in Educational Settings*. Buckingham: Open University Press.

Bates, I. (1998a) *The Competence and Outcomes Movement: The Landscape of Research*. Leeds: 14–19 Research Group, School of Education, University of Leeds.

Bates, I. (1998b) 'Resisting "empowerment" and realising power: an exploration of aspects of the GNVQ', *Journal of Education and Work*, 11 (2), 187–204.

Bates, I., Bloomer, M., Hodkinson, P. and Yeomans, D. (1998) 'Progressivism and the GNVQ: context, ideology and practice', *Journal of Education and Work*, 11 (2), 109–125.

Bauman, Z. (2000) *The Individualized Society*. London: Polity Press.

Beck, U. (1992) *The Risk Society: Towards a New Modernity*. London: Sage.

Bertram, T. (2005) 'Effective Early Years Practitioners: their distribution and characteristics', presented at SCETT seminar: *Preparing the Early Years Workforce Meeting the Challenge*, 10 February. NATFHE Conference Centre, London.

Bhabha, H. (1994) *The Location of Culture*. London: Routledge.

Bhabha, H. (1998) 'Culture's in between', in D. Bennett (ed.) *Multicultural States. Rethinking Difference and Identity*. London: Routledge.

Bhavani, K-K. and Phoenix, A. (eds) (1994) *Shifting Identities, Shifting Racism: A Feminism and Psychology Reader*. London: Sage.

Blackburn, P. (2004) *Children's Nurseries: UK Market Sector Report 2004*. London: Laing Buisson.

Blaise, M. (2005a) *Playing it Straight!: Uncovering Gender Discourses in the Early Childhood Classroom*. New York: Routledge Press.

Blaise, M. (2005b) 'A feminist poststructuralist study of children doing gender', *Early Childhood Research Quarterly*, 20, 85–108.

Blaise, M. and Andrew, Y. (2005) 'How "bad" can it be? Troubling gender, sexuality and early childhood teaching', in N. Yelland (ed.) *Critical Issues in Early Childhood Education*. London: Routledge.

Blunkett, D. (2000) 'Influence or irrelevance: can social science improve government?' *Research Intelligence*, 71: 12–21.

Boldt, G. (1997) 'Sexist and heterosexist responses to gender bending', in J. Tobin (ed.) *Making a Place for Pleasure in Early Childhood Education*. New Haven, CT: Yale University Press.

Bourdieu, P. (1986) *Distinction: A Social Critique of the Judgement of Taste*. London: Routledge.

Bourdieu, P. (2000) *Pascalian Meditations*. Cambridge: Polity Press.

Bowe, R., Ball, S.J. and Gold, A. (1992) *Reforming Education and Changing Schools: Case Studies in Policy Sociology*. London: Routledge.

Bowlby, J. (1978a) *Attachment and Loss: Vol. I, Attachment*. Harmondsworth: Penguin.

Bowlby, J. (1978b) *Attachment and Loss, Vol.II, Separation, Anxiety and Anger*. Harmondsworth: Penguin.

Bradley, B. (1989) *Visions of Infancy: A Critical Introduction to Child Psychology*. Oxford: Blackwell.

Bradley, H. (1996) *Men's Work, Women's Work*. Cambridge: Polity Press.

Brah, A. (1992) 'Difference, diversity and differentiation', in J. Donald and A. Rattansi (eds) *Race, Culture and Difference*. London: Sage.

Brannen, J. and Moss, P. (1991) *Managing Mothers: Dual Earner Households After Maternity Leave*. London: Unwin Hyman.

Brannen, J. and Moss, P. (1998) 'The polarisation and intensification of parental employment in Britain: consequences for children, families and the community', *Community, Work and Family*, 1, 229–247.

Brannen, J. and Moss, P. (2002) *Re-thinking Children's Care*. Buckingham: Open University Press.

Brooker, L. (2005) 'Learning to be a child: cultural diversity and early years ideology', in N. Yelland (ed.) *Critical Issues in Early Childhood Education*. London: Routledge.

Burke, S., Homer, N., Lines, C., Tarazona, P., Graham, K. and Mills, C. (2002) *Child's Play: New Mutual Models of Childcare Report*. London: Mutto.

Burn, E. and P. Holland (2000) 'Listening to Students: studying for a part-time degree in early childhood studies'. Paper presented at EECERA Conference: Complexity, diversity and multiple perspectives in early childhood at Institute of Education, London.

Burr, V. (1995) *An Introduction to Social Constructionism*. London: Routledge.

Butler, J. (1990) *Gender Trouble: Feminism and the Subversion of Identity*. London: Routledge.

Butler, J. (2004) *Undoing Gender*. London: Routledge.

Butler, J. (2005) *Giving an Account of Oneself*. New York: Fordham University Press.

Cameron, C. (2006) 'Men in the nursery revisited: issues of male workers and professionalism', *Contemporary Issues in Early Childhood*, 7 (1), 68–79.

Cameron, C. (1997) 'A review of staffing in childcare centres in six countries', *Early Child Development and Care*, 137: 47–67.

Cameron, C., Mooney, A. and Moss, P. (2002) 'The Childcare Workforce: Current Conditions and Future Directions', *Critical Social Policy*, 22 (4), 572–595.

Cameron, C., Moss, P. and Owen, C. (1999) *Men in the Nursery: Gender and Caring Work*. London: Sage Publications.

Cannella, G.S. (1997) *Deconstructing Early Childhood Education: Social Justice and Revolution*. New York, Peter Lang.

Cannella, G.S. and Grieshaber, S. (2001) 'A way forward: re-invented identities', in S. Grieshaber and G.S. Cannella (eds) *Embracing Identities in Early Childhood Education: Diversity and Possibilities*. New York: Teachers College Press.

Caproni, P. (2004) 'Work/life balance: you can't get there from here', *The Journal of Applied Behavioral Science*, 40 (2), 208–218.

Carabine, J. (2001) 'Unmarried motherhood 1830–1990: a genealogical analysis' in M. Wetherell, S. Taylor and S.J. Yates (eds) *Discourse as Data: A Guide for Analysis*. London: Sage Publications with the Open University.

Casper, V., Cuffaro, H.K., Shultz, S., Silin, J.G. and Wickens, E. (1998) 'Towards a most thorough understanding of the world: sexual orientation and early childhood education', in N. Yelland (ed.) *Gender in Early Childhood*. London: Routledge.

Centre for Economic and Social Inclusion (2006) Report prepared for UNISON: Qualifications, Pay and Quality in the Childcare Sector. Accessed 12 September 2006 at http://www.unison.org.uk/acrobat/B2773.pdf.

Chaplin, D.D., Hofferth, S.L. and Wissoker, D.A. (1996) 'Price and quality in childcare choice: a revision', *Journal of Human Resources*. 31, 703–706.

Chasnoff, D. and Cohen, H. (1997) *It's Elementary: Talking about Gay Issues in Schools*. (film) San Francisco: Women's Educational Media.

Chodorow, N.J. (1978) *The Reproduction of Mothering: Psychoanalysis and the Sociology of Gender*. London: University of California Press.

Claxton, G. (1999) 'The anatomy of intuition', in T. Atkinson and G. Claxton (eds) *The Intuitive Practitioner: On the Value of Not Always Knowing What One is Doing*. Buckingham: Open University Press.

Cohen, B., Moss, P., Petrie, P. and Wallace, J. (2004) *A New Deal for Children? Re-forming Education and Care in England, Scotland and Sweden*. Bristol: Policy Press.

Colley, H. (2006) 'Learning to labour with feeling: class, gender and emotion in childcare education and training', *Contemporary Issues in Early Childhood*, 7 (1), 15–29.

Collins, B. (2004) 'My nursery nightmare', *Daily Mail online*, London.

Crompton, R. (2001) 'The gendered restructuring of the middle-classes: employment and caring', in R. Crompton,. F. Devine., M. Savage and J. Scott (eds) *Renewing Class Analysis*. Oxford: Blackwell.

CWDC (2007a) Be a Leader: Early Years Professional Status. www.cwdcouncil.org. uk/pdf/Early%20Years/EYP_Prospectus_0407.pdf .

CWDC (2007b) Prospectus: Early Years Professional Status. www.cwdcouncil.org. uk/pdf/Early%20Years/EYP_Prospectus_0407.pdf.

CWDC (2008a) Early Years Professional Status. www.cwdcouncil.org.uk/eyps.

CWDC (2008b) *Early Years Professional Status, Providers' Handbook: A Guide to the Gateway Review and the Assessment Process*. Phase Two: revised on 8 June. Leeds: CWDC.

Dahlberg, G. and Moss, P. (2005) *Ethics and Politics in Early Childhood Education*. London: RoutledgeFalmer.

Dahlberg, G., Moss, P. and Pence, A. (1999) *Beyond Quality in Early Childhood Education and Care: Postmodern Perspectives*. London: Falmer Press.

Daily Telegraph, The (2004) 'BBC attacked after exposing "abuse" at nursery', London.

Daily Telegraph, The (2006) 'Helper suspended for wearing veil in class'. www. telegraph.co.uk/news/uknews/1531418/Helper-suspended-for-wearing-veil-in-class.html.

David, M.E. (1980) *The State, the Family and Education*. London: Routledge.

Davies, B. (1989) *Frogs and Snails and Feminist Tales. Pre-school Children and Gender*. Sydney: Allen Unwin.

Davies, B. (1992) 'Women's subjectivity and feminist stories', in C. Ellis and M. Flaherty (eds) *Investigating Subjectivity: Research on Lived Experience*. Newbury Park, CA: Sage.

Davies, B. (1993) *Shards of Glass: Children Reading and Writing Beyond Gendered Identities*. Sydney: Allen Unwin.

Davies, B. (1994) *Poststructuralist Theory and Classroom Practice*. Geelong, Vic.: Deakin University Press.

Davies, B. (2000) *A Body of Writing 1990–1999*. Oxford: AltaMira Press.

Davies, B. (2003) 'Death to critique and dissent? The policies and practices of new managerialism and of "evidence-based practice"', *Gender and Education*, 15 (1), 91–103.

Davies, H.T.O., Nutley, S.M. and Smith, P.C. (eds) (2000) *What Works? Evidence-based Policy and Practice in the Public Services*. Bristol: Policy Press.

Dean, H. (2001) 'Working parenthood and parental obligation', *Critical Social Policy*, 21 (3), 267–286.

Denscombe, M. (1998) *The Good Research Guide for Small-scale Social Research Projects*. 3rd Edition. Buckingham: Open University Press.

Department of Health (1989) *The Children Act*. London: HMSO.

Derrida, J. (1972) *Positions*. Chicago, IL: University of Chicago Press.

Derrida, J. (1976) *Of Grammatology* (translated by G.C. Spivak). Baltimore: John Hopkins University.

DfEE (1997) *Excellence in Schools*, Cmnd.3681. London: Department for Education and Employment.

DfES (1997) *Meeting the Childcare Challenge: The National Childcare Strategy*. London: HMSO.

DfES (2003a) *Every Child Matters* (Green Paper), Cm.5860. HMSO: London.

DfES (2003b) *Childcare Workforce Surveys 2002*. London: HMSO.

DfES (2005) *Children's Workforce Strategy: Building a World-Class Workforce for Children, Young People and Families*. London: DfES.

DfES (2006a) *Children's Workforce Strategy: Building a World-Class Workforce for Children, Young People and Families. The Government's Response to the Consultation*. London: DfES.

DfES (2006b) *Children's Workforce Strategy: Building an Integrated Qualifications*.

Diamond, I. and Quinby, L. (eds) (1988) *Feminism and Foucault: Reflections on Resistance*. Boston, MA: Northeastern University Press.

Dilworth, J. and Kingsbury, N. (2005) 'Home-to-job spillover for Generation X, Boomers and Matures: a comparison', *Journal of Family and Economic Issues*, 26 (2), 267–281.

Du Gay, P. (1996) *Consumption and Identity at Work*. London: Sage.

Dyck, I., Lynam, J.M. and Anderson, J.M. (1995) 'Women talking: creating knowledge through difference in cross-cultural research', *Women's Studies International Forum*, 18, 5–6, 611–626.

Ehrenreich, B. and Hochschild, A.R. (2003) *Global Woman: Nannies, Maids and Sex Workers in the New Economy*. London: Granta.

Eichenbaum, L. and Orbach, S. (1982) *Outside In…Inside Out: Women's Psychology: A Feminist Psychoanalytic Approach*. London: Pluto Press.

Elfer, P. (1994) *Parental Views on the Development of Day Care and Education Services for Children Under Eight in England*. London: National Children's Bureau.

Elfer, P., Goldschmied, E. and Selleck, D. (2003) *Key Persons in the Nursery: Building Relationships for Quality Provision*. London: David Fulton.

Epstein, D. (1994) *Challenging Lesbian and Gay Inequalities in Education*. Buckingham: Open University Press.

Epstein, D. (1999) 'Sex play: romantic significations, sexism and silences in the schoolyard', in D. Epstein and J.T. Sears. (eds) *A Dangerous Knowing: Sexuality, Pedagogy and Popular Culture*. London: Cassell.

Epstein, D. (2001) 'Boys and girls come out to play: making masculinities and femininities in primary playgrounds', in D. Epstein, M.J. Kehily, M. Mac an Ghaill and P. Redman, *Men and Masculinities. Special Issue: Disciplining and Punishing Masculinities*, 4 (2), 158–72.

Epstein, D. with Steinberg, D.L. and Johnson, R. (1997) *Border Patrols: Policing the Boundaries of Heterosexuality*. London: Cassell.

Equal Opportunities Commission (EOC) (2006) *Facts About Men and Women in Great Britain*. London: EOC.

Fairclough, N. (2001) 'The discourse of New Labour: critical discourse analysis', in Wetherell, M., Taylor, S. and Yates, S.J. (eds) *Discourse as Data: A Guide for Analysis*. London: Sage Publications with the Open University.

Fenech, M. and Sumsion, J. (2007) 'Early childhood teachers and regulation: complicating power relations using a Foucauldian lens', *Contemporary Issues in Early Childhood*, 8 (2), 109–122.

Fleer, M. (2003) 'Early childhood education as an evolving "community of practice" or as lived "social reproduction": researching the "taken-for-granted"', *Contemporary Issues in Early Childhood*, 4 (1), 64–79.

Forrester, G. (2000) 'Professional autonomy versus managerial control: the experience of teachers in an English primary school', *International Studies in Sociology of Education*, 10 (2), 133–151.

Foucault, M. (1972) *The Archaeology of Knowledge* (translated by A. Sheridan). London: Tavistock.

Foucault, M. (1978) *The History of Sexuality: Volumes I–III*. New York: Pantheon.

Foucault, M. (1979) *Discipline and Punish: The Birth of the Prison*. Harmondsworth: Penguin.

Foucault, M. (1980) *Power/Knowledge: Selected Interviews and Other Writings 1972–1977*, London: Routledge.

Foucault, M. (1983) 'The subject and power: afterward', in H. Dreyfus and P. Rabinow (eds) *Michel Foucault: beyond structuralism and hermeneutics*. Chicago, IL: Chicago University Press.

Foucault, M. (1994) *Power: Essential Works of Foucault 1954–1984, Volume 3*. James D. Faubion (ed.) (translated by Robert Hurley). London: Penguin.

Francis, B. (1999) 'Modernist reductionism or post-structuralist relativism – can we move on? An evaluation of the arguments in relation to feminist educational research', *Gender and Education*, 11 (4), 381–393.

Francis, B. (2001) 'Commonality AND difference? Attempts to escape from theoretical dualisms in emancipatory research in education', *International Studies in Sociology of Education*, 11 (2), 157–172.

Francis, B. (2002) 'Relativism, realism and feminism – an analysis of some theoretical tensions in research on gender identity', *Journal of Gender Studies*, 11 (1), 39–54.

Francis, B. (2003) 'The creation and dissemination of feminist research in education: facts and fictions?' in C. Hughes (ed.) *Disseminating Qualitative Research in Educational Settings: a critical introduction*. Buckingham: Open University Press.

Francis, B. and Archer, L. (2005) 'British–Chinese pupils' and parents' constructions of the value of education', *British Educational Research Journal*, 30 (1), 89–108.

Fraser, N. (1989) *Unruly Practices: Power, Discourse and Gender in Contemporary Social Theory*. Cambridge: Polity Press.

Friedan, B. (1963) *The Feminine Mystique*. London: Penguin.

Friere, P. (1999) *Pedagogy of the Heart*. New York: Continuum Publishing.

Fuqua, R.W. and Labensohn, D. (1986) 'Parents as consumers of childcare', *Family Relations*. 35, 295–303.

Furedi, F. (2008) *Paranoid Parenting: Why Ignoring the Experts May Be Best for Your Child*. London: Continuum Press.

Gatrell, C. (2005) *Hard Labour*. Maidenhead: Oxford University Press.

Gee, J.P. (1999) *An Introduction to Discourse Analysis: Theory and Method*. London: Routledge.

Gee, J.P., Hull, G. and Lankshear, C. (1996) *The New Work Order: Behind the Language of the New Capitalism*. Sydney; Allen and Unwin.

Gewirtz, S. (2001) 'Cloning the Blairs: New Labour's programme for the re-socialisation of working-class parents', *Journal of Education Policy*, 16, 365–378.

Giudici, C., Rinaldi, C., Krechevsky, M. (eds) (2001) *Making Learning Visible: Children as Individual and Group Learners*. Reggio Emilia, Italy: Reggio Children.

Giroux, H. (1992) *Border Crossings: Cultural Workers and the Politics of Education*. New York: Routledge.

Gittins, D. (1998) *The Child in Question*. London: Macmillan.

Goodfellow, J. (2004) 'Documenting professional practice through the use of a professional portfolio', *Early Years*, 24 (1), 63–74.

Goodson, I.F. and Sikes, P. (2001) *Life History Research in Educational Settings: Learning from Lives, Doing Qualitative Research in Educational Settings Series*. Buckingham: Open University Press.

Gray, J. (2007) '(Re)considering voice', *Qualitative Social Work*, 6 (4), 411–430.

Grieshaber, S. (2001) 'Constructing the gendered infant', in N. Yelland (ed.) *Gender in Early Childhood*. London: Routledge.

Grieshaber, S. (2002) 'A national system of childcare accreditation: Quality Assurance or a technique of normalisation?' in G.S. Cannella and J.L. Kincheloe (eds) *Kidworld: Childhood Studies, global perspectives and education*, 161–180.

Guardian, The (2006a) 'Nurseries "fostering generation of Vicky Pollards"'. Accessed 3 October 2006 at http://www.guardian.co.uk/education/2006/aug/02/schools.uk3?INTCMP=SRCH.

Guardian, The (2006b) 'Tribunal dismisses case of Muslim woman ordered not to teach in veil'. Accessed 20 October 2006 at http://www.guardian.co.uk/uk/2006/oct/20/politics.schools1.

Hakin, C. (2001) *Work-lifestyle Choices in the Twenty-first Century*. Oxford: Oxford University Press.

Hall, S. (1992) *New Ethnicities*, in J. Donald and A. Rattansi (eds) *Race, Culture and Difference*. London: Sage.

Hall, S. (1996) 'Introduction: who needs "identity"? in P. Duy (ed.) *Representation: Cultural Representation and Signifying Practices*. London: Sage.

Hall, S. (2001) 'Foucault: power, knowledge and discourse', in M. Wetherell, S. Taylor and S.J. Yates (eds) *Discourse, Theory and Practice: A Reader*. London: Sage in association with the Open University.

Hammersley, M. (2000) 'If the social world is how qualitative researchers say it is, what impact can their work have on policy making and practice?', *Current Issues in Qualitative Research*, Centre for Applied Research in Education, University of East Anglia.

Harding, S. (1987) *Feminism and Methodology*, Milton Keynes: Open University Press.

Hays, S. (1996) *The Cultural Contradictions of Motherhood*. New Haven: Yale University Press.

Hearn, J.R. and Parkin, P.W. (2001) *Gender, Sexuality and Violence in Organizations: The Unspoken Forces of Organization Violations*. London: Sage.

Helsby, G. (1995) 'Teachers' construction of professionalism in England in the 1990s', *Journal of Education for Teaching*, 21 (3), 317–332.

HM Government (2003) *Every Child Matters*. London: HMSO.

HM Treasury, Department for Education and Skills, Department for Work and Pensions and Department for Trade and Industry (2004) *Choice for Parents, the Best Start for Children: A Ten-Year Strategy for Childcare*. London: Her Majesty's Stationery Office.

Hey, V. (1996) '"A game of two halves" – a critique of some complicities between hegemonic and counter hegemonic discourses concerning marketisation and education', *Discourse: Studies in Cultural Politics of Education*, 17 (3), 351–362.

Hey, V. (1997) 'Northern accent and Southern comfort: subjectivity and social class', in P. Mahoney and C. Zmroczek (eds) *Class Matters: Working-Class Women's Perspectives on Social Class*. London: Taylor & Francis. Chapter 13, pp. 140–151.

Hey, V. and Bradford, S. (2006) Re-engineering Motherhood? Sure Start in the Community, *Contemporary Issues in Early Childhood*, 7 (1), 5367.

Hilton, G. (1991) 'Boys will be boys – won't they? The attitudes of playgroup workers to gender and play experiences', *Gender and Education*, 3 (3), 311–313.

Hochschild, A.R. (1983) *The Managed Heart: The Commercialisation of Human Feeling*. Berkley: University of California Press.

Hochschild, A.R. (2003) *The Commercialization of Intimate Life: Notes from Home and Work*. California: University of California Press.

Hock, E., Christman, K. and Hock, M. (1980) 'Factors associated with decisions about return to work in mothers of infants', *Developmental Psychology*, 16, 383–402.

Hodkinson, P., Sparkes, A.C. and Hodkinson, H. (1996) *Triumphs and Tears: Young People, Markets and Transition from School to Work*. London: David Fulton.

Holloway, S. (1998) 'Local childcare cultures: moral geographies of mothering and the social organisation of pre-school education', *Gender, Place and Culture*, 5 (10), 29–53.

Hollway, W (1984) 'Gender difference and the production of subjectivity', in J. Henriques, W. Hollway, C. Urwin, C. Venn and V. Walkerdine, *Changing the Subject: Psychology, Social Regulation and Subjectivity*. London: Methuen.

Homan, R. (1991) *Ethics in Social Research*. Harlow: Longman.

hooks, b. (1981) *Ain't I a Woman? Black Women and Feminism*. London: Pluto Press.

hooks, b. (1984) *Feminist Theory: From Margin to Center*. London: Pluto Press.

hooks, b. (2000a) *Feminism is for Everybody: Passionate Politics*. London: Pluto Press.

hooks, b. (2000b) *Where We Stand: Class Matters*. London: Routledge.

Hughes, A. and Menmuir, J. (2002) 'Being a student on a part-time early years degree', *Early Years*, 22 (2), 147–161.

Hughes, S. (2005) 'Bringing emotion to work: emotional intelligence, employee resistance and the reinvention of character', *Work, Employment and Society*, 19 (3), 603–625.

Hutchison, S. (ed.) (1993) *Mark Twain: Critical Assessments*. London: Routledge.

Irwin, S. (2004) 'Attitudes, care and commitment: pattern and process', *Sociological Research On-line*, 9 (3). www.socresonline.org.uk/9/3/irwin.html.

James, A. and James, A.L. (2004) *Constructing Childhood: Theory, Policy and Social Practice*. London: Palgrave.

James, A. and Prout, A. (eds) (1990) *Constructing and Reconstructing Childhood: Contemporary Issues in the Sociological Study of Childhood*. London: Falmer Press.

James, A., Jenks, C. and Prout, A. (1998) *Theorising Childhood*. London: Polity Press.

Jenks, C. (1996) *Childhood*. London: Routledge.

Jensen, J.J. (1996) *Men as Workers in Childcare Services: A Discussion Paper*. European Commission Network on Childcare and other measures to reconcile Employment and Family Responsibilities for Women and Men. Brussels: European Equal Opportunities Unit.

Jones, L. and Osgood, J. (2007) 'Mapping the fabricated identities of childminders: pride and prejudice', *Contemporary Issues in Early Childhood*, 8 (4), 289–300.

Jones, L., Holmes, R. and Powell, J. (2005) *Early Childhood Studies: A Multi-Professional Perspective*. Maidenhead: Open University Press.

Jordan, B., Redley, M. and James, S. (1994) *Putting the Family First: Identities, Decisions and Citizenship*. London: UCL Press.

Katz, L. (1995) *Talks with Teachers of Young Children*. New Jersey: Ablex.

Kelleher, S. (2000) *Alternative Education Provision at Key Stage Four*. Local Government Association, Research Report 11. Slough: NFER.

Kilderry, A. (2006) 'Early childhood education and care as a community service or big business?', *Contemporary Issues in Early Childhood*, 7 (1), 80–83.

Lather, P. (1988) 'Feminist perspectives on empowering research methodologies', *Women Studies International Forum*, 11 (6), 569–81.

Lawler, S. (2000) *Mothering the Self: Mothers, Daughters, Subjects*. London: Routledge.

Lawler, S. (2008) *Identity: Sociological Perspectives*. Cambridge: Polity.

Levitas, R. (1998) *The Inclusive Society? Social Exclusion and New Labour*. London: Macmillan Press.

Lewis, J. (2003) 'Developing early years childcare in England 1997–2002: the choices for (working) mothers', *Social Policy and Administration*, 37 (3), 219–238.

Luck, P. (2008) 'How do early years leaders and managers experience the process of professionalisation in the context of the early years professional status initiative in England?' Paper presented at *EECERA 18th Annual Conference*, Stavanger, Norway.

Luke, A. (1995) 'Text and discourse in education: an introduction to critical discourse analysis', *Review of Research in Education*, 21, 3–47.

Luke, A. and Luke, C. (1999) 'Theorizing interracial families and hybrid identity: an Australian perspective', *Educational Theory*, 49 (2), 223–49, Spring.

Luke, A. and Luke, C. (2001) 'Editorial: calculating the teacher', *Teacher Education*, 12 (1), 5–10.

MacLure, M. (2003) *Discourse in Educational and Social Research*. Buckingham: Open University Press.

MacNaughton, G. (1998) 'Improving our gender equity "tools": a case for discourse analysis', in N. Yelland. (ed) *Gender in Early Childhood*, London: Routledge.

MacNaughton, G. (2000) *Rethinking Gender in Early Childhood Education*. Sydney: Allen and Unwin.

MacNaughton, G. (2001) 'Silences, sex-roles and subjectivities: 40 years of gender in the Australian Journal of Early Childhood', *Australian Journal of Early Childhood*, March, 40 (4), no page.

Maguire, M. (1997) 'Missing links: working-class women of Irish descent', in P. Mahony and C. Zmroczek (eds) *Class Matters: Working Class Women's perspectives on Social Class*. London: Taylor & Francis.

Maguire, M. and Ball, S.J. (1994) 'Discourses of educational reform in the United Kingdom and USA and the work of teachers', *British Journal of In-service Education*, 20 (1), 5–16.

Mahony, P. and Hextall, I. (2000) *Reconstructing Teaching*. London: RoutledgeFalmer.

Mahony, P. and Zmroczek, C. (1997) (eds) *Class Matters 'Working-Class' Women's Perspectives on Social Class*. London: Taylor & Francis.

Manion, C. (2006) 'Feeling, thinking, doing: emotional capital, empowerment and women's education', in I. Epstein (ed.) *Recapturing the Personal: Essays on education and embodied knowledge in comparative perspective*. London: Sage.

McGillivray, G. (2008) 'Constructs of childhood: Enduring or open to change? early years students' reflections or first hand experiences of childhood and early years education in a different country and culture'. Paper presented at *EECERA 18th Annual Conference*, Stavanger, Norway.

McKie, L., Bowlby, S. and Gregory, S. (2001) 'Gender, caring and employment in Britain', *Journal of Social Policy*, 30 (2), 233–258.

McNay, L. (2000) *Gender and Agency: Reconfiguring the Subject in Feminist and Social Theory*. Cambridge: Polity Press.

McQuail, S. and Pugh, G. (1995) *Effective Organisation of Early Childhood Services*. London: National Children's Bureau.

Middleton, S. (1992) *Feminist Pedagogy: A Life-history Approach*. New York: Teachers College Press.

Miller, L. (2008) 'Developing professionalism within a regulatory framework in England: challenges and possibilities', in L. Miller. and C. Cable (eds) *Professionalism in the Early Years*. London: Hodder Arnold.

Miller, L. and Cable, C. (eds) (2008) *Professionalism in the Early Years*. London: HodderArnold.

Moll, L.C. and Greenberg, J. (1990) 'Creating zones of possibilities: combining social contexts for instruction', in L.C. Moll (ed.) *Vygotsky and Education*. Cambridge: Cambridge University Press, 319–348.

Moll, L.C., Amanti, C., Neff, D. and Gonzalez, N. (1992) 'Funds of knowledge for teaching: using a qualitative approach to connect homes and classrooms', *Theory into Practice*, 31, 2, Qualitative Issues in Educational Research (Spring), 132–141.

Mooney, A. and Munton, A. (1997) *Research and policy in Early Childhood Services: Time for a New Agenda*. Institute of Education: University of London.

Moss, P. (2006) 'Structures, understandings and discourses: possibilities for re-envisioning the early childhood worker', *Contemporary Issues in Early Childhood*, 7 (1), 30–41.

Moss, P. and Petrie, P. (2002) *From Children's Services to Children's Spaces: Public Policy, Children and Childhood*. London: Falmer Press.

Moyles, J. (2001) 'Passion, paradox and professionalism in early years education', *Early Years*, 21 (2), 81–95.

Nelson, M. (1989) 'Negotiating care: relationships between family daycare providers and mothers', *Feminist Studies*, 15 (1), 7–33.

Nelson, M. (1990) 'Mothering others children: the experiences of family daycare providers', in E.K. Abel and M.K. Nelson (eds) *Circles of Care: Work and Identity in Women's Lives*. New York: SUNY Press. Chapter 10, 210–231.

Nias, J. (1999) 'Primary teaching as a culture of care', in J. Prosser (ed.) *School Culture*. London: Paul Chapman.

Nicolson, P. (1996) *Gender, Power and Organisation*. London: Routledge.

Nicolson, P. (2002) *Having It All? Choices for Today's Superwoman*. London: John Wiley.

Nilsen, T. and Manum, L. (1998) 'Masculine care: the nursery school as a man's workplace', in C. Owen., C. Cameron. and P. Moss (eds) *Men as Workers in Services for Young Children: Issues of a mixed gender workforce*. Bedford Way Papers, Institute of Education: University of London.

Novinger, S. and O'Brien, L. (2003) 'Beyond "boring, meaningless shit", in the academy: early childhood teacher educators under the regulatory gaze', *Contemporary Issues in Early Childhood*, 4 (1), 4–18.

Nowotny, H. (1981) 'Women in public life in Australia', in C. Fuchs Epstein and R. Laub Coser (eds) *Access to Power: Cross National Studies of Women and Elites*, London: Allen Unwin.

Nursery World (2008) 'Organisations give verdict on EYP', 8 June. pp. 12–14.

Oakley, A. (2005) *Gender, Women and Social Science: A Reader*. London: Polity Press.

Osgood, J. (2003) *Developing the Business Skills of Childcare Professionals: An Evaluation of Business Support Programmes*. London: Department for Education and Skills.

Osgood, J. (2004) 'Time to get down to business? The responses of early years practitioners to entrepreneurial approaches to professionalism', *Journal of Early Childhood Research*, 2 (1), 5–24.

Osgood, J. (2005) 'Who cares? The classed nature of childcare', *Gender and Education*, 17 (3), 289–303.

Osgood, J. (2006a) 'Professionalism and performativity: the paradox facing early years practitioners', *Early Years*, 26 (2), 187–199.

Osgood, J. (2006b) 'Editorial: rethinking "professionalism" in the early years: English perspectives', *Contemporary Issues in Early Childhood*, 7 (1), 1–4.

Osgood, J. (2006c) 'Deconstructing professionalism in the early years: resisting the regulatory gaze', *Contemporary Issues in Early Childhood*, 7 (1), 5–14.

Osgood, J. (2008) 'Professionalism and performativity: the paradox facing early years practitioners', in E. Wood. (ed) *The Routledge Reader in Early Childhood Education*. London: Routledge.

Osgood, J. and Stone, V. (2002) *Assessing the Business Skills of Early Years, Childcare and Playwork Providers.* London: Department for Education and Skills.

Osgood, J., Francis, B. and Archer, L. (2006) 'Gendered identities and work placement: why don't boys care?' *Journal of Education Policy,* 21 (3), 305–321.

Osgood, J., Stone, V. and Thomas, A. (2002) *Delivering a Work-focused Service: Views and Experiences of Clients.* Department for Work and Pensions. Research Report No. 167, CDS: Leeds.

Owen, C., Cameron, C. and Moss, P. (eds) (1998) *Men as Workers in Services for Young Children: Issues of a Mixed Gender Workforce.* Bedford Way Papers, Institute of Education, University of London.

Ozga, J. (1995) 'Deskilling a profession: professionalism, deprofessionalisation and the new managerialism', in H. Busher and R. Saran (eds) *Managing Teachers as Professionals in Schools.* London: Routledge.

Ozga, J. (2000) *Policy Research in Educational Settings: Contested Terrain.* Buckingham: Open University Press.

Palmer, S. (2006) *Toxic Childhood: How the Modern World is Damaging our Children and What We Can Do About It.* London: Orion.

Parker, I. (1998) (ed) *Social Constructionism, Discourse and Realism.* London: Sage.

Payne, J. (2006) *What's Wrong with Emotional Labour?* SKOPE Research Paper 65, Oxford: University of Oxford.

Pearson, A. (2003) *I Don't Know How She Does It.* London: Vintage.

Penguin English Dictionary, The (2000) London: Penguin.

Penn, H. (1997) *Comparing Nurseries: Staff and Children in Italy, Spain and the UK.* London: Paul Chapman Publishing.

Penn, H. and McQuail, S. (1996) *Childcare as a Gendered Occupation,* Report for DfEEE/OECD.

Phoenix, A. (1994) 'Practising feminist research: the intersection of gender and "race" in the research process', *Researching Women's Lives from a Feminist Perspective.* London: Taylor & Francis.

Potter, J. and Wetherell, M. (1992) *Discourse and Social Psychology: Beyond Attitudes and Behaviour.* London: Sage.

Pungello, E.P. and Kurtz-Costes, B. (1999) 'Why and how working women choose child care: a review with a focus on infancy', *Developmental Review,* 19 (1), 31–96.

Pungello, E.P. and Kurtz-Costes, B. (2000) 'Working women's selection of care for their infants: a prospective study', *Family Relations,* 49, 245–255.

Purves, L. (2004) *How Not to be the Perfect Mother.* London: Harper Collins.

Rabinow, P. (1991) *The Foucault Reader.* London: Penguin.

Rahilly, S. and E. Johnston (2002) 'Opportunity for childcare: the impact of government initiatives in England upon childcare provision', *Social Policy and Administration,* 36 (5), 482–495.

Ramazanoglu, C. (ed) (1994) 'Introduction', in *Up Against Foucault: Explorations of Some Tensions Between Foucault and Feminism.* London: Routledge.

Ramazanoglu, C. with Holland, J. (2002) *Feminist Methodology: Challenges and Choices.* London: Sage.

Rancière, J. (1991) *The Ignorant Schoolmaster: Five Lessons in Intellectual Emancipation.* Stanford, CA: Stanford University Press.

Randall, V. (2000) *The Politics of Child Daycare in Britain.* Oxford: University Press.

Reay, D. (1996) 'Dealing with difficult differences: reflexivity and social class in feminist research', *Feminism and Psychology*, 6 (3), 443–456.

Reay, D. (1997) 'The success of failure or the failure of success?' in P. Mahony and C. Zmroczek (eds) *Class Matters: Working-class Women's Perspectives on Social Class*. London: Taylor & Francis.

Reay, D. (1998) 'Rethinking social class: qualitative perspectives on class and gender', *Sociology*, 32 (2), 259–275.

Reay, D. (2000) 'A useful extension of Bourdieu's conceptual framework? Emotional capital as a way of understanding mothers' involvement in their children's education', *The Sociological Review*, 4, 568–585.

Reay, D. (2001) 'Finding or losing yourself? Working-class relationships to education', *Journal of Education Policy*, 16 (4), 333–346.

Reay, D. (2004) 'Qualitative perspectives on gender and social class', in S. Nagy Hess-Biber and M. Yaiser (eds) *Feminist Perspectives on Social Research*. New York: Oxford University Press.

Reay, D. and Ball, S.J. (2000) 'The essentials of female management: women's ways of working in the education market place?' *Educational Management and Administration*, 28 (2), 145–158.

Renold, E. (2005) *Girls, Boys and Junior Sexualities: Exploring Children's Gender and Sexual Relations in the Primary School*. London: RoutledgeFalmer.

Rhedding-Jones, J. (2005a) 'Questioning diversity', in N. Yelland (ed.) *Critical Issues in Early Childhood Education*. London: Routledge.

Rhedding-Jones, J. (2005b) *What is Research? Methodological Practices and New Approaches*, Oslo: Universiteforgalet.

Rhedding-Jones, J. (2008) 'How is European early education addressing implications of the Islamic Diaspora?' Paper presented at *EECERA Annual Conference*, September. Stavanger, Norway.

Riceour, P. (1991) 'Narrative identity' (translated by D. Wood), in D. Wood (ed.) *On Paul Riceour: Narrative and Interpretation*. London: Routledge.

Rich, A. (1977) *Of Woman Born: Motherhood as Experience and Institution*. London: Virago.

Riley, D. (1983) *War in the Nursery: Theories of the Child and Mother*. London: Virago.

Rinaldi, C. (2006) *In Dialogue with Reggio Emilia*. London: Routledge.

Rizvi, F. and Lingard, B. (1996) 'Forward', in J.P. Gee, G. Hull and C. Lankshear (eds) *The New Work Order: Behind the language of the New Capitalism*. St Leonards: Allen Unwin.

Robinson, K. (2002) 'Making the invisible visible: gay and lesbian issues in early childhood education', *Contemporary Issues in Early Childhood*, 3 (3), 415–434.

Robinson, K. (2005a) '"Queerying" gender: heteronormativity in early childhood education', *Australian Journal of Early Childhood*, 30 (2), 19–28.

Robinson, K. (2005b) 'Doing anti-homophobia and anti-heterosexism in early childhood education. Moving beyond immobilising impacts of "risk", "fears" and "silences". Can we afford not to?' *Contemporary Issues in Early Childhood Education*, 6 (2), 175–188.

Robinson, K. and Jones-Diaz, C. (1999) 'Doing theory with early childhood educators: understanding difference and diversity in personal and professional contexts', *Australian Journal of Early Childhood*, 24 (4), 33–41.

Robinson, K. and Jones-Diaz, C. (2006) *Diversity and Difference in Early Childhood Education: Issues for Theory and Practice*. Maidenhead: Open University Press.

Rolfe, H. (2005) 'Building a stable workforce: recruitment and retention in the child care and early years sector', *Children and Society*, 19, 54–65.

Rose, S. (1999) *Powers of Freedom: Reframing Political Thought*. Cambridge: Cambridge University Press.

Runte, M. and Mills, A. (2004) 'Paying the toll: a feminist post-structural critique of the discourse bridging work and family', *Culture and Organisation*, 10 (3), 237–249.

Ryan, S. (2005) 'Freedom to choose: examining children's experiences in choice time', in N. Yelland (ed.) *Critical Issues in Early Childhood Education*. Buckingham: Open University Press.

Ryan, S. and Grieshaber, S. (eds) (2005) *Practical Transformations and Transformational Practices: Globalisation, Postmodernism and Early Childhood Education*. New York: Elsevier.

Sachs, J. (2000) 'The Activist Professional', *Journal of Educational Change*, 1, 77–95.

Sachs, J. (2001) 'Teacher Professional Identity: competing discourses, competing outcomes', *Journal of Education Policy*, 16 (2), 149–161.

Sataoen, S.O. (1998) 'Men as workers in services for young children', in: C. Owen, C. Cameron and P. Moss (eds) *Men as Workers in Services for Young Children: Issues of a Mixed Gender Workforce*. Bedford Way Papers, Institute of Education, University of London.

Saugeres, L. and Duncan, S. (2002) 'Choice and ideology in mothers' worker-life decisions'. Paper presented at the ISA Conference August, Brisbane, Australia.

Sawicki, J. (1991) *Disciplining Foucault: Feminism, Power and the Body*. London: Routledge.

Segal, L. (1987) *Is the Future Female? Troubled Thoughts on Contemporary Feminism*. London: Virago Press.

Segal, L. (1994) *Straight Sex*. London: Virago.

Seo, S. (2003) 'Early child care choices: a theoretical model and research implications', *Early Child Development and Care*, 173, 637–650.

Sevenhuijsen, S. (1998) *Citizenship and the Ethics of Care: Feminist Considerations on Justice, Morality and Politics*. London: Routledge.

Sheridan, M. (1997) *From Birth to Five Years: Children's Developmental Progress*. London: Routledge.

Siann, G., Riley, S., Wilson, F. and Callaghan, M. (2000) 'Gender at home and work: continuities and changes', *Journal of Applied Social Psychology*, 30 (12), 2491–2512.

Silin, J. (2005) 'Who can speak? Silence, voice and pedagogy', in N. Yelland (ed.) *Critical Issues in Early Childhood Education*. London: Routledge.

Sinclair, A. (1996) 'Leadership in administration: rediscovering a lost discourse', in P. Weller and G. Davis (eds) *New Ideas, Better Government*. NSW: Allen and Unwin.

Singer, E. (1992) *Childcare and the Psychology of Development* (translated by A. Porcelijn). London: Routledge.

Skeggs, B. (1995) 'Situating the production of feminist ethnography', in M. Maynard and J. Purvis (eds) *Researching Women's Lives from a Feminist Perspective*. London: Taylor & Francis.

Skeggs, B. (1997) *Formations of Class and Gender*. London: Sage.

Skeggs, B. (2003) *Class, Self, Culture*. London: Routledge.

Smithson, J. and Stokoe, E.H. (2005) 'Discourses of work–life balance: negotiating "genderblind" terms in organizations', *Gender, Work and Organization*, Volume 12, Number (2), 147–168.

Spivak, G.C. (1987) *In Other Worlds: Essays in Cultural Politics*. London: Metheun.

Spivak, G.C. (1999) *A Critique of Postcolonial Reason: Toward a History of Vanishing Present*. Cambridge: Harvard University Press.

Stanley, L. and Wise, S. (1990) 'Method, methodology and epistemology in feminist research processes', in L. Stanley (ed.) *Feminist Praxis: Research, Theory and Epistemology*. London: Sage.

Steedman, C. (1982) *The Tidy House: Little Girls Writing*. London: Virago.

Steedman, C. (1986) *Landscape of a Good Woman*. London: Virago.

Strathern, M. (1987) 'Out of contexts: the persuasive fictions of anthropology', *Current Anthropology*, 28, 251–281.

Strathern, (2000) 'The tyranny of transparency', *British Educational Research Journal*, 26, 310–332.

Strober, M., Gerlach-Downie, S. and Yeager, K. (1995) 'Childcare centres as workplaces', *Feminist Economics*, 1 (1), 93–119.

Stronach, I., Corbin, B., McNamara, O. Stark, S. and Warne, T. (2003) 'Towards an uncertain politics of professionalism: teacher and nurse identities in flux', *Journal of Education Policy*, 17 (1), 109–138.

Sumsion, J. (2005) 'Putting postmodern theories into practice in early childhood teacher education', in Ryan, S. and Grieshaber, S. (eds) *Practical transformations and Transformational Practices: Globalisation, Postmodernism and Early Childhood Education*. New York: Elsevier.

Sure Start Unit (2005) 'Birth to three matters: an introduction to the framework'. http://www.surestart.gov.uk/_doc/P0000285.pdf.

Sylva, K., Melhuish, E., Sammons, P., Siraj-Blatchford, I., Taggart, B. and Elliot, K. (2003) *The Effective Provision of Pre-school Education (EPPE) Project: Findings from the Pre-school Period*. London: DfES.

Tamboukou, M. and Ball, S.J. (eds) (2003) 'Genealogy and ethnography: fruitful encounters or dangerous liaisons?' in *Dangerous Encounters: Genealogy and Ethnography (Eruptions, V. 17)* London: Peter Lang.

Taylor, R. (2004) 'Four nursery staff sacked after BBC documentary', The *Guardian*, London.

Taylor, S. (2001) 'Locating and conducting discourse analytic research', in M. Wetherell, S. Taylor and S.J. Yates (eds) *Discourse as Data: A Guide for Analysis*, Buckingham: Open University Press.

Taylor, S., Rizvi, F., Lingard, B. and Henry, M. (1997) *Educational Policy and the Politics of Change*. London: Routledge.

Tickell, C. (2011) *The Early Years: Foundations for Life, Health and Learning: An Independent Report on the Early Years Foundation Stage to Her Majesty's Government*. London: HMSO.

Tomlinson, S. (1997) *Education 14–19: Critical Perspectives*. London: Athlone Press.

Troyna, B. (1993) *Racism and Education: Research Perspectives*. Buckingham: Open University Press.

Troyna, B. and Carrington, B. (eds) (1988) *Children and Controversial Issues: Strategies for the Early and Middle Years*. London: Falmer Press.

Troyna, B. and Hatcher, R. (1992) *Racism in Children's Lives: Study of Mainly-white Primary Schools*. London: Routledge.

Tuominen, M. (2003) *We Are Not Babysitters. Family Childcare Providers Redefine Work and Care*. New Brunswick, NJ: Rutgers University Press.

Uttal, L. (1996) 'Custodial care, surrogate care and co-ordinated care: employed mothers and the meaning of childcare', *Gender and Society*, 10, 291–311.

Uttal, L. (1997) '"Trust your instincts": racial ethnic and class-based preferences in employed mothers childcare choices', *Qualitative Sociology*, 20 (2), 253–274.

Uttal, L. (2002) *Making Care Work: Employed Mothers in the New Childcare Market*. New York: Rutgers University Press.

Vincent, C. and Ball, S.J. (2001) 'A market in love? Choosing pre-school childcare', *British Educational Research Journal*, 27 (5), 633–651.

Vincent, C. and Ball, S.J. (2006) *Childcare, Choice and Class Practices*. London: Taylor & Francis.

Vincent, C. and Ball, S.J. and Kemp, S. (2003) 'Metropolitan mothers: mothers, mothering and paid work'. Paper presented at the British Educational Research Association Conference, Heriot-Watt University, September.

Vogt, F. (2002) 'A caring teacher: explorations into primary school teachers' professional identity and ethic of care', *Gender and Education*, 14 (3), 251–264.

Walby, S. (1990) *Theorising Patriarchy*. Cambridge: Polity Press.

Walby, S. (1997) *Gender Transformation*. London: Routledge.

Walkerdine, V. (1990) *Schoolgirl Fictions*. London: Verso.

Walkerdine, V. (1997) *Daddy's Girl: Young Girls and Popular Culture*. London: MacMillan.

Walkerdine, V. (2003) 'Reclassifying upward mobility: femininity and the neo-liberal subject', *Gender and Education*, 15 (3), 237–248.

Walkerdine, V. and Lucey, H. (1989) *Democracy in the Kitchen: Regulating Mothers and Socialising Daughters*. London: Virago.

Walkerdine, V., Lucey, H. and Melody, J. (2001) *Growing Up Girl*. London: Palgrave.

Walters, S. (2005) 'Making the best of a bad job? Female part-timers' orientations and attitudes to work', *Gender, Work and Organization*, 12 (3), 193–216.

Walzer, S. (1997) 'Contextualizing the employment decisions of new mothers', *Qualitative Sociology*, 20 (2), 211–227.

Warren, T. (2000) 'Women in low-status, part-time jobs: a class and gender analysis', *Sociological Research Online*, 4 (4). www.socresonline.org.uk/4/4/warren.html.

Warren, T. (2003) 'A privileged pole? Diversity in women's pay, pensions and wealth in Britain', *Gender, Work and Organization*, 10 (5), 605–628.

Warren, T. (2004) 'Working part-time: achieving a successful work-life balance?' *British Journal of Sociology*, 55 (1), 99–122.

Weedon (1987) *Feminist Practice and Post-structuralist Theory*. Oxford: Blackwell.

Wenger, E. (1998) *Communities of Practice: Learning, Meaning and Identity*. Cambridge: Cambridge University Press.

Williams, F. (1999) 'Good-enough principles for welfare', *Journal of Social Policy*, 28 (4), 667–687.

Winnicott, D.W. (1965) *The Family and Individual Development*. London: Tavistock.

Witz, A. (1992) *Professions and Patriarchy*. London: Routledge.

Wolf, A. (1995) *Competence-based Assessment*. Buckingham: Open University Press.

Woollet, A. and Phoenix, A. (1991) 'Motherhood: social construction, politics and psychology', in A. Phoenix, A. Woollet and E. Lloyd (eds) *Motherhood: Meanings, Practices and Ideologies*. London: Sage.

Yelland, N. and Kilderry, A. (2005) 'Against the tide: new ways in early childhood education', in N. Yelland (ed) *Critical Issues in Early Childhood Education*. London: Routledge.

Index

DATE DUE